1846
Portrait of the Nation

America in 1846

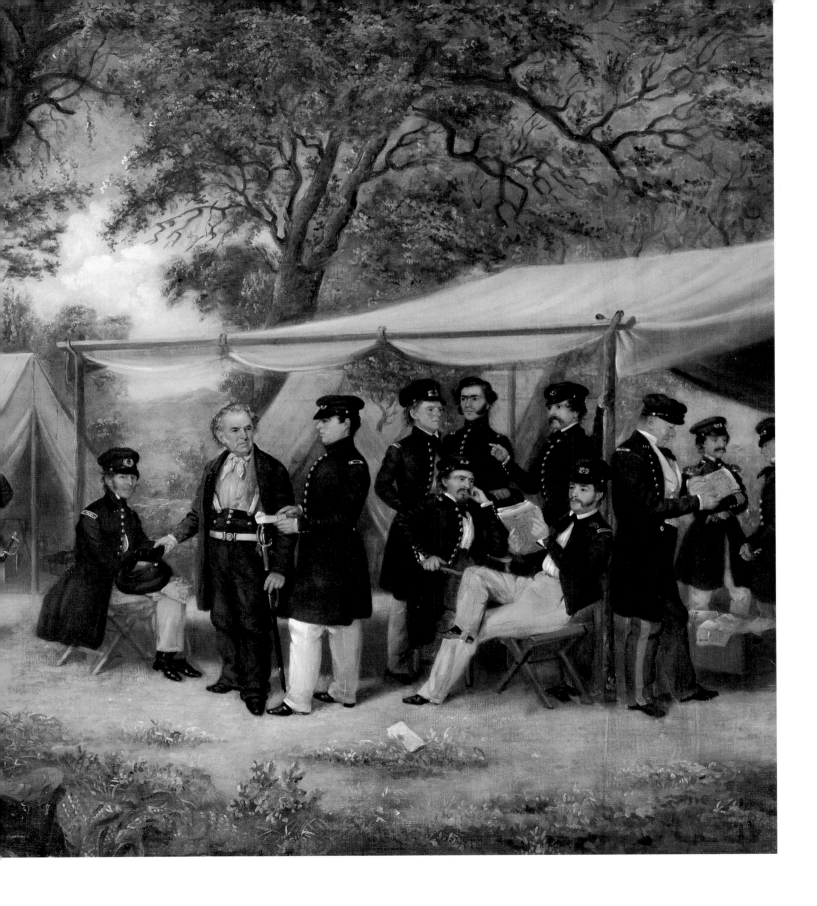

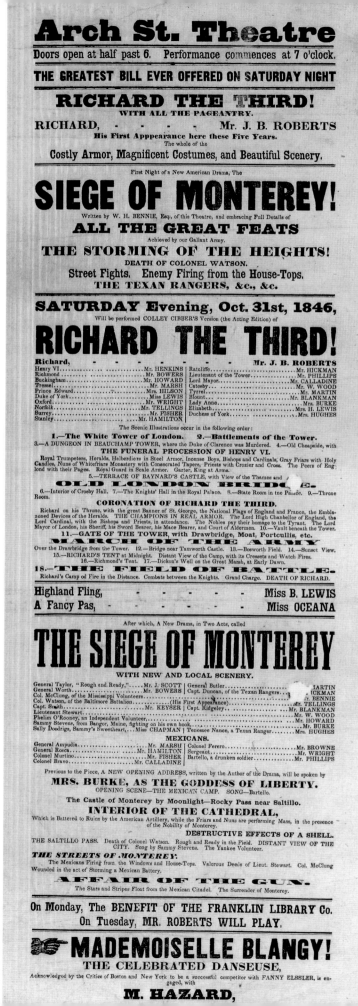
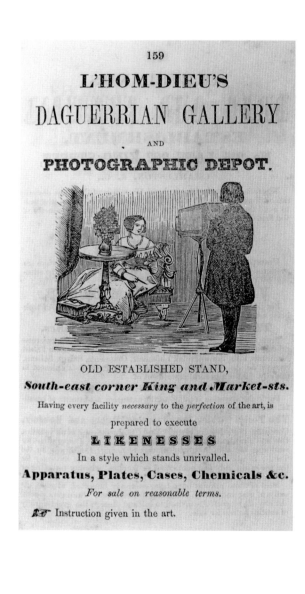

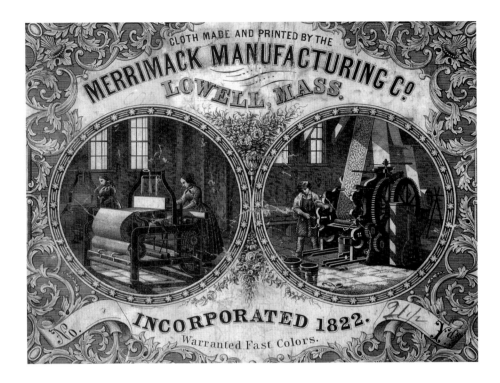

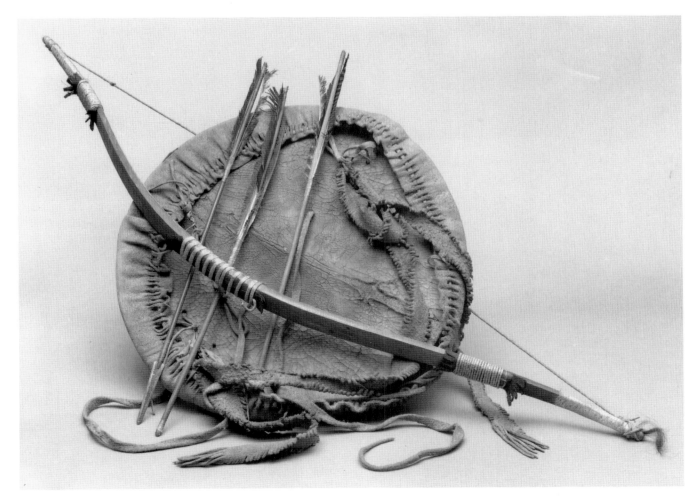

of twenty one years, or intestate, I then bequeath the whole of my property subject to the annuity of one hundred pounds to John Fitall and for the security and payment of which, I mean stock to remain in this country to the united states of america, to found at Washington, under the name to the Smithsonian institution, an establishment for the increase & diffusion of Knowledge among men.

I think proper here to state that all the money which will be standing in the French five per cents, at my death in the names of the father of my above mentioned nephew, Henry James Hungerford & all that in my names, is the property of my said nephew being what he inherited from his father, or what I have laid up for him from the saving upon his income.

James Smithson.

1846

Portrait of the Nation

Margaret C. S. Christman

In celebration of the 150th anniversary
of the founding of the Smithsonian Institution

Published by the Smithsonian Institution Press
for the National Portrait Gallery

Washington, D.C., and London

An exhibition at the National Portrait Gallery
commemorating the 150th anniversary of the founding
of the Smithsonian Institution
April 12–August 18, 1996

This exhibition has been made possible by a grant from
the Smithsonian Institution Special Exhibition Fund.

Library of Congress Cataloging-in-Publication Data
Christman, Margaret C. S.
    1846 : portrait of the nation / Margaret C. S. Christman.
        p.   cm.
    Includes bibliographical references and index.
    ISBN 1-56098-674-3 (alk. paper)
    1. United States—Civilization—1783–1865. 2. Smithsonian
Institution—History. I. Title.
E166.C5   1996
973.6—dc20   95-52390

British Library Cataloguing-in-Publication Data is available

Manufactured in the United States of America
03 02 01 00 99 98 97 96   5 4 3 2 1

♾ The paper used in this publication meets the minimum re-
quirements of the American National Standard for Information
Sciences—Permanence of Paper for Printed Library Materials
ANSI Z39.48-1984.

Illustrations from "America in 1846" are re-illustrated on pages 57,
63, 77, 89, 100, 102, 111, 113, 116, 158, 162, and 190.

The frontispiece is re-illustrated on page 13.

Page viii:

Playbill for *Richard III* and *Siege of Monterey*, the Arch Street
Theatre, Philadelphia, October 31, 1846. Folger Shakespeare
Library, Washington, D.C.

Advertisement for L'Hom-Dieu's Daguerrian Gallery. The
Charleston Museum, Charleston, South Carolina.

Cover:

Background: *Map of Oregon and Upper California* (detail), 1848. Geography and Maps Division, Library of Congress, Washington, D.C.

Clockwise from upper left: Frederick Douglass (detail) by an unidentified artist. National Portrait Gallery, Smithsonian Institution,
Washington, D.C.

Elias Howe's original patent model of sewing machine. Textile
Division, National Museum of American History, Smithsonian
Institution, Washington, D.C.

Doll carried to California by Martha Reed in 1846. Sutter's Fort
State Historic Park, California Department of Parks and Recreation, Sacramento

John Charles Frémont (detail) by William S. Jewett. National
Portrait Gallery, Smithsonian Institution, Washington, D.C.

John Charles Frémont's personal flag. Southwest Museum,
Los Angeles, California

Clipper Ship Sea Witch Coming to Anchor at Whampoa (detail) by
an unidentified artist. Peabody Essex Museum, Salem, Massachusetts

Daniel Webster (detail) by George Peter Alexander Healy. National
Portrait Gallery, Smithsonian Institution, Washington, D.C.

Antislavery banner. Massachusetts Historical Society, Boston

Contents

Foreword

The American is a mechanic by nature," observed a traveler from abroad, quoted by Robert Remini in his essay here. The creative energies of these mechanics had brought so many working models to the United States Patent Office by the 1830s that a larger space was required to house them. William P. Elliot, a draftsman in the Patent Office, prepared the design and Robert Mills, who had designed the Treasury Building, was engaged to supervise the construction. The space provided was at a prime location on Pierre L'Enfant's plan of the city, a place originally designated as a "proper shelter for such monuments as were voted by the late Continental Congress, for those heroes who fell in the cause of liberty, and for such others as may hereafter be decreed by the voice of a grateful nation." Ground was broken in 1836.

I find a special suitability in the fact that I am writing these lines in the building originally occupied by the Patent Office. Today the National Portrait Gallery occupies a portion of the building, at last fulfilling L'Enfant's vision, but in 1846—the year on which this book is centered—portraits were only a portion of what could be seen in the monumental classical structure. The main attraction was the display of patent models. The newly opened Model Hall attracted crowds of visitors, who came to reflect on the potential of ingenious machines to improve life, make agriculture and manufacturing more efficient, facilitate communication, and create wealth.

For the American of the 1840s, mechanics and science were not far apart, so science naturally had its place in the Patent Office. The National Institute was given space in the display rooms for objects brought back by the western exploring parties as well as mounted birds and animals collected by natural scientists. These were shown alongside collections of significant artifacts of the political and military history of America, and works of the visual arts assembled by public-minded collectors. Botanical specimens, including those collected by the Wilkes expedition to the South Seas, were shown in a large greenhouse adjoining the Patent Office on the north. In effect, America's first national museum had opened in the center of downtown Washington in the space today occupied by the Smithsonian's National Portrait Gallery.

Not far from the Patent Office, Samuel F. B. Morse had set up a telegraph office to demonstrate the power of this new electrical medium to transmit information over long distances instantaneously. Morse was later given rooms in the building just constructed for the General Post Office, facing the Patent Office across F Street; there, the Regents of the newly established Smithsonian Institution held their first meeting in 1846 to chart the program of the new Institution and to select a Secretary as its head. Their choice would be a physical scientist from Princeton, Joseph Henry, whose experiments in electricity had already brought him prominence in the nation. Away from Washington, John James Audubon, settled in his new home north of New York City, published the second volume of the *Viviparous Quadrupeds of North America* in 1846 with his friend and collaborator, John Bachman. Audubon's eyesight and energies were failing, but his confidence in the desire of Americans to subscribe to important

studies in natural science was unabated. This spirit also motivated the Smithsonian Regents and their new Secretary in planning for the new Institution "for the increase and diffusion of knowledge."

But the city of Washington, for all its newly built monumental government structures, was still a place of muddy streets and undeveloped areas. The Mall was largely woodland, the marshy bank of the Potomac came close to the south gates of the White House, most of the members of Congress lived in boardinghouses, and slaves were traded in nearby Alexandria. Shipping came into Georgetown and Alexandria, but most travelers to the city came by coach or on horseback. Such roads as existed were unreliable at best; trips between the major towns took days, if not weeks; and accommodations were makeshift.

Today the streets of Washington are paved and busy, three major airports serve the region, and the town has grown in size and sophistication beyond the wildest dreams of its founders. But the portion of the Patent Office that existed in 1846 today fulfills the function L'Enfant envisioned. Long after the Patent Office had vacated the building, when Congress proposed to demolish it to make way for a parking lot, President Eisenhower was prevailed upon to save the handsome building. In 1962 President Kennedy signed the law establishing the National Portrait Gallery within the Smithsonian Institution, and decreed that it would occupy a portion of the building once designated as "a proper shelter for . . . monuments." In 1968 the Portrait Gallery opened to the public as a free public museum for the "exhibition and study of portraiture . . . [of] men and women who have made significant contributions to the history, development, and culture of the people of the United States" and for the study of the art of portraiture. Since that time, the Gallery has devoted itself to collecting portraits of as many notable Americans as it could find, and has presented a series of exhibitions and published enduring books focused on these people and their accomplishments. This is the latest in the series, and it has a particular resonance in linking together the year in which the Smithsonian was founded (as virtually Congress's final act before it adjourned) with the politicians, social reformers, artists, writers, and scientists who were active then, and with the building that occupied such a central place in the nation's capital.

In the pages that follow, Robert Remini has splendidly set the stage for Margaret Christman's admirable evocation of the texture of life, thought, and politics in 1846. The complexities of the long debate preceding passage of the Smithsonian's enabling legislation reflected the complexities of the nation at that watershed time. Science and technology were seen as the most powerful guides to a modern society. Not yet appreciated for their abstract qualities, art and literature were valued primarily for their power to improve the moral fiber of audiences, as well as for their ability to reflect the appearance of the world and to suggest how the diversity of divine creation was embodied in a land of special qualities. Education was so highly valued that it was withheld from slaves, lest they gain from it the knowledge and power to overturn the system.

Yet just as the rude buildings of necessity were being replaced by thoughtfully designed structures, and just as formal gardens began to replace the barely cultivated plots cleared from the wilderness, so the establishment of the Smithsonian sprang from the newly sophisticated, confidently optimistic view that the gathering, interpretation, and sharing of knowledge would contribute to the greatness of a nation that had, at last, passed beyond the early stages of settlement.

Alan Fern
Director, National Portrait Gallery

Acknowledgments

In the forefront of those to whom I have cause to be grateful is National Portrait Gallery Director Alan Fern, who conceived the idea of celebrating the 150th anniversary of the Smithsonian's founding through a look back at the America of 1846.

Provided with a theme, the search for portraits began, a task made immeasurably easier by the Gallery's Catalog of American Portraits, which has amassed information on upwards of one hundred thousand images. But for the CAP and the help of its staff, headed by Keeper Linda Thrift, I fear I would have been, as it was with the Donner party, hacking my way through a roadless canyon and bogged down in the unmeasured desert.

Next came the great joy of research in the Gallery's library, where I had the assistance of Librarian Cecilia Chin's helpful and agreeable crew. Particular mention should be made of Assistant Librarian Pat Lynagh, who somehow secured from hither and yon every single thing I requested.

Early on, as I sought out the feel and look of 1846, I found a ready welcome at the Museum of American History's Division of Costume. To Curator Claudia Kidwell and Museum Specialist Shelly Foote go special thanks for their aid, both with this book and with the exhibition.

Throughout, my mainstay has been Curator of Exhibitions Beverly Cox. Simply put, I could not have managed without her. Assistant Curator of Exhibitions Claire Kelly has been, as always, a steady source of support.

At the moment when I most needed help came Alice Padwe to track down all manner of things, to research matters that were often arcane, to look for illustrations, to arrange for photographs. All of this and more she undertook with great cheer.

My longtime and much-valued editors, Publications Officer Frances Stevenson and Managing Editor Dru Dowdy, have done their best to keep me comprehensible and within bounds. Unrelenting in their diligence, they are nearly impossible to outwit. Editorial intern Kirsten Williams, with her extraordinary eagle eye, has caught more errors than I care to acknowledge.

Finally, an inscription to the rising generation, in my case Andrea and Abigail; Erin; and our latest acquisition, little Newtie. They must learn to be worthy of their heritage.

Margaret C. S. Christman
National Portrait Gallery, Summer 1995

Lenders to the Exhibition

American Antiquarian Society, Worcester, Massachusetts

Amon Carter Museum, Fort Worth, Texas

Aurora Historical Society, Aurora, Illinois

Beinecke Rare Book and Manuscript Library, Yale University, New Haven, Connecticut

Berkshire Athenaeum, Pittsfield, Massachusetts

The Trustees of the Boston Public Library, Massachusetts

The Brooklyn Museum, New York

Laurie and John Bullard

Castle Collection, AHHP, Smithsonian Institution, Washington, D.C.

Chicago Historical Society, Illinois

Decatur House, a Property of the National Trust for Historic Preservation, Washington, D.C.

George Eastman House, Rochester, New York

Fishburn Library, Hollins College, Roanoke, Virginia

Folger Shakespeare Library, Washington, D.C.

Framingham State College, Framingham, Massachusetts

Georgetown University Library, Washington, D.C.

Gilman Paper Company Collection, New York City

Hargrett Rare Books and Manuscripts Library, University of Georgia, Athens

The Historic New Orleans Collection, Louisiana

Hood Museum of Art, Dartmouth College, Hanover, New Hampshire

Matthew R. Isenburg

The Library Company of Philadelphia, Pennsylvania

Library of Congress, Washington, D.C.

City of Lowell, Massachusetts

The Lynn Historical Society, Inc., Massachusetts

Manoogian Foundation, Taylor, Michigan

Massachusetts General Hospital, Boston, through Harvard University Art Museums, Cambridge, Massachusetts

Massachusetts Historical Society, Boston

The Metropolitan Museum of Art, New York City

Missouri Historical Society, Saint Louis

Mount Holyoke College Library, South Hadley, Massachusetts

Museum of American Folk Art, New York City

Museum of American Textile History, Lowell, Massachusetts

Museum of Church History and Art, Salt Lake City, Utah

Museum of Fine Arts, Boston, Massachusetts

Museum of the City of New York, New York

National Archives, Washington, D.C.

National Gallery of Art, Washington, D.C.

National Museum of American Art, Smithsonian Institution, Washington, D.C.

National Museum of American History, Smithsonian Institution, Washington, D.C.

National Museum of the American Indian, Smithsonian Institution, Washington, D.C.

National Park Service, Longfellow National Historic Site, Cambridge, Massachusetts

National Portrait Gallery, Smithsonian Institution, Washington, D.C.

New-York Historical Society, New York City

New York Public Library, New York City

The People of Missouri

The Philbrook Museum of Art, Tulsa, Oklahoma

The Phillips Collection, Washington, D.C.

James K. Polk Memorial Association, Columbia, Tennessee

Enoch Pratt Free Library, Baltimore, Maryland

Princeton University, New Jersey

Private collection

Harry Ransom Humanities Research Center, The University of Texas at Austin

The Saint Louis Art Museum, Missouri

The Schlesinger Library, Radcliffe College, Cambridge, Massachusetts

Shelburne Museum, Vermont

Smithsonian Institution Libraries, Washington, D.C.

Society for the Preservation of New England Antiquities, Boston, Massachusetts

The Society of the Cincinnati at Anderson House, Washington, D.C.

Southwest Museum, Los Angeles, California

The J. B. Speed Art Museum, Louisville, Kentucky

State Historical Society of Iowa, Des Moines

Sutter's Fort State Historic Park, California Department of Parks and Recreation, Sacramento

Earl Gregg Swem Library, College of William and Mary, Williamsburg, Virginia

Terra Museum of American Art, Chicago, Illinois

Thiel College, Greenville, Pennsylvania

Constance Fuller Threinen

University of Virginia Library, Charlottesville

Mrs. Robert Blake Watson

Wellesley College Library, Massachusetts

Wentworth-Coolidge Commission, Portsmouth, New Hampshire

Trustees of the John Greenleaf Whittier Homestead, Haverhill, Massachusetts

Estate of William Woodville VIII

1846: Portrait of the Nation

The Smithsonian! The name itself resounds with the triumphs and trials, the discoveries and culture, the history and achievements the American people have produced over the centuries, which have lifted the nation to a rank in power, wealth, and distinction second to none. Sprawled like a pride of lions near and around and beyond the Mall in the District of Columbia, this vast collection of museums preserves the many artifacts that explain who Americans are, what they look like, where they came from, and what they are about.

The Smithsonian has been called the nation's attic, but that is a distinct disservice to what it has provided in terms of research and education since its founding in 1846—150 years ago. It never was and never will be a static place, such as an attic might imply, because its founder, James Smithson, in providing the money to create this institution, expressly stated in his will that he wanted "an establishment for the increase and diffusion of knowledge among men."

The Smithsonian's Sesquicentennial, then, provides a wonderful opportunity to look back at its beginning and reflect upon what it has preserved, recorded, and interpreted during these intervening years. This anniversary also provides an opportunity to think back on the year of its founding and try to evoke a portrait of the nation as it existed in 1846.

Bernard DeVoto declared 1846 to be the "Year of Decision" in a book by that title. Indeed, it was a year in which the nation began to move in a new direction, a direction that would eventually produce civil war and the emergence of a transcontinental power of such economic strength that it rivaled the great nations of the world.

The year began, in a manner of speaking, on January 3, 1846, in the House of Representatives during a debate over a dispute with Great Britain concerning the boundary line between the United States and Canada in the far Northwest. Robert C. Winthrop of Boston rose in the House and declared derisively that there was a "new revelation" of the "right" of this nation to spread itself to the Pacific Ocean. "I mean that . . . which has been designated as *the right of our manifest destiny to spread over the continent. . . .* The right of our manifest destiny!"

Manifest Destiny—a doctrine first enunciated just a few months earlier in an essay by John L. O'Sullivan, editor of *The Democratic Review*—was one that many Americans immediately espoused. O'Sullivan argued that the vast stretch of western land reaching to the Pacific Ocean belonged to this country "by right of our manifest destiny to overspread and to possess the whole of the continent which Providence has given us for the development of the great experiment of liberty and federative self-government entrusted to us." God had appointed the American people, according to O'Sullivan, to bring liberty and democratic rule across a wide continent. Imbued with the belief that their experiment in republican self-government should become available to all, Americans echoed this "new spirit of nationalism" around the country, even though it collided with the territorial claims of other countries, most notably Mexico and Great Britain.

As a matter of fact, this imperialistic impulse had already received wide publicity during the presidential election of 1844, when the Democratic Party nominated as their candidate the first "dark horse" in American history, James Knox Polk of Tennessee, on a platform calling for "the reoccupation of Oregon and the reannexation of Texas at the earliest practicable period." "54°40′ or Fight" had been the Democratic rallying cry during the election. These expansionists demanded the entire Oregon country, clear up to the southern border of Alaska. And they believed that Texas was part of the Louisiana Purchase and therefore rightfully belonged to the United States.

In that election, the Whig Party nominated one of this nation's greatest statesmen, Henry Clay of Kentucky, who opposed the annexation of Texas and the occupation of the Oregon territory as likely to lead to war with either Mexico or Britain, or both. In the ensuing election, he went down to ignominious defeat.

In 1846 the nation was obsessed with territorial expansion, despite the external conflict it could cause and despite the internal discord it had already generated over the slavery question. More and more, the leading politicians in the country—such figures as Daniel Webster, John C. Calhoun, Henry Clay, and Thomas Hart Benton—had expressed their views about whether slavery should be restricted to the states where it already existed or allowed to expand into the territories. As the nation rushed westward to possess a continent, the quarrel over this issue stirred fears that it could all culminate in bloody, fratricidal conflict.

Capitalizing on the spirit of Manifest Destiny and the victory of the Democrats at the polls in 1844, President John Tyler, in the closing days of his administration, helped arrange the passage of a joint resolution in Congress by which Texas, having already won its independence from Mexico, was annexed. On December 29, 1845, Texas became the twenty-eighth state to enter the Union. It entered as a slave state.

But President Polk hungered for more than Oregon and Texas. He wanted California, with its magnificent seaports fronting the Pacific Ocean and inviting expanded trade with the Orient. Still, he understood the danger of simultaneously provoking both England and Mexico, so he abandoned his party's extravagant claims to Oregon and agreed with Great Britain that the forty-ninth parallel would separate Canada from the United States in the Northwest. The Senate ratified the treaty on June 15, 1846.

Then, when Mexico again refused to sell California, Polk decided to move American troops stationed along the Nueces River to the Rio Grande, thereby intruding into a kind of no-man's-land separating Texas from Mexico. That action virtually invited Mexican attack, and it came on April 25, 1846. Mexican troops crossed the Rio Grande, ambushed an American scouting party, and killed sixteen men. Polk immediately notified Congress that American blood had been shed on "American soil." In response, both houses promptly voted a declaration of war, which Polk signed on May 13, 1846.

That decision set events in motion that ultimately brought the United States title to a huge territorial expanse. General Zachary Taylor won notable victories at Palo Alto and Buena Vista as he advanced into Mexico from the north, while General Stephen W. Kearny marched westward with 1,700 men from Fort Leavenworth, captured Santa Fe, and drove on to

California, where John C. Frémont and other Americans had raised the Bear Flag and declared California independent of Mexico. General Winfield Scott invaded Mexico from the Gulf of Mexico at Vera Cruz and captured Mexico City in September 1847. In a little more than a year, American forces had annihilated Mexican resistance.

The Treaty of Guadalupe Hidalgo, which ended the war, ceded the territories of California and New Mexico, out of which the present states of California, Nevada, Utah, Arizona, New Mexico, and parts of Wyoming and Colorado were eventually carved. Less than two thousand Americans were killed in battle, but more than twelve thousand died of disease. Both Henry Clay and Daniel Webster, who had opposed the war, lost sons in the conflict. The treaty of peace was ratified by the Senate on March 10, 1848.

The year of decision had initiated a war; it also exacerbated the continuing quarrel between the North and the South as to whether this vast territory would be opened to slavery. On August 8, 1846, David Wilmot, a Democratic congressman from Pennsylvania, introduced an amendment to an appropriations bill, which stated that slavery would never exist in any territory acquired by the United States as a result of the war. The House of Representatives passed this Wilmot Proviso, as it was called, but it died in the Senate. Nevertheless, it continued to be debated and argued over for the next four years, with southerners threatening to secede from the Union if it became law.

However important, the Mexican War and the spirit of Manifest Destiny were only two aspects of life in the United States in 1846. Other impulses shaped the various ways in which Americans behaved and thought. Many of those impulses had roots that extended back several years but were becoming ever more visible, especially to foreign visitors. For example, the continuing growth of democracy, the ongoing evolution of industrialism, an expanding transportation and communication system, the steady rise of the cities, the creative bursts that produced new inventions and great works of literature, plus the fierce desire by Americans to reform social conditions so that they might improve the quality of their lives and the lives of others—all these, and more, presented a picture of such towering energy and enthusiasm that visitors to this country marveled in disbelief.

"The whole continent presents a scene of *scrambling*," commented one visitor, "and roars with greedy hurry. Go ahead! is the order of the day." "Go ahead" is the "real motto of the country," said another. No one could miss it. It vibrated everywhere. "Our age is wholly of a different character from the past," declared Daniel Webster. "Society is full of excitement."

Just so. It had taken the first European settlers to this country more than a hundred and fifty years to move from the sheltering shores of the Atlantic Ocean to the Allegheny Mountains. Now, in their eagerness and excitement, Americans had scampered across three thousand miles in less than thirty years to create their dream—a new society, stretching from ocean to ocean and dedicated to equality and freedom.

Jacquard double-woven coverlet (detail) depicting the United States Capitol as it appeared in 1846. Division of Textiles, National Museum of American History, Smithsonian Institution, Washington, D.C.

That society consisted of more than 20 million people, of whom about 15 percent lived in urban areas. The potato famine in Ireland in 1846 sent thousands of Irish immigrants rushing to America to escape their poverty. They helped swell the population of the cities, operate the factories, build the railroads, and manage the households of wealthy industrialists. Immigration from Scandinavian countries during the 1840s also increased markedly, with the greatest number going to Wisconsin and Minnesota.

Because of the increased labor supply provided through immigration, and because of the great natural resources of the country, like iron, coal, and water power, large-scale industrial growth reached the "take-off" stage of development. The number of corporations increased rapidly in the 1840s, while the number of banks tripled and sent the amount of money in circulation soaring to nearly $100 million. A national banking system for the country had been the subject of intense political dispute since the first administration of George Washington, but on August 6, 1846, Congress passed the Independent Treasury Act, by which government funds were separated from private banks. This legislation remained in effect until 1920, when the Federal Reserve System replaced it.

Increased tariff rates had also sparked numerous political controversies. They even led directly to the threat of secession by South Carolina in 1832–1833. But on July 30, 1846, Congress passed the Walker Tariff, which moderated protection on many items, reducing them to about 25 percent and thereby eliminating one contentious sectional issue.

The transportation revolution of the past twenty-five years had brought roads, bridges, highways, turnpikes, canals, and railroads to many parts of the country, providing a constant flow of people and goods from city to town to rural communities and pumping economic life to all the areas they served. Henry Clay took more than three weeks to reach Washington from his home in Lexington, Kentucky, when he first went to Congress in 1806, using boats, carriages, and horses. By 1846, thanks to the railroad, he could traverse the distance in four days. And the invention of the telegraph by Samuel F. B. Morse in 1844 sparked a communication revolution that continues to this day.

To a very large extent, commented one foreign observer, "the American of the North and Northwest, whose character now sets the tone in the United States, is permanently a man of business." Since the nation was still primarily an agrarian society, that remark did not exclude farmers, many of whom cultivated large tracts of land and shipped their excess produce to the growing cities. Northern farmers produced corn, wheat, dairy products, wool, fruit, and vegetables for urban workers. More and more, they adopted scientific methods of farming and began to adopt large-scale production of cash crops that could be sold in the cities and abroad. In the South, a plantation system, consisting of three million black slaves working alongside a white population of approximately five million—only a fraction of whom owned slaves—produced cotton, corn, wheat, sugar, rice, and tobacco. The production of cotton had spread so rapidly over the preceding forty years that by 1846 nearly two million bales were grown. At the outbreak of the Civil War, the South produced two-thirds of the world's total supply of cotton.

What Americans had achieved since winning independence from Great Britain in encompassing a continent astonished the world. How to explain it? "No one else [but Americans] can conform so easily to new situations and circumstances," declared one foreigner. "Where in Europe young men write poems or novels, in America . . . they invent machines and tools." The American "is a mechanic by nature." As a matter of fact, in 1846 alone, Elias Howe invented the sewing machine, Richard M. Hoe invented the rotary printing press, and Dr. William T. G. Morton first administered ether in a surgical operation. These became part of a long history of American invention, starting with the cotton gin, the cast-iron plow, the smallpox vaccination, the steamboat, the railroad locomotive, the reaper, the revolver, and the vulcanization process for rubber. And even more exciting inventions would come in the latter half of the century.

Many believed that the secret of Americans' success was their firm commitment to the Puritan work ethic. "Work and at eighteen you shall get . . . more than a captain in Europe," wrote one shrewd observer. "You shall live in plenty, be well clothed, well housed, and able to save." From this premise all else followed. "Be attentive to your work, be sober and religious, and you will find a devoted and submissive wife; you will have a more comfortable home than many of the higher classes of Europe. . . . Work, and

1846: Portrait of the Nation

if the fortunes of business should be against you and you fail, you shall soon be able to rise again, for a failure is nothing but a wound in battle."

In 1846 most young American men were earning a living by the age of fifteen. By their early twenties they were expected to have established themselves, married, and started families. "He who is an active and useful member of society," wrote one man, "who contributes his share to augment the national wealth and increase the numbers of the population, he only is looked upon with respect and favor."

These hard-working, energetic Americans of 1846 were also extremely optimistic about their future. They were the product of a romantic age that preached the perfectibility of men and women and their ability to advance "the progress of the whole human race." Alexis de Tocqueville, in his classic work, *Democracy in America*, commented that most Americans of this era believed the philosophical theory "that man is endowed with an indefinite faculty for improvement." Such literary figures as Ralph Waldo Emerson, Margaret Fuller, Henry Thoreau, Orestes Brownson, and others went beyond the simple belief in human perfectibility and goodness and emphasized man's likeness to God. Called Transcendentalists, they contended that men and women, through their intuitive faculties, could "transcend" experience and reason and discover the mysteries of the universe. They looked out at the world and saw the majesty, the wonder, and the beauty of God.

Transcendentalists saw beauty in nature. So, too, did the visual artists of the age. The so-called Hudson River School of landscape painting, led by such great artists as Asher B. Durand, Thomas Cole, George Inness, and others, captured in their works the sublime grandeur of the American landscape. Those works now decorate the walls of every major art museum in the United States. In architecture, the Greek Revival style of the 1820s and 1830s was slowly giving way to a Gothic revival, of which the original Smithsonian Castle building on the Mall is an excellent example.

But Americans saw the rampant ugliness in society as well and felt compelled to do something about it. The impulse to violence and war, the territorial rapaciousness of Manifest Destiny, the abomination of slavery, the materialism and greediness that obsessed those caught up in the Industrial Revolution, the wretched working conditions in many factories, the limited rights of women, and the ghastly living conditions in the slums of the cities, in prison, in asylums, and other institutions horrified many and spurred their efforts at reform. In his famous essay "Man the Reformer," Emerson declared: "What is man born for but to be a Reformer, a Re-Maker of what man has made, a renouncer of lies; a restorer of truth and goodness, imitating that great Nature which embosoms us all?"

So Americans, who fervently believed in volunteerism, formed associations to initiate the reforms that would eradicate slavery; promote women's rights, temperance, and world peace; and improve labor conditions, education, and the treatment of the insane and those in prison—such associations as the American Anti-Slavery Society, the American Temperance Union, the American Peace Society, and many others. The extraordinary number of men and women who volunteered their services to advance these causes, and the talents, determination, and enthusiasm they brought to their work, virtually guaranteed success. And although it took years, decades, and more than a century to convince the rest of the country of the need and importance of some of these reforms, on balance they achieved an extraordinary record of success.

The urgency of many Americans, in every section of the country, to re-shape society came in large measure from their religious beliefs. "It is part of Christian duty," declared one clergyman, to assist those in need and in want. "It becomes Christians to . . . seek the good of those who are careless of their own good." Americans in 1846 were a deeply religious people, and throughout this period church attendance climbed. New religious sects emerged, which founded communities where men and women and their families might pursue their particular creeds without interference or persecution.

The Rappites, led by George Rap, founded New Harmony in Indiana as a settlement for German pietists. It was later purchased by Robert Owen, a humanitarian textile owner in Scotland. The Shakers, founded by Mother Ann Lee, established numerous communities throughout the Northeast and Midwest and are generally credited with inventing the circular saw, the flat (as opposed to the round) broom, the clothespin, and the washing machine. John Humphrey Noyes began a community in Oneida, New York, where the members specialized in manufactured products.

One of the most important new religious sects was the Church of Jesus Christ of Latter-Day Saints, more commonly known as the Mormons, founded by Joseph Smith, called the Prophet by his followers. Born in Vermont and raised in Palmyra, New York, Smith claimed to have supernatural visions. He said he was instructed by the angel Moroni to unearth a book written on golden plates and buried in a stone box. *The Book of Mormon*, published in 1830, purports to account for the lost tribes of Israel. The charismatic Smith gathered a following, organized a religious oligarchy and a cooperative settlement, and led the faithful from New York to Ohio, then Missouri, and finally Nauvoo, Illinois, where some ten thousand persons settled. The hostility of neighboring towns, because of the success of the Mormon community as well as the practice of polygamy by some of the leaders, led to Smith's murder in 1844 by a mob in Carthage, Illinois. The leadership of the church then fell to Brigham Young. To escape mounting persecution and criticism of their beliefs, some fifteen thousand Mormons abandoned their community in Nauvoo and in 1846 followed Young on the long trek across the plains to the Rocky Mountains, which eventually brought them to Salt Lake City, where they established the flourishing Mormon state of Deseret, now Utah.

In 1846 the American world was rapidly expanding in every conceivable direction. It was a world on the verge of economic greatness, and a world on the verge of a calamitous Civil War, a world beset with intractable problems that would haunt later generations.

But there was something special that marked 1846: the Smithsonian. From that date forward, this institution began to record and preserve the past and make available for the edification of the world every facet of American life as its people moved confidently into the future. Today this educational wonder consists of sixteen museums and galleries as well as the National Zoological Park, the largest collection of cultural and scientific artifacts to be found anywhere. It is a triumphant expression of the American spirit and the American Dream. It is a proud presentation of the extraordinary heritage of the American people.

Robert V. Remini
The University of Illinois at Chicago

James Smithson (1765–1829), whose wealth had enabled him to devote his life to chemistry and mineralogy, had, as far as could be determined, no connection with the United States. "So strange is this donation of a half a million of dollars for the noblest of purposes," wrote John Quincy Adams, "that no one thinks of attributing it to a benevolent motive." The American chargé d'affaires in London, recorded Adams, "intimates . . . that the man was supposed to be insane." The English chargé d'affaires in Washington thought that Smithson "must have had republican propensities; which is probable. . . . Why he made this contingent bequest to the United States of America, no one can tell."

James Smithson (detail) by Henri-Joseph Johns (1761–1843), tempera on paperboard, 1816. National Portrait Gallery, Smithsonian Institution, Washington, D.C.; transfer from the Division of Political History, National Museum of American History, Smithsonian Institution

Chapter 1

August 10, 1846

The Twenty-ninth Congress had been in session since December 1845—eight long and contentious months. Texas was admitted to the union by joint resolution; the Oregon boundary was settled by compromise; war began with Mexico; "a tariff of abominations" (according to the Whigs) was passed; an independent treasury was established (to the satisfaction of the Democrats); a harbor and river improvement bill was stopped by presidential veto. "Do what you have to do, gentlemen! and go home to your wives," exhorted Walt Whitman, Democratic editor of the *Brooklyn Eagle*.

On Monday, August 10, Congress hurried to bring its business to a close. "The adjournment was fixed at noon for the convenience of members, many of whom departed in the railway cars for Baltimore at that hour," recorded Massachusetts representative John Quincy Adams. "The day, like all the last days of a session of Congress, was a chaos of confusion." President James K. Polk stood by in the Capitol ready to sign any bills that might be passed. Signed into law on that day was the act establishing the Smithsonian Institution.

"The most gratifying act of the whole of the session was the unexpected passage of the Smithsonian Institution bill," reported the *New York Evening Post*. It had been a very long time in coming. A decade had passed since Congress, over the protests of some, had voted to accept James Smithson's half-million-dollar bequest to establish an institution in Washington for the "increase and diffusion of knowledge among men."

———

James Smithson, the illegitimate son of the first Duke of Northumberland, died in 1829, leaving his estate, if his nephew died without heirs, to the United States government. This occurred in 1835, and President Andrew Jackson, claiming that the Chief Executive had no authority to act in the matter, turned it over to Congress.

South Carolina Senator John C. Calhoun had immediately dismissed the bequest on constitutional grounds. If Congress accepted this fund, said the state's other senator, William C. Preston, "every whippersnapper vagabond that had been traducing our country might think proper to have his name distinguished in the same way. It was not consistent with the dignity of the country."

Richard Rush, who had been secretary of state to James Monroe and secretary of the treasury to John Quincy Adams, was sent to England in July 1836 to see the matter through Chancery. Two years later, on September 1, 1838, Rush returned with the then-enormous sum of $515,169 in gold.

No one took a greater interest in the Smithson bequest than John Quincy Adams, who became the conscience for the fund. To his complete disgust, the money was taken from the Treasury and invested in bonds of Michigan and Arkansas, which were soon in default. "The chief obstacle," Adams wrote in his diary, "will now be to extricate the funds from the fangs of the State of Arkansas."

On December 7, 1838, Adams was appointed chairman of a House select committee on the bequest, and he proceeded "with a heavy heart, from a presentiment that this noble and most munificent donation will be filtered to nothing, and wasted upon hungry and worthless political jackals."

But then the question remained for Adams and the committee: How should the money be used to "increase and diffuse knowledge"? The committee received support for establishing an institution to carry on experiments in physical sciences and several more to establish an agricultural institution or farm school, as well as a petition asking that the fund be applied to the instruction of women. Most of the communications, Adams noted, "contemplated Institutes for education and the expenditure of the Capital

Draft of a portion of James Smithson's will, in his own hand. Smithsonian Institution Archives, Washington, D.C.

I James Smithson son to Hugh first Duke of Northumberland & Elizabeth heiress of the Hungerfords of Studley & niece of Charles the Proud Duke of Somerset now residing in Bentinck Street Cavendish Square, do this twenty third day of October one thousand eight hundred & twenty six, make this my last will and Testament. I bequeath the whole of my property of every nature & kind soever to my bankers Messrs Drummonds, of Charing-cross, in trust, to be disposed of in the following manner; and I desire of my said executors to put my property under the management of the court of Chancery.

To John Fitall formerly my servant, but now employed in the London docks and residing at No 27 Jubilee Place North mile End old town, in consideration of his attachment and fidelity to me & the long and great care he has taken of my effects & my having done but very little for him I give and bequeath the annuity or annual sum of one hundred pounds Sterling for his life to be payed to him quarterly free of legacy duty and all other deductions the first payment to be made to him

at the expiration of three months after my death.

I have at diverse times lent sums of money to Henry Honoré Sailly formerly my servant but now keeping the Hungerford Hotel in the rue Caumartin at Paris & for which sums of money, I have undated bills or bonds signed by him, now I will and direct that if he desires it these sums of money be let remain in his hands at an interest of five per cent for five years after the date of the present will.

To Henry James Hungerford my nephew, heretofore called Henry James Dickinson, son to my late brother Lieutenant Colonel Henry Louis Dickinson, now residing with Mr Auboin at Bourg la Reine near Paris, I give and bequeath for his life the whole of the income arising from my property, of every nature and kind whatever, after the payment of the above annuity, & after the death of John Fitall that annuity likewise, the payments to be made to him at the time of the interests or dividends become due on the stocks or other property from which their income arises X turn the next!

Should the said Henry James Hungerford have a child or children, legitimate or illegitimate, I leave to such child or children his or their heirs, executors & assigns, after the death of his, or her or their father, the whole of my property of every kind, absolutely and for ever to be divided between them, if there is more than one, in the manner their father shall judge proper, or in case of his omitting to decide this, as the Lord Chancellor shall judge proper. Should my said nephew Henry James Hungerford marry, I empower him to make a jointure.

In the case of the death of my said nephew without leaving a child or children, or of the death of the child or children he may have had under the age of twentyone years, or intestate, I then bequeath the whole of my property, subject to the annuity of one hundred pounds to John Fitall and for the security and payment of which I mean stock to remain in this country, to the united states of america, to found at X

Washington, under the name to the Smithsonian institution, an establishment for the increase & diffusion of knowledge among men.

I think proper here to state that all the money which will be standing in the French five per cents, at my death in the names of the father of my above mentioned nephew, Henry James Hungerford & all that in my names, is the property of my said nephew, being what he inherited from his father, or what I have laid up for him from the saving upon his income.

James Smithson

In February 1846 John Quincy Adams (1767–1848) posed for Moses Billings, a portrait painter from Erie, Pennsylvania, whose congressman had secured him the use of a committee room at the Capitol for the sitting.

That month Adams was much engaged in committee meetings about the Smithsonian bequest, and he held two principles uppermost in his mind: the protection of the fund's capital and the stipulation that no part of the money be applied "for the endowment of any school, college, university, institution of education or ecclesiastical establishment." Adams stood firm that Smithson's "express purpose" was "not the education of children or of youth, but the increase *and diffusion of knowledge among men."*

John Quincy Adams by Moses Billings (1809–1884), oil on canvas, 1846. Thiel College, Greenville, Pennsylvania

fund, instead of annual appropriations from the accrueing income." Adams himself believed that the best use of Smithson's money would be to establish an astronomical observatory, with salaries provided for an astronomer and an assistant.

In 1839, as chairman of a joint congressional committee, Adams won agreement that the first appropriation from the Smithson funds—but not all of the money—should be used for an observatory. Since the letter and spirit of Smithson's bequest embraced "the improvement of all the arts and sciences," Adams was willing to also consider proposals for "a botanical garden, a cabinet of natural history, a museum of mineralogy, conchology, or geology, a general accumulating library." Even though James Smithson's personal preference may have been for natural sciences, no branch of human knowledge was to be excluded.

But what Adams would not consider was retiring Rhode Island Senator Asher Robbins's "mean and selfish" plan "to found a university," with Robbins himself as its president. When the Senate adopted this scheme, Adams angrily protested, saying that it superseded all of the House of Representatives' work and that such an institution would not only absorb the entire fund but would also call for a large appropriation of public money to keep it going. Several meetings of the joint committee failed to resolve the conflict between the observatory and the university. With no concurrence possible, separate bills were prepared; nothing came of either of them.

In the Senate, the task of wrestling with the Smithsonian bequest had been assigned to the Library Committee, where Benjamin Tappan of Ohio took the lead in drafting a bill. Tappan, the son of a Northampton, Massachusetts, goldsmith, had gone from being an aspiring artist to being a frontier lawyer and was an enthusiastic Jacksonian Democrat, as well as a collector of geological specimens. Also on the committee was Rufus

In August 1846 proofs of an engraving of the United States Senate, offered for sale at $10 a copy by Anthony, Clark and Company of New York, were placed on view in the lobby of the Senate and the House of Representatives. Nearly four years in the making, the picture was a composite of daguerreotypes taken over the past three sessions of Congress especially for the purpose. "It marks an era in American art, and reflects the highest credit upon every one connected with its production," pronounced the Washington National Intelligencer. "In delicacy and strength this engraving rivals the finest mezzotints of Europe, while its size and in number of accurate likenesses it has never been equalled."

United States Senate Chamber by Thomas Doney (active 1844–1870s), after James A. Whitehorne, after daguerreotypes by Victor Piard at Anthony, Clark and Company, mezzotint and etching, 1846. National Portrait Gallery, Smithsonian Institution, Washington, D.C.

"Does not the whole history of civilization concur to declare that a various and ample library is one of the surest, most constant, most permanent, and most economical instrumentalities to increase and diffuse knowledge?" asked Rufus Choate (1799–1859) in the debate over the Smithsonian bequest. "There this would be—durable as liberty, durable as the Union, a vast storehouse, a vast treasury, of all the facts which make up the history of man and nature."

Choate retired from political office at the close of his Senate term in 1845, but accepted appointment to the Smithsonian's first Board of Regents.

Rufus Choate attributed to Henry Willard (1802–1855) or William Willard (1819–1904), oil on canvas, not dated. National Portrait Gallery, Smithsonian Institution, Washington, D.C.; on loan from the University of Michigan Museum of Art, Ann Arbor; bequest of Henry C. Lewis, 1895.45

Choate, a descendant of the Puritans, a founder of the Whig Party of Massachusetts, and a man who had found in the legal profession a consuming passion exceeded only by his appetite for books—his library numbered eight thousand volumes. Tappan and Choate would prove to have very different ideas about how best to "increase and diffuse knowledge."

Tappan's bill, introduced on December 12, 1844, provided for a building "of plain and durable materials and structure without unnecessary ornament, and of sufficient size and with suitable rooms for the reception and arrangement of objects of natural history, a chemical laboratory, and lecture room or rooms." Allowance was made for taking ten acres out of the public ground called the Mall for horticultural and agricultural experiments. A twelve-member Board of Managers, appointed by joint congressional resolution, would oversee an institution for the teaching of natural history, chemistry, astronomy, and such other fields "as the wants of science may require."

In the debate on the bill, Choate noted that Tappan's program would result in "a pretty energetic diffusing of the fund; not much diffusion of knowledge." Choate instead proposed a program of lectures by visiting luminaries in science and literature, to be held during sessions of Congress for the benefit of an audience of public men of mature years and first-rate minds. The cost for this would be less than $5,000 a year, and the rest of the money would be spent "accumulating a grand and noble public library; one which, for variety, extent and wealth, shall be, equal to any now in the world." Choate suggested a $20,000 annual expenditure for purchasing books and manuscripts. Tappan agreed to add the library provision onto his bill, even though the expenditure of much of the bequest's accrued interest for books would leave little money for carrying out his own proposals.

Tappan's bill, topped by Choate's library requirement, passed the Senate on January 21, 1845, and was the first bill on the Smithsonian bequest to pass either branch of Congress. It was also the swan song for Tappan and Choate, both of whom were retiring from Congress at the close of the Twenty-eighth Congress in March. When this bill reached the House of Representatives, Indiana Democrat Robert Dale Owen moved to add a teacher-training provision, "an absurd amendment," thought John Quincy Adams as he succeeded in tabling the bill.

Owen's interest in the Smithsonian bequest was probably kindled by his visionary father, who was full of schemes for improving the world. The senior Owen had previously approached Adams with a proposition "for universal education, for which the Smithsonian Fund may provide the means."

The younger Owen was determined to bring the Smithsonian matter to resolution during the Twenty-ninth Congress. Owen's bill, he declared to Tappan, was "your child, which I have merely had taken to have dressed & decorated a little." Owen had added a provision for a normal school, which he knew would meet with Tappan's approval. To mollify John Quincy Adams, he named astronomy *as one of the branches to be taught, and, in the description of the building, have specified "a tower suitable for astronomical observations." If the old man is not satisfied with that, we shall have to carry it over his head; which I don't doubt but that we can do.* It turned out that Adams was satisfied with the recent establishment of an astronomical observatory in Washington under the direction of the navy; he would, however, raise other objections to Owen's bill.

As soon as the Twenty-ninth Congress convened, Robert Dale Owen gave notice of the bill to establish the Smithsonian Institution. His bill was read on December 19 and referred to a select committee, of which he was chairman. The Philadelphia *North American* was skeptical, observing that his bill was "the wildest and strangest of all, being no less than a project of converting the Smithsonian Institution into a college to train up *Common-School Teachers*, with a sort of *model* farm *annexed*." On February 28, 1846, Owen asked that the Smithsonian bill be

"The House of Representatives is a beautiful and spacious hall, of semi-circular shape, supported by handsome pillars," wrote Charles Dickens, who visited Washington in 1842. "The chair is canopied, and raised considerably above the floor of the House; and every member has an easy chair and a writing desk to himself; which is denounced by some people out of doors as a most unfortunate and injudicious arrangement, tending to long sittings and prosaic speeches. It is an elegant chamber to look at, but a singularly bad one for all purposes of hearing."

The House of Representatives *by Thomas Mann Baynes (1794–1854) after a sketch by E. T. Coke, lithograph, circa 1832. Architect of the Capitol Collection, Prints and Photographs Division, Library of Congress, Washington, D.C.*

Robert Dale Owen (1801–1877), the "Scotch atheist" or the "Scotch infidel from Lanark" as John Quincy Adams variously referred to him, had come from New Lanark, Scotland, in 1825, with his father Robert Owen to set up a communal colony in New Harmony, Indiana. The experiment fell apart by 1827, and the younger Owen gravitated to New York, where he was involved with publishing a freethinking newspaper and anticlerical tracts. In 1830 Owen published Moral Physiology; or, a Brief and Plain Treatise on the Population Question, which contained practical advice on contraception. Advertisements for the tract in 1846 proclaimed, "Were this book carefully read by every married person, and its advice strictly followed, we are persuaded that a different state of society from the present would exist." Owen returned to New Harmony in 1833, served in the state legislature, and was elected to Congress as a Democrat in 1843.

When it came to the drafting of the Smithsonian bill, no section was closer to Owen's heart than that providing for a teacher-training institution.

Robert Dale Owen by an unidentified photographer, daguerreotype, circa 1847. National Portrait Gallery, Smithsonian Institution, Washington, D.C.; gift of Andrew Oliver

brought before Congress on the second Tuesday in April. Debate began in the Committee of the Whole House on April 22.

George W. Jones, a Democrat from Tennessee and a strict constructionist of the Constitution, in an attempt to reverse the decision to accept the bequest, stood up to say that he would vote to return the money to the English Chancery. Owen replied that although he did not share Jones's constitutional objections, he, too, would vote to send the money back if action was delayed much longer.

Alexander Sims of South Carolina "opposed the bill in every shape and form it could assume." He asked Adams "by what power Congress [is] authorized to accept and administer this fund." Adams countered that if Sims would "point me to the power in the Constitution *to annex Texas* I will answer his question." By a vote of 123 to 8, the House of Representatives declined to return the money.

Ironically, John Quincy Adams, for so long the great champion of the Smithsonian bequest, tried to postpone the whole matter indefinitely when he offered an amendment that accepted in principle the establishment of the Smithsonian Institution, but denied any appropriation until Arkansas and Michigan made payment on their defaulted securities. Democrat Hannibal Hamlin of Maine countered that "the money should properly be considered as in the Treasury, and if it was not there the Government was bound for it, principal and interest." Adams's amendment was defeated on a vote of 74 to 57.

In an hour-long speech emphasizing the provision for the normal school, Robert Dale Owen declared, "I hold it to be a democratic duty to elevate, to the utmost of our ability, the character of our common-school instruction. I hold this to be a far higher and holier duty than to give additional depth to learned studies, or supply curious authorities to antiquarian research."

Adams, holding to his contention that "increase of Knowledge should be by new discovery" and not by common education, protested that there was nothing more remote from James Smithson's intent than "the communication of knowledge already possessed." He would rather see "the whole money thrown into the Potomac than to appropriate one dollar for that purpose."

Vermont Whig George Perkins Marsh, a close friend of Rufus Choate since their days together at Dartmouth, suggested that for a reasonable period of time the entire income should be used for a great library. Owen protested, "In the first place Smithson's own pursuits were scientific, not antiquarian. In the second, had he desired to merely found a library it is reasonable to suppose he would have said so."

But Adams warmly embraced Marsh's proposal on the library, no doubt motivated by his opposition to the normal school, which he succeeded in striking out on a vote of 72 to 42. Owen attempted to recoup by inserting a provision calling for professors in science and arts to educate teachers in the useful sciences, and allowing for the printing and circulation of elementary works for the promotion of education. His amendments were rejected. "So, it was settled that the institution should have nothing to do with instruction," reported the *New York Tribune*.

On April 28, as debate on the Smithsonian bill resumed, William J. Hough, a first-term Democrat from the Oswego district of New York, offered a substitute for the entire bill. It retained the lectures, the publication of popular tracts, prize essays, and other aids to education—and the encouragement of scientific research generally—but omitted the teaching establishment.

But before the substitute bill could be passed, up rose George Perkins Marsh to eliminate all of Hough's programs and increase the library appropriation to $25,000. The apparent effect of Marsh's amendments was to give complete victory to the library men. John Quincy Adams thought as much, recording on April 29, the day the House passed Hough's bill with Marsh's amendments, "Thus nearly the whole proceeds of the Bequest are devoted to the annual accumulation of a great National Public Library. The best disposal of the Fund, which it has been practicable to obtain." The final vote was 85 to 75, with more than a quarter of the House not voting. Of the forty-two congressmen from the Deep South, all but six voted against the bill, reflecting John Quincy Adams's prediction that John C. Calhoun's mentality "will be persisted in by the South Carolina school of politics and morals to the last, without any idea of returning the money, but with the purpose of defeating any useful application of it."

There was no sign that the Senate intended to take up the Smithsonian bill. Massachusetts lawyer and man of letters George S. Hillard, speaking before the American Unitarian Association in May, declared, "In a moment Congress votes millions of money to carry on this wicked and most unchristian war [with Mexico], but how slowly does a measure, which has for its object the diffusion of truth [to] men, toil and lag through that body!"

As the August recess approached and no action had been taken by the Senate, the *New York Post*'s Washington correspondent reported that it was feared the Senate did not intend to pass any bill regarding the Smithsonian bequest. "If they do not, then a blasting, burning shame upon the country will be perpetuated. The manner in which that bequest has been so far treated is a national disgrace, as utterly dishonorable to the country as an open, bare-faced swindle."

Robert Dale Owen had given up hope that the Senate would take up the Smithsonian bill, but spurred on by a letter from his father, he made a final attempt to rally support in the upper house. When the Senate gathered on August 10, Maine Whig George Evans proposed the Smithsonian bill as the first order of business, and "in a few well directed and effective words, urged its passage without amendment." Democrat John Adams Dix of New York promptly seconded him, and the bill passed without debate on a vote of 26 to 13—with John C. Calhoun and Thomas Hart Benton among those voting no. President James K. Polk immediately signed the bill.

"The great object is achieved in getting the ball started," observed the *New York Herald*'s James Gordon Bennett. But what in reality was the Smithsonian Institution to be? Before 1846 had ended, some answers were forthcoming.

29th Congress. Begun and held at the city of Washington in the District
1st Session of Columbia, on Monday, the first day of December, eighteen hundred and forty-five.

An Act to establish the "Smithsonian Institution" for the increase and diffusion of knowledge among men.

James Smithson, esquire, of London, in the kingdom of Great Britain, having by his last will and testament, given the whole of his property to the United States of America to found at Washington, under the name of the "Smithsonian Institution," an establishment for the increase and diffusion of knowledge among men; and the United States having, by an act of Congress, received said property, and accepted said trust:

Therefore,
For the faithful execution of said trust according to the will of the liberal and enlightened donor;

Be it Enacted
By the Senate and House of Representatives of the United States of America in Congress Assembled.

That, the President and Vice President of the United States, the Secretary of State, the Secretary of the Treasury, the Secretary of War, the Secretary of the Navy, the Postmaster General, the Attorney General, the Chief Justice, and the Commissioner of the Patent Office of the United States, and the mayor of the city of Washington, during the time for which they shall hold their respective offices, and such other persons as they may elect honorary members, be and they are hereby constituted an "establishment," by the name of the "Smithsonian Institution" for the increase and diffusion of knowledge among men; and by that name shall be known and have perpetual succession, with the powers, limitations, and restrictions hereinafter contained, and no other.

An Act to Establish the Smithsonian
Institution, August 10, 1846. National
Archives, Washington, D.C.

Sec. 9. And be it further enacted, That of any other moneys which have accrued, or shall hereafter accrue, as interest upon the said Smithsonian fund, not herein appropriated, or not required for the purposes herein provided, the said managers are hereby authorized to make such disposal as they shall deem best suited for the promotion of the purpose of the testator, any thing herein contained to the contrary notwithstanding.

Sec. 10. And be it further enacted, That the author or proprietor of any book, map, chart, musical composition, print, cut, or engraving, for which a copy=right shall be secured under the existing acts of Congress, or those which shall hereafter be enacted respecting copy=rights, shall, within three months from the publication of said book, map, chart, musical composition, print, cut, or engraving, deliver or cause to be delivered one copy of the same to the Librarian of the Smithsonian institution, and one copy to the Librarian of Congress Library for the use of the said Libraries.

Sec. 11. And be it further enacted, That there is reserved to Congress the right of altering, amending, adding to or repealing any of the provisions of this act. Provided, That no contract, or individual right, made or acquired under such provisions, shall be thereby divested or impaired.

John W Davis   Speaker of the House of Representatives

David R Atchison   President of the Senate Pro tempore.

Approved August 10. 1846

James K Polk

Although burdened with the duties of his office and plagued daily by a procession of office-seekers, President James K. Polk (1795–1849) devoted an astonishing amount of time to sitting for George Peter Alexander Healy, who had been commissioned by King Louis-Philippe of France to paint the portraits of American statesmen. Polk agreed to pose at the behest of

his old Tennessee friend, Supreme Court Justice John Catron. The President sat for about two hours a session on seven occasions, grumbling constantly that he "could but illy spare the time" and declaring over and over again, "I think it is the last sitting for my portrait which I will submit to during a Session of Congress." Healy finished the portrait on February 9. "I am

heartily rejoiced at it," Polk recorded, but at the end of the month he submitted to eight more sittings, so that the artist might retain his own copy. Healy's first portrait of Polk is on exhibition here.

James K. Polk (detail) by George Peter Alexander Healy (1813–1894), oil on canvas, 1846. James K. Polk Memorial Association, Columbia, Tennessee

Chapter 2

President Polk's Washington

Washington on New Year's Day 1846 was unusually fair for the season. According to custom, President James K. Polk received "ladies and gentlemen, and persons of all ages and sexes, without distinction of rank or condition in life." A thousand or more streamed through the East Room to shake the President's hand and then walked across Lafayette Park to pay respects to the venerable but still buoyant former first lady, Dolley Madison. On F Street, near the Executive Mansion, former President John Quincy Adams—the "Old Man Eloquent" of the House of Representatives—recorded that a considerable portion of those who called on him were "members of Congress, among which a small number are of politics opposite to mine." In July Adams would turn eighty and, drawn by irresistible impulse, he took a swim at his old bathing spot on the banks of the Potomac.

The Twenty-ninth Congress, which had convened in December, was heavily Democratic, but Democratic President James K. Polk would not have an easy year of it. Polk, the first dark-horse candidate in American history, was derided by the Whigs (the political party born out of opposition to Democrat Andrew Jackson) as an "accidental president." A former Speaker of the House of Representatives, Polk had

Educated at the respected Moravian Academy in Salem, North Carolina, Sarah Childress Polk (1803–1889) was a charming conversationalist. Antislavery Whig Charles Sumner, on a visit from Boston in early April, although completely out of sympathy with the Democratic Polk administration, wrote upon his return home, "Among the pleasant recollections of Washington is Mrs Polk, whose sweetness of manner, won me entirely."

A pious Presbyterian, Sarah Polk frowned upon frivolous amusements, among which she included the popular pastime of dancing. But despite the effects of the temperance movement across the country, wine had not been banished from the President's table. "The glassware was very handsome," noted one White House dinner guest, "blue and white finely cut, and pink champagne, gold sherry, green hock, madeira, the ruby port, and sauterne, formed a rainbow around each plate."

Sarah Childress Polk by George Peter Alexander Healy (1813–1894), oil on canvas, 1846. James K. Polk Memorial Association, Columbia, Tennessee

won nomination—over the hopes of former President Martin Van Buren—at the 1844 Democratic convention. His victory over Whig candidate Henry Clay was in great part due to the small, antislavery Liberty Party, which drew off enough votes to cost the Whigs the state of New York.

Polk came to the presidency with certain objectives—the resolution of the United States claim to Oregon, where some five thousand American citizens had already settled; the acquisition of California; and reduction in the protective tariff of 1842. A determined man without a trace of humor, Polk seemed bent on working himself to death. Pledged to serve but one term in office, he lived with the suspicion that he was surrounded by those who would like to become President.

Every Tuesday and Friday evening, the President received visitors informally in the parlor from 8:00 until 11:00 or 12:00, while the Marine band played in the outer hall. He found these occasions to be very agreeable, but most important, they made it possible for him to devote the remaining evenings to business. Polk's sole indulgence was a walk around the President's square every morning shortly after sunrise and every evening about sunset.

By her husband's side, as she had been throughout his political career, was Sarah Childress Polk. Varina Davis, the twenty-year-old wife of Democratic Congressman Jefferson Davis of Mississippi, reporting on her first dinner at the Executive Mansion, wrote: "Mrs. P. came up dressed to death—she is a very handsome woman is too entertaining for my liking—talks too much a la Presidents wife—is to anxious to please. Polk is an insignificant looking little man. I don't like his manners or any thing else—we had about fifty courses it seemed to me."

The Davises did not go often to the White House, Varina recalled, because their boarding house on Capitol Hill was too distant for walking; they did not keep a carriage, and "a livery carriage meant $1.50 an hour." Mrs. Davis's fondest memory was of intimate parties at the Coast Survey, "a large old-fashioned barrack of a house, on the edge of Capitol hill, overlooking Pennsylvania Avenue." Here Professor Alexander Dallas Bache, head of the Coast Survey, gathered a convivial circle that included his brother-in-law, Treasury Secretary Robert Walker, and Jefferson Davis—a trio given to trading reminiscences of their West Point days. "About nine

The Polks posed with Dolley Madison, Secretary of State James Buchanan (extreme left) with his niece Harriet Lane, Postmaster General Cave Johnson (fourth from left), and Secretary of the Treasury Robert Walker (between President and Mrs. Polk). The young woman next to Mrs. Polk was probably one of the nieces who were very often at the White House.

By an unidentified photographer, daguerreotype (detail), circa 1845–1846. George Eastman House, Rochester, New York

1846: Portrait of the Nation

"In the midst of a large open square, on a piece of high ground overlooking the Potomac, though about a quarter of a mile back from it, is the President's House, or the 'White House,' as it is more generally called," noted Scottish visitor Alexander Mackay. "It is a spacious and elegant mansion, surrounded by soft sloping lawns, shaded by lofty trees and dotted with shrubbery."

The President's House by John Plumbe Jr. (1809–1857), daguerreotype, 1846. Prints and Photographs Division, Library of Congress, Washington, D.C.

An 1828 graduate of West Point, Jefferson Davis (1808–1889) served in the regular army for seven years before he resigned in 1835 to marry—against her father's wishes—the daughter of his commanding officer, Colonel Zachary Taylor. The couple took up life on a Mississippi plantation, but within three months Sara Knox Taylor was dead of malaria. In 1846, after Davis left Congress to assume command of the First Mississippi Regiment, his former father-in-law wrote to him, "I can assure you I am more than anxious to take you by the hand, & to have you & your command with or near me."

Davis, who had served on the select committee to consider the Smithsonian bequest, was named a regent of the Smithsonian Institution in December 1847 and reappointed in 1851.

Jefferson Davis by George Lethbridge Saunders (1807–1863), watercolor on ivory, 1849. National Portrait Gallery, Smithsonian Institution, Washington, D.C.; gift of Joel A. H. Webb and Varina Webb Stewart

o'clock we were ushered pell-mell into a long, unfurnished room," Mrs. Davis wrote, "the walls of which were hung everywhere with scientific instruments . . . old telescopes, with all the paraphernalia of adjuncts to scientific investigation; and, in the middle of the room was a great table laden with everything good and appetizing that Washington could furnish." Terrapins and canvasback ducks were "in profusion. The perfume of the long-necked bottle of Rhine wine filled the room, which the Professor opened himself, there being no servants present, and the gentlemen pledged us and each other in a glass, and the quip and jest flew from one to another."

Another who enjoyed Bache's hospitality was his fellow scientist Joseph Henry, a professor at Princeton, who at Bache's request came to Washington in July for consultation on field work concerning the Chesapeake and the Delaware Bay. Henry looked around the Capitol and wrote home, as

Married in February 1845 to widower Jefferson Davis, who was eighteen years her senior, Varina Howell (1826–1906) was almost immediately introduced to public life when her husband was elected to Congress from Mississippi. Traveling to Washington in December, the Davises had a horrendous journey by steamboat, sled, and stagecoach—"three weeks of peril, discomfort, and intense cold," Varina wrote, "during which we were obliged to eat our life-long supply of worst with maple syrup for a condiment." They took rooms in a boarding house on Pennsylvania Avenue, where they ate their meals with others of like political persuasion. Mrs. Davis later recounted that she was kept busy assisting her husband in his correspondence with his constituents.

🖤 *Varina Howell Davis by John Wood Dodge (1807–1893), watercolor on ivory, 1849. National Portrait Gallery, Smithsonian Institution, Washington, D.C.; gift of Varina Webb Stewart*

"The front of the Capitol was turned to the east; but the town having taken the contrary direction, the legislative palace has the appearance of turning its back upon it," wrote Scottish barrister Alexander Mackay, who was visiting Washington in 1846. "But notwithstanding this, it has a most imposing effect, rising, as it does, in classic elegance from its lofty site, over the greensward and rich embowering foliage of the low grounds at its base."

🖤 *East Front of the Capitol by John Plumbe Jr. (1809–1857), daguerreotype, 1846. Prints and Photographs Division, Library of Congress, Washington, D.C.*

most visitors did, about Horatio Greenough's twenty-ton statue of George Washington, commissioned for the Rotunda but now residing on the east lawn and protected by a kind of hut. "It is an immensely large figure of blueish marble in a sitting posture delivering up a sword," Henry told his wife. "It is naked to the waist and does not strike one favourably at first although the impression becomes greater and the effect better the longer you gaze on it." The statue had been the subject of much attention, mostly ridicule, since its arrival from Italy in 1843. "The most abominable thing I have seen in Washington is the statue of Washington," Varina Davis scoffed. It "is sitting on a high pedestal, half naked with a little roman (potatoe masher Col Roberts says) broad sword in his hand—it is the most ridiculous looking thing I ever saw."

Mrs. Davis was eager to take in all the sights of Washington and to share her experiences with her family in Mississippi. "We went down to-day,"

The General Post Office, assessed Alexander Mackay, was "the choicest architectural bijou in Washington, being a neat classic structure built of white marble. . . . Its beauties are, however, almost lost from defect of site."

The two pairs of wires visible in the upper left are probably from the house on Pennsylvania Avenue at Sixth Street,

where Samuel F. B. Morse's telegraph office was located.

✺ *The General Post Office from the corner of Seventh and E Streets by John Plumbe Jr. (1809–1857), daguerreotype, 1846. Prints and Photographs Division, Library of Congress, Washington, D.C.*

In 1846 Samuel F. B. Morse (1791–1872) had the satisfaction of seeing telegraph lines pushed forward in all directions. "All physical and scientific difficulties are vanquished," he wrote in October. "Washington, Baltimore, Philadelphia, Harrisburg, New York, New Haven, Hartford, Springfield, Boston, Albany, Troy, Utica, Auburn, Rochester, Syracuse, and Buffalo are now in communication with each other," exulted the National Intelligencer, *"and for business purposes, all these cities are formed into one great community, holding instantaneous correspondence with each other."*

Horatio Greenough executed what he pronounced "an excellent likeness" of his fellow artist when Morse was in Italy, preparing himself to produce a great historical canvas for the Capitol Rotunda, a commission he would never receive.

✺ *Samuel F. B. Morse by Horatio Greenough (1805–1852), marble, 1831. National Museum of American Art, Smithsonian Institution, Washington, D.C.; gift of Edward L. Morse*

she related, "to see Mr. Morse's machine make the wires talk, and repeat messages from one town to another." Samuel F. B. Morse's telegraph office was on Pennsylvania Avenue at Sixth Street, and Varina noted, *There are small wires stretched from Baltimore to this place, and they are brought into the windows of a house on the Avenue. Inside of a little stall a man sits and sends messages and receives the answers. I think it is a trick, but paid my two-bits to get a message "that it was a fine day."*

At the Capitol, young Eastman Johnson, just getting his start as an artist, was given the use of a committee room. He recounted that Dolley Madison "wandered in of her own account and I asked her to let me make a sketch of her to which she easily assented." Another who posed for Johnson was eighty-nine-year-old Elizabeth Schuyler Hamilton, who was in

Elizabeth Schuyler Hamilton (1757–
1854) "is one of the most interesting
women, perhaps in America," wrote Walt
Whitman. "So old—connected to the men
and things of a past age—Mrs. H. seems
to us one of the characters of what may be
called a beginning to American history."
On the forty-second anniversary of the
death of her husband, Alexander Hamilton, the bill for the acquisition of his papers passed the Senate, but was subsequently lost in the rush to adjournment.

Elizabeth Schuyler Hamilton (detail)
by Eastman Johnson (1842–1906), crayon on
paper, 1846. The New-York Historical Society, New York City

Dolley Madison (1768–1849) was a favorite with the Polks and almost everyone
else in Washington. Present at a "brilliant
soiree at the White House" on January
21, 1846, Madison "enjoyed the fete with
all the buoyancy of youth; she talked for
hours with her friends and appeared to
relish a hearty laugh as well as a lass of
eighteen. She walked amongst the throng
supported on the President's arm for a
long time, and without any apparent ex-
haustion."

The remarkable widow of ex-President
Madison, the Philadelphia Evening
News informed its readers, "is one of the
persons most visited by strangers in Washington, and those who visit her are always
deeply impressed with her agreeable manners, her wonderful memory, and her dignified bearing." She was described by one
who saw her during the spring of 1846 as
"a tall, dignified woman, with a full face,
blue eyes and somewhat florid complexion,
and is apparently over seventy years of
age. Her dress was black, and in a style
that comported well with her years; and
upon her head she wore a white turban."

Dolley Payne Madison by William S.
Elwell (1810–1881), oil on canvas, 1848.
National Portrait Gallery, Smithsonian
Institution, Washington, D.C.

the process of petitioning Congress for help in publishing the works of her husband, Alexander Hamilton, with the idea of presenting the manuscripts to the government when the task was completed. "The intended publication will be the pride of her old age, as her distinguished husband was of her earlier years," editorialized Cornelia Walter of the *Boston Evening Transcript*, "and she justly may regard it as a monument to his enlightened patriotism and elevated system of national policy." With the tariff-reduction bill just then under consideration, the New England editor pointed out that Hamilton had been "a strenuous advocate for protection to commerce, encouragement to manufactures and improvement in agriculture, and for all other measures in accordance with the expansive destinies of the United States."

———

"At best, Washington is but a small town, a fourth-rate community as to extent, even in America," assessed Alexander Mackay, a Scottish barrister and journalist who spent several months in the city. "When Congress is not sitting, it is dull and insipid to a degree, its periodical excitements disappearing with the bulk of its population." When Congress was in session, *what a motley heterogeneous assemblage does Washington then contain! . . . the semi-savage 'Far Western,' the burly backwoodsman, the enterprizing New-Englander, the genuine Sam Slick, the polished Bostonian, the adventurous New Yorker, the staid and prim Philadelphian, the princely merchant from the seaboard, the wealthy manufacturer, the energetic farmer, and the languid but uncertain planter.*

Most members of Congress lived in hotels and boarding houses, although about 19 of the 56 senators and 71 of the 230 members of the House of Representatives had their families with them. A few, such as Whig Senator Daniel Webster of Massachusetts and Democratic Senator Thomas Hart Benton of Missouri, had taken houses.

Webster, according to New York Whig Philip Hone, "lives pleasantly in one of the back streets, in his own house as a gentleman should . . . where a bottle of cool wine, strawberries, a quiet house, and most agreeable conversation awaited us." Webster's lifestyle was made possible by an annuity set up for his benefit by Boston Whigs. Webster suggested that a similar arrangement might be made to alleviate the poverty of his dear friend Dolley Madison, but upon learning of this plan, Madison put a stop to it.

Thomas Hart Benton, dubbed by John Quincy Adams "the doughty knight of the stuffed cravat," lived in a house on C Street near the Capitol,

"From morning till night the bar rooms of the hotels are full; the bar, indeed, being the chief source of the hotel-keepers' revenue," observed Scottish visitor Alexander Mackay. "Amongst those who frequent them is generally to be found a large sprinkling of members of Congress." Mackay related that a subscription had been raised for the purpose of presenting two silver cups "to one of the bar-keepers of the National Hotel, whose fame as a compounder of gin sling and mint julep was almost coextensive with the bounds of the republic. Amongst the ornaments of the bar was a portrait of this functionary, exhibiting his adroit manipulations in the more critical operations of his calling."

The National Hotel, Washington City *by James Barton Longacre (1794–1869), engraving, circa 1846. Prints and Photographs Division, Library of Congress, Washington, D.C.*

Right:
In the political circles of 1846, no portrait painter was more in demand than George Peter Alexander Healy. He was the choice of the fifteen New York Whigs—the dining group known as the Hone Club—to depict their champion, Daniel Webster (1782–1852). Philip Hone had feared that Healy "is so much in vogue that the time and price required for our picture may be be-yond our patience and money." To their immense pleasure, however, Healy accepted the commission at a cost of $550, which included the frame. Webster posed in Washington as the long-winded debate about Oregon's boundary got under way, and the exhausted senator at times dozed off during the sittings. The portrait was received in New York on April 25. "This 'counterfeit presentment' of our honorary member, the distinguished Massachusetts senator," wrote Hone, "is a great picture—the best that has been done of him."

Daniel Webster by George Peter Alexander Healy (1813–1894), oil on canvas, 1846. National Portrait Gallery, Smithsonian Institution, Washington, D.C.; transfer from the National Gallery of Art; gift of Andrew W. Mellon, 1942

"54°40' or Fight"

The dispute with England over the Oregon boundary was the preoccupation of Washington in the spring of 1846. "The great subject now is Oregon & whether we shall have war," wrote Benjamin Brown French, clerk of the House of Representatives. "I have not a doubt the President will stand, firm as a rock, for the whole of Oregon, & if England does not yield, & chooses to have a war about it she can be gratified." President Polk, in keeping with the Democratic platform, publicly insisted that America's claim to Oregon extended all the way to Alaska, that is, to 54°40'. Privately, however, with war against Mexico over the annexation of Texas impending, Polk maneuvered to have the Oregon boundary settled by compromise at the forty-ninth parallel.

Democrats in Congress were divided, however. "54°40' or Fight" continued to be the cry of the radical "Loco Foco" Democrats (called such after a match of that name), exemplified by Midwest Senators Lewis Cass of Michigan, Sidney Breese of Illinois, and William Allen of Ohio. On the other hand, Democrat John C. Calhoun of South Carolina, whose appetite for expansion had been satisfied by the annexation of Texas, had returned to the Senate with the prime objective of keeping peace with Great Britain. The President fumed, "The truth is that in all this Oregon discussion in the Senate, too many Democratic Senators have been more concerned about the Presidential election in '48, than they have been about settling Oregon either at 49 or 54 40."

With some notable exceptions, the Whigs stood back from demanding all of Oregon, because of the risk of war with England. But John Quincy Adams caused excitement and astonishment when he went against his party and supported 54°40'. And abolitionist Joshua Giddings of Ohio, outraged by the annexation of slaveholding Texas, declared in a furious speech "that he had two sons, whose blood he would rather see spilt in the contest for Oregon, than to see the balance of power where the annexation of Texas had placed it." An indignant correspondent wrote to the *Cleveland Daily Plain Dealer* that Giddings, "the miserable traitor, hopes that a war with England, and a negro insurrection in the southern States, will dissolve the Union."

During the debate about Oregon, Massachusetts Whig Robert C. Winthrop spoke of "Manifest Destiny"—a phrase brought into currency by Democratic editor John L. O'Sullivan late in 1845—for the first time in the House of Representatives when he derided "that new revelation of right which has been designated as *the right of our manifest destiny to spread over this continent.*" Winthrop, a descendant of the Puritan fathers, snorted, *The right of our manifest destiny! There is a right for a new chapter in the law of nations; or rather for the special laws of our own country; for I suppose the right of a manifest destiny to spread, will not be admitted to exist in any nation except the universal Yankee nation!*

Winthrop was answered by Edward D. Baker of Illinois (the victor over Abraham Lincoln for the Whig nomination for Congress), who protested, "That man must be poor in discernment who could see nothing like a destiny of freedom, of wealth and power, in a country such as ours, inhabited by twenty millions of such a population." Manifest Destiny "is a thought that leaps forth from the American heart like a bright

War! Or No War *by Frances Palmer (1812–1876), lithograph, 1846. Prints and Photographs Division, Library of Congress, Washington, D.C.*

WAR! OR NO WAR

Jhe ! say the 49 th d lets settle it amircably   *Xo Sir – ree Igees for the hull of Oregon or none... I do t dent do nor thin else*

sword from its scabbard. There was such a thing as a destiny for the American race—a destiny that would yet appear upon the great chart of human history."

Thomas Hart Benton (1782–1858), in a speech that lasted for three days—dwelling at length on the value of Oregon and the march of American civilization—took his position alongside Calhoun and most Whigs in favor of a compromise that would avoid war with England. Benton, the longtime advocate of western settlement, would later say that he knew his constituents were expecting a boundary line at 54°40′, but he relied "upon their equity and intelligence to give him a fair hearing and a safe deliverance."

The *New York Mirror* proclaimed on April 9, *We have now Mr Webster, the Atlas of the East, Mr Calhoun, the* great embodiment *of the South, and Mr Benton, the* great exponent *of the West, all against 54 40: and we may, therefore, consider 54 40, with a war at the end of the dispute, as having a very poor chance—54 40 makes in fact at present a very sorry figure.*

On June 10 the Senate went into a closed session to settle the Oregon boundary at the forty-ninth parallel. This was ratified by a vote of 41 to 14 on June 12, and three days later it was signed by Secretary of State James Buchanan and British Minister Edward Pakenham.

PRESENT PRESIDENTIAL POSITION.

Present Presidential Position *by Edward Williams Clay (1799–1857), lithograph, 1846. Prints and Photographs Division, Library of Congress, Washington, D.C.*

Thomas Hart Benton by Ferdinand Thomas Lee Boyle (1820–1906), oil on canvas, circa 1861. National Portrait Gallery, Smithsonian Institution, Washington, D.C.

which had a rear garden enclosed by walls. With him was his twenty-two-year-old daughter Jessie, whose husband, Captain John C. Frémont, was on a government-sponsored exploring expedition that would take him to California. During the summer of 1842, Frémont, in charge of a scientific expedition instigated by Senator Benton, had been sent to explore the trail to Oregon. A second venture the following year took him across the Sierra Nevada into California. It was her "most happy life work," Mrs. Frémont said, to be able to assist her husband in writing the accounts of his expeditions, and their literary polish and dramatic style are attributed to Jessie. "Fremont has particularly touched my imagination," Henry Wadsworth Longfellow was moved to write in his journal. "What a wild life, and what a fresh kind of existence! But, ah, the discomforts."

In her memoirs Jessie Benton Frémont (1824–1902) recalled that during her childhood she was often at the Capitol with her father, Missouri Senator Thomas Hart Benton, "pastured" in the chamber that housed the Library of Congress, where she was free to browse among Thomas Jefferson's books and John James Audubon's bird plates. At home in St. Louis she became proficient in Spanish and French, and her education was completed at Miss English's Female Seminary in Georgetown. Her elopement at seventeen to John Charles Frémont, a handsome army surveyor of illegitimate birth, enraged her father. He soon forgave the pair, however, and Jessie later declared, "We could count on each other—my father Mr. Frémont and I, as one."

Jessie Benton Frémont by Thomas Buchanan Read (1822–1872), oil on canvas, 1856. Southwest Museum, Los Angeles, California

Congress ordered twenty thousand copies of the combined reports printed, and Jessie proudly wrote to her husband on June 16, "As for your Report, its popularity astonished even me, your most confirmed and oldest worshipper."

In March General Samuel Houston, lately president of the Republic of Texas, took his seat as a senator from the new state. The *Alexandria Gazette* reported that he came "dressed in an odd looking suit of gray, embroidered with black braid and enveloped in his red Mexican blanket. His singular appearance seemed to attract considerable attention." Varina Davis observed that Houston "was considerably over the ordinary height—six feet four at least. He had a noble figure and handsome face." His manner she found to be "very swelling and formal. When he met a lady he took a step forward, then bowed very low, and in a deep voice said, 'Lady, I salute you.' It was an embarrassing kind of thing, for it was performed with the several motions of a fencing lesson." President Polk was particularly pleased to see Houston, with whom he had served in Congress twenty years before: "I found him thoroughly Democratic and fully determined to support my administration."

The traffic in Indian delegations was heavy during 1846, and $50,000 had been provided for their reception. "Every Indian that comes to Washington costs the Treasury as much as a member of Congress," quipped a writer to the *Boston Evening Transcript*, "and in nine cases out of ten, he is just as profitable."

On July 1 Polk received "between 40 & 50 chiefs and braves of the Comanche and other bands and tribes of wild Indians from the prairies in the North of Texas." The President recorded in his diary, "Their visit to the U.S. will no doubt have a fine effect in impressing them with our numbers and power, and may be the means of preserving peace with them." Mrs. Polk was dubbed the "great Mother" by the Comanche delegation, the only presidential wife to be accorded that distinction.

The most famous of the visiting Indians was the Cherokee chief John Ross. Ross had bitterly opposed the faction of his nation that had signed the 1837 treaty selling their ancestral lands to the government. But once removal became inevitable, he had led his people to the designated land west of the Mississippi, a territory already occupied by Cherokee "old settlers," who had agreed to leave their eastern land in 1817 and 1819. Conflict between the three factions of the Cherokee Nation—the "Ross party," the "treaty-party," and the "old settlers"—was inevitable, with

"Two classes of people," a Nashville belle observed, "pursued Sam Houston all his life—artists and women." Others have attributed the abundance of images of Houston (1793–1864) to his well-known vanity. In any case, one of Houston's finest portraits was executed by twenty-seven-year-old Martin Johnson Heade, an artist who became known for his depictions of flowers and hummingbirds. And if the painting is uncharacteristic of the artist, the elegant but conventional attire is likewise uncharacteristic of a sitter often given to flamboyant costume. Houston posed for Heade at the time he came to Washington to represent the new state of Texas in the Senate.

Samuel Houston by Martin Johnson Heade (1819–1904), oil on canvas, 1846. The Texas Governor's Mansion Collection, Austin

charges of treason and murder of three principal chiefs of the "treaty party" ensuing. All three groups appealed to the federal government, and President Polk, with the agreement of the House Committee on Indian Affairs, proposed the division of the Cherokee into separate tribes. Ross, however, who wanted a unified nation above all, persuaded the President to appoint commissioners to settle the difficulties among the three factions and to look into their complaints against the federal government. The controversies were settled by compromise, with Ross agreeing to the legitimacy of the 1837 treaty and the old settlers conced-

1846: Portrait of the Nation

In February 1845, at the insistence of Secretary of War William L. Marcy, President Polk began sittings with John Gadsby Chapman, in preparation for medals to be cast for presentation to the various Indian tribes. Chapman, a painter rather than a medalist, had executed the Baptism of Pocahontas *for the Capitol Rotunda.*

☀ *James K. Polk Indian peace medal by John Gadsby Chapman (1808–1889), silver, 1845. National Museum of the American Indian, Smithsonian Institution, Washington, D.C.*

Cherokee Chief John Ross (1790–1866) was the son of a Scottish father and a mother who was one-fourth Cherokee. "He does not seem to have a drop of Indian blood in his veins," wrote one who saw him in Washington, "and you would take him to be an honest tradesman, shrewd and prudent at making a bargain, and well to do in the world, rather than a powerful chieftain of a border tribe, who has exercised more real authority, and is possessed of more wealth, than any individual of the aboriginal race since the days of Tecumseh."

When Ross posed for his portrait by John Neagle in 1848, he chose to be shown holding a scroll inscribed "TREATY between the Cherokee Nation and the United States 1846," indicating his satisfaction that the differences between the three Cherokee factions had been settled without dividing the nation as originally proposed by the President and the House Committee on Indian Affairs.

☀ *John Ross by John Neagle (1799– 1865), oil on canvas, 1848. The Philbrook Museum of Art, Tulsa, Oklahoma*

In September Elias Howe was awarded a patent for a sewing machine that utilized the eye-pointed needle and sewed a lock-stitch using two threads, one from a spool and one from a bobbin in a shuttle. Finding no support for his "sewing jenny" in America, where it was viewed as a threat to the livelihood of seamstresses, Howe sent a machine to England in October, where it was sold to a large manufacturer of corsets, shoes, and umbrellas. Subsequently, Howe found several American companies selling machines that followed his design, and he began five years of litigation over patent infringement, which ended with him winning legal recognition as the sewing machine's primary inventor.

✳ *1846 model for Elias Howe's sewing machine. Textile Collection, Division of Social History, National Museum of American History, Smithsonian Institution, Washington, D.C.*

✳ *Patent for Howe's sewing machine, September 10, 1846. National Archives, Washington, D.C.*

ing that the Ross party had a right to lands in the West. A general amnesty was to be put into effect.

The agreed-upon treaty was confirmed by the Senate on August 8, and five days later the Cherokee delegation arrived at the White House for an exchange of the ratification. "John Ross, the Principal Chief, addressed me & said they were all now in harmony and were satisfied," Polk recorded in his diary. The harmony, however, would last no more than a decade.

———

From May 21 to June 3, a great National Manufacturers Fair took place in Washington, set up in a very large temporary building that occupied nearly two squares on C Street. "Almost every State sent earnest of its industry and ingenuity," remembered Varina Davis years later. Her husband found her a place around a crowded stand where she could see "a small box, and through a slot on the top was slowly pushed two narrow edges of cloth, and a needle with an eccentric motion played laterally through the cloth and sewed a pretty good seam." The exhibitor "plunged into a state of unintelligible terminology in which slots, tensions, headpieces, spirals, cylinders, cogs, and what not made havoc with his audience." Although Mrs. Davis does not name the exhibitor, he apparently was Elias Howe, who would be awarded a patent for a sewing machine on September 10.

Horace Greeley, editor of the *New York Tribune*, went to the fair and told his readers, "It is a vast and gratifying exhibition. Of cotton goods, and indeed of woven textures generally, there has been no previous exhibition equal in extent and variety on this continent if anywhere. . . . There are at least five hundred varieties of American calicoes or prints ranging from 6 to 20 cents per yard; some at 7 cents which no lady need be ashamed to wear."

Among those participating in the fair was John Plumbe Jr. of

Twenty-seven-year-old Elias Howe (1819–1867) was in Washington in May 1846, demonstrating a "new and useful machine for sewing seams" for which he applied for a patent. The machine, reported the Boston Evening Transcript, "is said to be able to sew up the seam of a pair of pantaloons, from ankle to hip in three minutes, and to do it better than any tailor can!" The writer cautioned, "In view of the success of such an instrument, what is to become of the poor seam-stresses?"

Elias Howe by an unidentified artist, after Charles Loring Elliott, oil on canvas, not dated. Division of Political History, National Museum of American History, Smithsonian Institution, Washington, D.C.; gift of Elias Howe Stockwell

Among the manufacturers whose products were on prominent display at the great National Manufacturers Fair, and who passed through the city as the tariff reduction bill came under heavy debate, was Abbott Lawrence (1792–1855), a former member of Congress and a principal spokesman for the American textile industry. A leader among the cotton Whigs of Massachusetts, Lawrence sought to stifle antislavery rhetoric in the interest of cooperation with southern planters. "Cotton thread holds the Union together; united John C. Calhoun and Abbott Lawrence," wrote Ralph Waldo Emerson in his journal shortly before July 4, 1846. "Patriotism for holidays and summer evenings, with music and rockets, but cotton thread is the Union."

Abbott Lawrence by Chester Harding (1792–1866), oil on canvas, circa 1840–1845. Museum of Fine Arts, Boston, Massachusetts; gift of the Misses Aimée and Rosamond Lamb

There was no doubt that John Plumbe Jr. (1809–1857), who had turned from railroad promotion to the new art of the daguerreotype, had an abundance of the 'go ahead' spirit of 1846. He had daguerreotype establishments in Boston, New York, Philadelphia, Baltimore, New Orleans, Saratoga, St. Louis, Dubuque, Louisville, and Newport, as well as Paris and Liverpool. In Washington Plumbe's National Daguerrian Gallery was in Concert Hall, on Pennsylvania Avenue between Sixth and Seventh Streets.

In 1846 Plumbe touted the new process of plumbeotyping, his term for the lithographs done after his daguerreotype plates. "This great and beautiful improvement, or strictly speaking new invention," he advertised, "enables every one, not only to possess a Daguerreotype likeness of himself or his friend; but also any number of portraits on paper, at a price for each, scarcely exceeding that of a common newspaper." A plain portrait on paper could be had for seven cents and a colored one for ten cents. Judging by the handful of surviving "plumbeotypes," Plumbe's project to have prints made from his daguerreotype plates was short-lived.

John Plumbe Jr. by an unidentified artist, after a self-portrait daguerreotype, lithograph, 1846. Contained in The National Plumbeotype Gallery (Philadelphia, 1847). National Portrait Gallery, Smithsonian Institution, Washington, D.C.

Daguerreotypist John Plumbe Jr. promised to publish "a daily Portrait of some interesting public character." One who lent himself to "plumbeotyping" was Secretary of the Navy George Bancroft (1800–1891), whose loyal service to the Polk administration was to be rewarded in September by appointment as minister to England, where he would be afforded the opportunity to continue research on his History of the United States.

George Bancroft by John Plumbe Jr. (1809–1857), daguerreotype, circa 1844. National Portrait Gallery, Smithsonian Institution, Washington, D.C.

George Bancroft by an unidentified artist, after a daguerreotype by John Plumbe Jr., hand-colored lithograph, 1846. Contained in The National Plumbeotype Gallery (Philadelphia, 1847). National Portrait Gallery, Smithsonian Institution, Washington, D.C.

Boston, who won a gold medal "for excelling all others in producing daguerreotype pictures." His hometown *Evening Transcript* trumpeted, "We believe the Professor has more medals, diplomas, etc presented him than any other 'live man.' Well, he deserved them all, and as many more, for he has made in certain more important discoveries in bringing the art to perfection than every other operator combined."

Plumbe had come to Washington earlier in the year to photograph its public buildings, with the idea of having lithographs made from his daguerreotype plates. "It is his intention to dispose of copies of these beautiful pictures, either in sets or singly," the press reported, "thus affording to all an opportunity of securing perfect representations of the government buildings." Only a single print has turned up—that of the Capitol—but five daguerreotypes still exist.

———

Before 1846 was out, the District of Columbia would lose a third of its territory when the portion of the ten-mile square across the Potomac was retroceded to Virginia. Citizens of Alexandria won approval for the return from the Virginia Assembly, and Congress consented, provided that a majority of white men in Alexandria County, including those without property, voiced their agreement. In early September a referendum was held, and retrocession was carried by a vote of 763 to 222, an event hardly noticed by those in Mr. Polk's Washington.

VIEW OF WASHINGTON CITY
AND GEORGETOWN

The inserts here show the main attractions of Washington in 1846, along with the Smithsonian building, soon to be under construction on the Mall, and the Washington Monument, begun in 1847 according to Robert Mills's design, although the circular base would never be incorporated.

View of Washington City and Georgetown *by Edward D. Weber Lithography Company (active 1835–1853), tinted lithograph with additional hand-coloring, 1849. I. N. Phelps Stokes Collection, The Miriam and Ira D. Wallach Division of Art, Prints and Photographs, The New York Public Library, New York City; Astor, Lenox and Tilden Foundations*

A Visit to the Patent Office

"The Patent Office in Washington is an object of much interest to every stranger," wrote a Scottish minister, in taking note of the patent models "arranged with much taste and elegance" on the first and second floors of the building located on the north side of F Street between Seventh and Ninth Streets. "I was struck by the endless variety of inventions for warming apartments. There seemed no end of models of heating apparatus, but few contrivances for ventilation." Scottish barrister Alexander Mackay remarked in 1846, "The American people discover an extraordinary talent for invention. The Patent-office in Washington is a most creditable monument to their inventive powers. They are also quick in the adoption of an improvement, no matter from what source it proceeds."

Robert Mills, who had supervised the construction of the Patent Office from 1836 to 1840, described it: *The principal entrance to this building is from the south, up a noble flight of granite steps, and through a magnificent portico of sixteen massive Doric columns, in double rows, into a spacious hall, at the end of which a double flight of marble steps lead to the grand exhibition room.*

The lion's share of this great vaulted hall, which Mills claimed was the largest room in the United States, was given over to the tons of specimens— animal, vegetable, and mineral—as well as artifacts from exotic cultures brought back by the United States Exploring Expedition, which had traveled the Pacific from 1838 to 1842 under the command of Lieutenant Charles Wilkes. Initially placed under the care of the private National Institution for the Promotion of Science (incorporated in 1842 as the National Institute), the collection was now under the jurisdic-

tion of the Joint Library Committee of the Congress, and Wilkes was put in charge of both the collections and the scientific reports of the expedition. The National Institute retained space for its own collection of minerals, fish, shells, insects, stuffed birds, bird skeletons, and works of art—mostly copies of old-master paintings and other European pictures—as well as the contents of John Varden's "Washington Museum," a miscellaneous assemblage that included two Egyptian mummies and other curiosities.

A separate section in the Great Hall was set aside for the effects of James Smithson, the Englishman who had inexplicably left his entire estate for the foundation in Washington of an institution to promote "the increase and diffusion of knowledge among men." After Congress had agreed to accept the Smithson bequest in 1836, Smithson's cabinet of gems and minerals, books, and personal effects, even his nightcaps and stockings, arrived in America along with bags of gold amounting to some half-million dollars. While Congress debated what should be done with the bequest, the Treasury invested the money in the state bonds of Arkansas and Michigan, and sent Smithson's possessions to the National Museum in the Patent Office.

Early on, the politically well-connected members of the National Institute had persuaded government agencies to contribute to the display at the Patent Office. From the War Department had come a hundred or so portraits painted by Washington resident artist Charles Bird King and assembled by Thomas McKenney during his tenure as commissioner of the United States Bureau of Indian Affairs from 1824 to

Patent Office by John Plumbe Jr. (1809–1857), daguerreotype, 1846. Prints and Photographs Division, Library of Congress, Washington, D.C.

PLAN
OF THE
NATIONAL GALLERY,
CONTAINING THE COLLECTIONS
OF THE
EXPLORING EXPEDITION.

1. War implements, &c., from the Feejee Islands.
2. Fishing implements, &c., from the Feejee Islands.
3. Pottery, Clothing, &c., from the Feejee Islands.
4. Personal ornaments, &c., from the Feejee Islands.
5. Implements, Manufactures, &c., from the Samoa or Navigator Islands.
6. "   "   "   from the Sandwich and Tonga Islands.
7. "   "   "   from the Kingsmill, Paumotu and Marquesas Islands.
8. "   "   "   from New Zealand.
9. "   "   "   from New Holland, Siam, Japan and China.
10. "   "   "   from the East India Islands and Tierra del Fuego,
    Also, Hieroglyphical Tablets from Central America, belonging to the National Institute Society.
11. Implements, Manufactures, &c., from Oregon and California.
12, 13. American Manufactures.
14. Minerals and Geological specimens from the Sandwich Islands.
15. Rocks and Earth from Icebergs near the Antarctic Land; Geological specimens from the Feejee Islands, Navigator Islands, Society Islands, Coral Islands, South Shetland, New Zealand, the Phillipines, Madeira and St. Helena.
16. Minerals and Geological specimens from New Holland.
17. "   "   "   from Brazil, Patagonia, Tierra del Fuego, Chili and Peru.
18. "   "   "   from Oregon and California.
    Also, on the lower shelf, specimens collected by Lieut. Fremont on an Official Expedition to the Rocky Mountains.
19. Corals and Sponges.
20, 21. Corals.
22. Geological specimens and Ores from Iowa, Wisconsin and Indiana, collected by D. D. Owen on a Government survey.
23. Personal effects of the late James Smithson, Esq., of England.

24. Original Declaration of Independence, Relics of Washington, Treaties with Foreign Powers, and Presents to officers under Government.
25, 26. Insects deposited by M. Castelnau with the National Institute Society.
27. American Manufactures.
28, 29. Insects collected by the Exploring Expedition, mostly not yet arranged. Also, collections belonging to M. Castelnau and the National Institute Society.
30, 31, 32, 33, 34, 35. Quadrupeds. (But few of the specimens have been, as yet, prepared for exhibition.)
36. Skeletons and Crania of Mammalia.
    Also, Skeletons of Birds belonging to the National Institute Society.
37. Peruvian Mummies and Human Crania from various regions.
    Also, two Egyptian Mummies, deposited by Mr. Varden.
38. Specimens in alcohol of Molluscs and Crustacea.
39. Specimens in alcohol of Fishes and Reptiles, (at present in cases 48 and 49.)
40, 41. Birds belonging to the National Institute Society, about 500 specimens; at present among those of the Exploring Expedition.
42, 43, 44, 45, 46, 47, 48, 49. Ornithological specimens of the Exploring Expedition, (1800 specimens; many not yet prepared.)
50. Specimens of Woods and Fruits.
51, 52, 53, 54. Herbarium of the Exploring Expedition, including upwards of 10,000 species of plants, (not yet arranged.)
55. } Crustacea.
56. } Below—Reptiles, (in part belonging to the National Institute Society.)
57. Echini and Star Fish.
    Below—Fishes, (in part belonging to the National Institute Society.)
58. Shells from the East Indies, including the Land Shells of Luzon.
    Below—Fishes, (in part belonging to the National Institute Society.)
59, 60, 61, 62, 63. Shells.

PAINTINGS
DEPOSITED IN THE HALL.

No. 1. Flemish Fruit Market.—By Francis Snyder.
2. Dead Christ.—By Martin de Vos.
3. Winter Landscape.—By Albert Van Everdingen.
4. Halt at the Inn, } By P. Wouvermans?
5. Traveller's Rest, }
6. Christ in the Garden.—By Carlo Dolci. (A copy.)
7. The Nativity.—By Rubens.
8. Portrait of Guizot, the Prime Minister of France.—By G. P. A. Healy. (Presented to the American Government by the Americans at Paris.)
9. Street in Venice. Deposited by Mrs. Poinsett.
10. Magdalen in a Swoon.—By Cavaliere Benedetto Luti. (A copy.)
11. Christ Bound.—By Guido Reni. (A copy.)
12. Virgin, Child and St. John.—By Andrea del Sarto. (A copy.)
13. Saint Sebastian.—De Moya.
14. The Martyrdom of Saint Sebastian.—Titian. (A copy.)
15. Massacre of the Innocents. Deposited by J. Varden.
16. Portrait. Deposited by J. Varden.
17. Italian Seaport.—By Claude Lorraine. (A copy.)
18. Landscape. Deposited by J. Gales, Esq.
19. Winter Scene. Deposited by J. Gales, Esq.
20. Landscape. Deposited by J. Gales, Esq.
21. Madonna de la Seggiola.—By Raphael. (A copy.) Deposited by Mrs. Poinsett.
22. Landscape.—By Teniers (?)
23. Boy and Dog. Deposited by Mrs. Poinsett.
24. Landscape.—By Hobbima (?)
25. Rialto at Venice. Deposited by Mrs. Poinsett.
26 & 27. Flemish Carousals. Deposited by Major Smith.

28. Moorish Battle Piece. Deposited by J. Varden.
29. Landscape. Deposited by Major Smith.
30. Portrait of the Hon. Wm. C. Preston.—By Healy.
31. Portrait of his Excellency John Tyler.—By Healy.
32. Landscape. Deposited by J. Gales, Esq.
33. Landscape. Deposited by J. Gales, Esq.
34. Marine View. Deposited by J. Gales, Esq.
35. Mother and Child. Deposited by Mrs. Poinsett.
36. Landscape. Deposited by J. Gales, Esq.
37. A Head.—By Tofanelli. (A copy.)
38. Landscape. Deposited by J. Gales, Esq.
39. Portrait of Captain Evans.
40. Turkish Bashaw. Presented by Commodore Rodgers to the National Institute Society.
41. The Gamesters. Deposited by Mrs. Poinsett.
42. Job and his Comforters.—By Spagnoletti.
43. Portrait of Don Vincent Guerrero, President of the Mexican Republic. Deposited by the National Institute Society.
44. Black Ben.
45. Portrait of Gen. Washington.—By Charles W. Peale. Deposited by Count De Menou.

NORTH AMERICAN INDIANS.

46. A Sioux Chief.
47. Okee-maa-kie-quid.
48. Fox Chief, Cut-tas-tasi-tla.
49. Black Hawk.
50. Kee-o-kuk.

51. Tshusick, or Cornelia Barbour
52. Red Jacket.
53. Tukosee-mathla.
54. Waa-na-tan.
55. Chippewa Squaw and Child.

1830. From the State Department, of which the Patent Office was a part, came the Declaration of Independence, historic treaties and archives, and a variety of gifts received from foreign governments. Near the Declaration of Independence, detailed the Scottish minister, "is the commission Washington received from the First Congress, to be Commander-in-Chief, signed by Hancock the President. The dress, sword, camp table, and cooking vessels of the General, were deposited as relics, along with his commission."

To the Patent Office John Quincy Adams had sent the ivory cane that he had received from Julius Pratt & Co. of Meriden, Connecticut, "to be kept in custody of the Commissioner among the curiosities of the office, until the right of petition shall be restored by the extinction of the gag-rule in the House of Representatives." After the gag rule—which had been enacted to put a stop to petitions calling for the abolition of slavery—was rescinded on December 3, 1844, Adams had this date added to the cane, and returned it to the Patent Office. Slavery and the slave trade, however, continued as usual in the District of Columbia.

Adjoining the building was a 148-foot greenhouse built to accommodate the live plants brought back by the exploring expedition—"curious Exotics," wrote one of the thousands of tourists, "embracing a very great variety of flowers now in full blow and shrubs, also the coffee tree."

With such a variety of exotic and peculiar curiosities, it is no wonder that Varina Davis expressed her intent to visit the Patent Office at her earliest opportunity and promised to send a long account to her family in Mississippi.

Ivory cane deposited by John Quincy Adams in honor of the repeal of the gag rule. Division of Political History, National Museum of American History, Smithsonian Institution, Washington, D.C.

Plan of the National Gallery *by an unidentified artist, lithograph, 1844–1849.* Smithsonian Institution Archives, Washington, D.C.

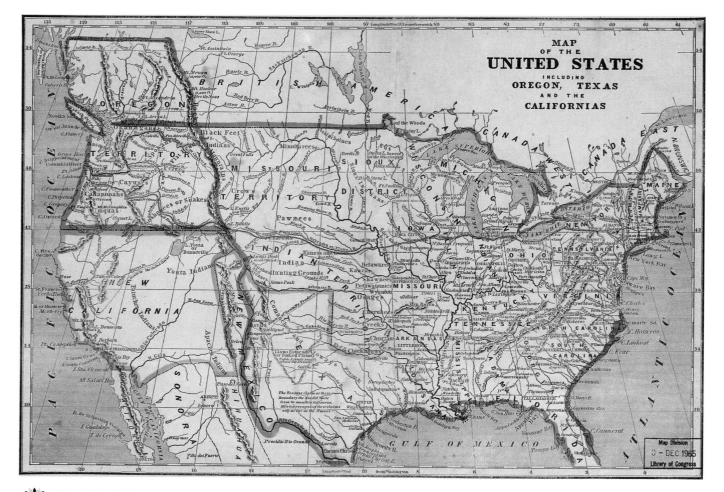

Map of the United States, Including Oregon, Texas, and the Californias *by John Haven (lifedates unknown); Haven & Emmerson, 1846. Geography and Map Division, Library of Congress, Washington, D.C.*

Chapter 3

Across the Fruited Plain

But what prospects open before us!" exclaimed James Gordon Bennett, editor of the *New York Herald,* as the year 1846 dawned—"a people of twenty millions, spread over a continent of immense surface, a wonder to ourselves and a wonder to the world!"

America was still predominantly a nation of plantations and farms—according to the 1840 census, fewer than eight hundred thousand were engaged in manufacture and trade, while those engaged in agriculture alone were nearly four million—but the fast growth was transforming the landscape. There was no holding back America in 1846—the "go-ahead" spirit was abroad in the land.

New York had become the fifth-largest city in the world, with a population of some 370,000, surpassing once-dominant Philadelphia by several hundred thousand. "Our good city of New York has already arrived at the state of society to be found in the large cities of Europe; overburdened with population," decried Philip Hone, former mayor of the city and incomparable diarist of the era. *The two extremes of costly luxury in living, expensive establishments, and improvident waste are*

presented in daily and hourly contrast with squalid misery and hopeless destitution. This state of things has been hastened in our case by the constant stream of European paupers arriving upon the shores of this land of promise.

Baltimore and New Orleans, positioned in different ways to take advantage of the expanding commerce of the nation, vied for third and fourth place, after Philadelphia, in the country's population, with about 102,000 inhabitants each. Both easily surpassed Boston in growth and left the southern metropolis of Charleston far behind. Scottish visitor Alexander Mackay wrote that if Charleston "is not a receding, it has none of the appearance of an advancing town."

Mobile, Alabama, after New Orleans the most important American seaport on the Gulf of Mexico, Mackay noted, "now ships more cotton for the North, and for Europe, than either Charleston or Savannah, and bids fair soon immeasurably to out-distance as a commercial emporium both of these places."

The colonial port city of Newport, Rhode Island, had blossomed as a summer resort. Philadelphia lawyer Sidney George Fisher, visiting in July 1846, fretted that the "sociable, easy, quiet society of the place is destroyed by the influx of this immense crowd, chiefly from New York, of ultra fashionable people who live for dissipation & carry the winter habits of the city into the summer & the country."

On the banks of the Merrimack River in Massachusetts had arisen the industrial city of Lowell, where $10 million of capital had been invested. Textile pioneer Nathan Appleton, one of the founders of the Merrimack Manufacturing Company, recalled that when he and his partners first came upon the spot, with its thirty-foot waterfall, in November 1821, "We perambulated the grounds, and scanned the capabilities of the place; and the remark was made, that some of us might live to see the place contain twenty thousand inhabitants."

In St. Louis, the city most often mentioned to logically replace Washington as the capital of the expanding country, Philip Hone *"put up at the Planters' House—one of those great hotels which astonish us in the great West."* Walking along the riverfront, Hone recounted, *"The scene there represented is greater than I can describe.*

Fifty large steamboats, at least, lie head on, taking in and discharging their cargoes. . . . The whole of the levee is covered, as far as the eye can see, with merchandise landed or to be shipped; thousands of barrels of flour and bags of corn, hogsheads of tobacco, and immense piles of lead (one of the great staples), whilst foreign merchan-

dise and the products of the lower country are carried away to be lodged in the stores which form the front of the city."

St. Louis in 1846 *by Henry Lewis (1819–1904), oil on canvas, 1846. The St. Louis Art Museum, Missouri; Eliza McMillan Fund*

Alexander Mackay, arriving in New York in 1846, observed that the East River opposite Brooklyn "is alive with every species of floating craft, from the tiny wherry to the enormous steamer, ploughing her way to the New England coast." In this view—sketched by Fanny Palmer, who, said one of her admirers in 1847, "stands at the head of the art" of lithography—Commodore Cornelius Vanderbilt's steamboat Vanderbilt can be seen.

View of New York from Brooklyn Heights *by Frances Flora Bond Palmer (1812–1876) at Currier and Ives Lithography Company, colored lithograph, 1849. The Gerald LeVino Collection, Museum of the City of New York, New York (57.100.125)*

Despite discomfort and danger, Americans were perpetual travelers. Philadelphia lawyer Sidney George Fisher, for one, preferred the old-fashioned stagecoach to the train or steamboat. "The change of passengers, of drivers & horses; the stoppings at the country inns, where you see new faces & groups & a thousand indications of the character of the people, all interest & occupy the mind," he explained. "The journey is enlivened by conversation, and your interest and attention are awakened by the collision of ideas, the varieties of manner & exhibition of character."

The Stage Coach "Seventy-Six" of the Knickerbocker Line, Brooklyn *by Henry Boese (active 1844–1863), oil on canvas, circa 1850. Museum of the City of New York, New York; gift of Herbert L. Pratt (40.178)*

The growth of cities, the stirring of industry, the rush in transportation and communication notwithstanding, America remained overwhelmingly an agricultural nation.

This farmscape is inscribed across the bottom "An Indian summer view of the Farm & Stock of JAMES C. CORNELL Northampton Bucks county Pennsylvania. That took the Premium in the Agricultural society, october the 12, 1848/ Painted by

E. Hicks in the 69th year of his age." Among the several prizes won by Cornell was "The first premium of $5 for the best cultivated Farm over 100 acres, regard being had to the quality of produce, mode of cultivation, and general appearance."

🌿 The Cornell Farm by Edward Hicks (1780–1894), oil on canvas, 1848. National Gallery of Art, Washington, D.C.; gift of Edgar William and Bernice Chrysler Garbisch

The remote sylvan site chosen for the University of Georgia in 1801 and named Athens could be reached by railroad in 1841. The tracks, however, stopped at Carr's Hill, across the river from the town, subjecting the passenger to the "horrors of the long ride between the depot and the hotel, as he was pitched about in Saulter's old omnibus, splashed with mud or suffocated with dust, according to the season of the year."

View of Athens from Carr's Hill *by George Cooke (1793–1849), oil on canvas, 1845. Georgia Museum of Art, University of Georgia, Athens; on extended loan from the Hargrett Rare Books and Manuscripts Library, University of Georgia Libraries*

The dangerous but profitable business of whaling was in its heyday. From Atlantic ports—particularly New Bedford, Massachusetts, the center of the industry—ships set out on long, four- or five-year voyages. The crews harvested in the Pacific, discovering new whaling grounds in the Arctic Ocean in 1846. It was estimated that a fleet of some 650 vessels employing 40,000 men brought to market whale oil valued at more than $36 million.

Whale Fishing—Attacking a "Right" Whale and "Cutting In" *by Martens after Ambrose Louis Garneray, aquatint engraving, 1850. Shelburne Museum, Shelburne, Vermont*

"It is indeed a city of wonderful growth for its age, and is one of the proudest tokens of New-England enterprise and munificence," wrote a visitor to Lowell, Massachusetts, in February 1846. "Like almost every New England town of considerable size, Lowell abounds in associations for the intellectual and moral training of all," detailed a correspondent in the New York Tribune. "The Mechanics' Lyceum, a fine large building, erected purposely for the benefit of all classes, is the best in Lowell, and has beside its Lecture-room, a large reading room and Laboratory, and through the entire winter supports a weekly course of lectures by the most distinguished in the country." Ralph Waldo Emerson graced the 1846 season.

Lowell Letter Paper with a New View of the City by Franklin Hedge (life-dates unknown), woodcut, 1848. Division of Prints and Photographs, Library of Congress, Washington, D.C.

When in 1846 Nathan Appleton (1779–1861) posed for a portrait intended to hang in the Mechanics' Hall in Lowell, he proudly posed in front of a calico-printing machine. A quarter of a century earlier, Appleton had been convinced that despite the difficulties involved, the time had arrived "when the manufacture and printing of calicoes might be successfully introduced in this country," a conviction borne out by the prosperous operation of the Merrimack Manufacturing Company in Lowell. But Appleton, also a partner in manufacturing establishments in Lawrence, Massachusetts, and Manchester, New Hampshire—as well as an investor in banks and railroads—insisted, "My mind has always been devoted to many other things rather than money-making." Christian theology was a favorite study with him, as was geology. He was also prominent in the Whig Party, although it was with reluctance that he served two terms in Congress, where he helped frame the protective tariffs of 1832 and 1842.

Nathan Appleton by George Peter Alexander Healy (1813–1894), oil on canvas, 1846. City of Lowell, Massachusetts

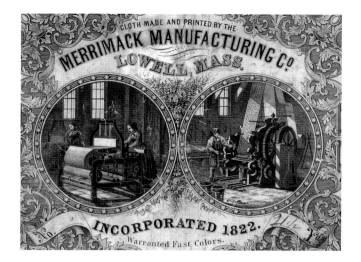

By 1846 other factories crowded the site, and Lowell's population had reached twenty-five thousand. Nine thousand girls from the surrounding countryside were employed in its twenty-seven textile factories, and they lived carefully controlled lives in the company boarding houses. The girls who came to work in Lowell were the object of wonder and admiration. "They dress well, going through the streets on Sunday in silk stockings and with a shawl and parasol," it was observed. "They save $150 or $200 some years and return to the bosom of their families ready to help defray the cost of establishing a new family." Female workers in Lowell received $1.75 per week; male workers $4 per week.

Traveling throughout the agricultural South, Alexander Mackay came upon a large establishment in Richmond, where crude tobacco was converted "into a form fit for chewing" and "packed in small cakes, in oblong boxes, labeled with the seductive name of 'Honeydew.'" Mackay detailed: *In all the departments of the factory the labour was performed by slaves, superintended by white overseers. They appeared to be very contented at their work, although the utmost silence was observed amongst them, except within certain hours of the day, when they were permitted to relieve their toil by singing, performing a succession of solos, duets, glees . . . in a way that was truly surprising, considering that they were entirely self-taught.*

Mackay observed that as he traveled south from Philadelphia, the proportion of blacks to whites increased in each successive town, and in no place were blacks more numerous in proportion than Charleston. *They are everywhere, in the capacity of domestic servants within and of labourers out of doors, about the wharves and shipping, and in the streets, toiling, singing or*

Some of the Lowell factory girls were not as content as visitors were led to believe. Four thousand of them petitioned the Massachusetts legislature in 1846, asking for a reduction in their hours on the grounds of health. A special committee came from Boston to look into the matter and determined that "the general health of the operatives was improved by the regularity of labor, diet" that the factory provided. The committee continued, "besides very many who work by the piece would prefer the hours lengthened, and many who signed the petition admitted that it was done to please those who called on them soliciting their names, not because they wished for a change." The committee concluded that the federal government should "regulate the hours of labor to one standard through the whole Union, so that Massachusetts factories for instance, need not be ruined under a ten hour system, by those of New Hampshire, or some other State which tolerates thirteen hours."

Merrimack Manufacturing Co. Trade Card. Warshaw Collection, Archives Center, National Museum of American History, Smithsonian Institution, Washington, D.C.

After the death of her husband in 1825, Rebecca Lukens (1794–1854) took over the commercial management of her family's Brandywine, Pennsylvania, iron-works, which was then close to bankruptcy. Surmounting litigation, transportation difficulties, the failure of water power when the Brandywine ran low, and a variety of other problems, Mrs. Lukens oversaw the successful manufacture of boilerplates to be used in ships and wood-burning locomotives. In 1846 Lukens, like the New England textile manufacturers, was concerned that the reduction in the tariff would be deleterious to her business, but the Brandywine Iron Works survived to be renamed, after her demise, the Lukens Steel Company.

Rebecca Webb Pennock Lukens by an unidentified artist, hand-colored photo-graph of an original oil on canvas, circa 1823. Courtesy Lukens Inc., Coatesville, Pennsylvania

whistling and grimacing. The practice of letting them out to hire is very prevalent in Charleston, many people making comfortable incomes in this way out of the labour of their slaves.

During the summer of 1846, William Cullen Bryant, editor of the *New York Evening Post*, traveled by way of the Great Lakes to visit his mother in Illinois, and for the edification of his readers he sent back descriptions of a growing America beyond the Atlantic seaboard. For example, Bryant found Cleveland to be "a thriving village yet to grow into a proud city of the lake country." But the *Cleveland Plain Dealer*, promoting a series of public lectures "to furnish entertainments of an intellectual character for the long winter evenings," exhorted in November, *Let us not be behind the spirit of the age. We are a community without reading rooms, without debating societies, without public libraries—a confession we must make, though it cost us not a little shame and confusion of face, because it furnishes a contrast so palpable, to almost every city either east or west of us.*

Nonetheless, the Western Reserve College had an impressive Egyptian Revival structure to house its medical department, with a museum

CITY OF CHICAGO,—South-West View, 1845.—Campbell & Co., Printers

New York Evening Post *editor William Cullen Bryant had trouble recognizing Chicago, which had grown in the last five years from five to fifteen thousand people:* "It has its long rows of warehouses and shops, its bustling streets; its huge steamers, and crowds of lake craft, lying at the wharves; its villas embowered with trees; and its suburbs, consisting of the cottages of German and Irish laborers, stretching northward along the lake, and westward into the prairies, and widening every day. The slovenly and raw appearance of a new settlement begins in many parts to disappear."

City of Chicago—South-West View 1845, *engraved by S. D. Childs and Roswell N. White (active 1832–1848), published in James Wellington Norris's* Business Advertiser and General Directory of the City of Chicago for 1845–6. *Prints and Photographs Division, Library of Congress, Washington, D.C.*

HAULING THE

Silhouettist William Henry Brown, on a visit to a cotton plantation near Vicksburg, Mississippi, cut and painted a five-foot-long collage showing the slaves as they went about their daily toil.

Hauling the Whole Week's Picking *by William Henry Brown (1808–1883), watercolor and paper mounted on cardboard, circa 1842. Museum/Research Center, The Historic New Orleans Collection, Louisiana (1975. 93.1–4)*

WEEKS PICKING

attached. "Among a thousand other things we saw an original letter of Gen. Washington, written while President, and the signatures of Jefferson, Koskiusko [*sic*], and General Knox, cut from original letters," detailed a visitor, "and also a cartridge box captured from the British at the battle of Bunker Hill. On the top of the College is a fine Observatory, which is now being completed for the reception of a large telescope."

Cincinnati—called Porkopolis in honor of its dominance in the meat-packing industry—had a population of some seventy-five thousand, making it the largest city west of the Appalachian Mountains. "It is one of the most orderly and industrious, and, for its size, one of the wealthiest towns in the Union," said Alexander Mackay.

Here lived Nicholas Longworth, a self-educated horticulturist and patron of the arts, who had come to the frontier town as a young lawyer in 1803 and bought up land around him. By midcentury, it was reported, only New York's John Jacob Astor paid more in real-estate taxes. Longworth had under cultivation, just above Cincinnati, a two-hundred-acre tract that he called the Garden of Eden, devoted to grapes, strawberries, and other fruit. According to Andrew Jackson Downing, editor of *The Horticulturist and Journal of Rural Art and Rural Taste*, Longworth "has established in the eyes of the world . . . that the banks of the Ohio can produce, in great abundance, pure wines, equal to the finest wines of the Rhine," and that "his favorite mode of cultivating the strawberry" made them abundant and cheap. It was Longworth's hope that laboring men would find his light wines to be a substitute for more potent drink. Sculptor Hiram Powers,

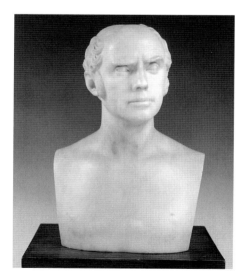

"There are few persons who have contributed as much to the agricultural improvement of the West" as Nicholas Longworth (1782–1863) of Cincinnati. "The fruit market of Cincinnati is not surpassed by any in the Union for the variety and excellence of its supplies," assessed the New Orleans Picayune *in August 1846. Longworth's name "is not only associated with the products of the earth, but . . . [his] liberality in patronizing the arts and artists of his native land has been the principal means of placing Hiram Powers in a position to illustrate the sculptural genius of the country."*

Powers modeled Longworth's bust in 1834, shortly before the young artist left Cincinnati, with a loan from Longworth, to seek national recognition in Washington, D.C.

Nicholas Longworth *by Hiram Powers (1805–1873), marble, after 1834 plaster. The Society of the Cincinnati Museum at Anderson House, Washington, D.C.*

one of the many artists whom Longworth befriended, declared that Longworth was "doing more for the cause of temperance than many preachers."

The Argentine visitor Domingo Faustino Sarmiento related that as he traveled down the Mississippi on the way to New Orleans, his first glimpse of that city was the dome of the St. Charles Exchange Hotel. "Here is the sovereign people who build palaces to shelter their heads for a night!" he exclaimed. "Every large city in the

While visiting Cincinnati in the 1840s, Domingo Faustino Sarmiento found that "from its port steamboats depart daily for Pittsburgh and downriver for St. Louis and New Orleans. In all directions, stagecoaches bridge the distance between neighboring cities. There are forty churches, a theater, a museum, an office for the sale of public lands, four markets, and a town hall." The Ohio River, which separated Ohio from Kentucky, was the boundary between freedom and slavery.

View of Cincinnati *by John C. Wild (circa 1804–1846), watercolor and gouache, circa 1835. Museum of Fine Arts, Boston, Massachusetts; M. and M. Karolik Collection*

In July the Horticulturist and Journal of Rural Art and Rural Taste *made its debut with editor Andrew Jackson Downing proclaiming, "Everywhere on both sides of the Alleganies, are our friends rapidly turning the fertile soil into luxuriant gardens, and crying out loudly for more light, and more knowledge." Adorning the frontispiece with a design for gothicizing an ordinary country house, Downing pointed out, "Already are the suburbs of our cities, and the banks of our broad and picturesque rivers, studded with the tasteful villa and cottage, where a charming taste in ornamental gardening is rapidly developing itself."*

Horticulturist and Journal of Rural Art and Rural Taste, *July 1846. Earl Gregg Swem Library, College of William and Mary, Williamsburg, Virginia*

FIG. 2. VIEW OF A COMMON COUNTRY HOUSE.

FIG. 3. VIEW OF THE SAME, IMPROVED.

Architect Alexander Jackson Davis, together with landscape gardener and architectural critic Andrew Jackson Downing, crusaded to change American taste away from the classical and toward the more picturesque Gothic. Around 1846 Davis drew up plans for a cottage built that year in New Bedford, Massachusetts, for William J. Rotch, a wealthy mill owner with a fondness for Sir Walter Scott. Downing, commenting on Rotch's house in his The Architecture of Country Houses, wrote, "The character expressed by the exterior of this design is that of a man or family of domestic tastes, but with strong aspirations after something higher than social pleasures."

Gothic Cottage of William J. Rotch by Alexander Jackson Davis (1803–1892), watercolor drawing, circa 1846. Laurie and John Bullard

This rendering of a Greek Revival house was probably done by Joseph Howard. He was for a brief time in partnership with Luther Briggs Jr., a young Boston architect who soon turned to Andrew Jackson Downing's picturesque pattern books and offered his clients adaptations of a cottage in the "Rural Gothic" style.

Elevation for a Cottage in the Greek Revival Style attributed to the firm of Luther Briggs Jr. and Joseph Howard, wash drawing, 1844–1846. Society for the Preservation of New England Antiquities, Boston, Massachusetts

Racecourses dotted the land, particularly in the South, where an appreciation for horses and the enjoyment of the social rituals of the racing season were particularly keen.

Oakland House and Race Course, Louisville, Kentucky, *by Robert Brammer (active 1838–1853) and Augustus Von Smith (active 1835–1848), oil on canvas, 1840. The J. B. Speed Art Museum, Louisville, Kentucky*

"With the exception of the Capitol in Washington no civil or religious monument in the United States is superior in size or good taste," wrote the Argentine traveler Domingo Faustino Sarmiento in describing New Orleans's St. Charles Exchange Hotel. The hotel's prodigious business is attested to by the daily consumption of some of the principal articles of food served to their customers: "500 lbs. fresh beef, 150 lbs. mutton, 24 turkeys, 50 chickens, 30 pairs wild ducks, 30 dozen robins or other small birds, 120 lbs ham, 6 to 10 thousand oysters, 120 to 130 dozen eggs. 75 gallons of milk, 350 loaves bakers' bread, 50 lbs. coffee, 10 lbs. tea, 225 lbs. sugar, 6 bbls. potatoes, 75 lbs. salt beef and pork, besides any quantity of venison, bear, grouse, and other items entirely 'too tedious to mention,' as they say in the advertisements."

In the busy winter season, "Seven hundred diners," Sarmiento noted, gathered around "three parallel mahogany tables that run the length of the room, a distance of a little less than half a block." Sarmiento's traveling companion exclaimed, "Everything should be pardoned a people who raise up monuments to the dining room and crown their kitchens with domes like this one!"

St. Charles Exchange Hotel *(detail)* *by B. W. Thayer and Co. (active 1840–1853), lithograph, 1845. Louisiana State Museum, New Orleans*

United States boasts of two or three monstrous hotels that compete among themselves in offering luxury and comfort to the public at the lowest prices." Boston had its Tremont House—not to mention the United States Hotel, which Alexander Mackay found had "a large wing on one side called Texas, and one in process of completion, on the other, to be called Oregon"—while New York boasted the mammoth Hotel Astor. "More money has been put into the Astor than into any church in that city," Sarmiento asserted.

Be that as it may, New York saw the completion of two notable churches in 1846. Richard Upjohn's Trinity Church, a landmark of Gothic design in America, was consecrated on May 21. Upjohn, a devout Episcopalian, had recently created a stir when he refused, on grounds of religious conviction, to design a Boston church for the Unitarians, causing the new humor magazine *Yankee Doodle* to jest, "This beats those tender-hearted abolitionists who refuse to eat sugar because it is the product of slave labor."

Grace Church, at the head of Broadway, was consecrated in March. The white marble Gothic structure was the first important commission undertaken by James Renwick, the son of a natural-history professor at Columbia College. The senior Renwick proudly told his friend Alexander Dallas Bache that he did not doubt that Grace "is the handsomest church in the United States, as well as least costly in proportion to its size. . . . It seats more persons than Trinity Church."

Among the popular resort hotels patron-
ized by those with means and leisure was
the Claremont Hotel, situated in what was
then the rural area of New York City and
is today the neighborhood of Grant's
Tomb—Riverside Drive and 124th Street.

The Claremont *by an unidentified
artist, oil on canvas, circa 1855. The Edward
W. C. Arnold Collection of New York Prints,
Maps, and Pictures, The Metropolitan
Museum of Art, New York City; bequest of
Edward W. C. Arnold, 1954*

"There is not a city on earth to which Trinity Church would not be a first-rate architectural accession," asserted Scottish barrister Alexander Mackay. Taking note of the "noble florid Gothic pile . . . built of dark brownish stone, which rises in such stately yet buoyant proportions at the head of Wall-street," Mackay commented, "There is something both curious and suggestive in its position. It stands, pointing loftily to heaven, on a spot visible from almost every point of that street where Mammon is most eagerly and unaffectedly worshipped in America."

Bird's-Eye View of Trinity Church, New York *by John Forsyth and E. W. Mimee (active dates unknown), lithograph, 1847. The J. Clarence Davies Collection, Museum of the City of New York, New York*

One of the new periodicals appearing in *1846 was* Yankee Doodle, *an American humor magazine patterned after the English* Punch, *which made its long-anticipated debut on October 10. In an apt delineation of the national character of 1846, the editors announced that the character Yankee Doodle had as "his hobby . . . the American Continent. He wishes to see his opinions, people, towns, churches, pictures, statues, books, newspapers, filling it from one end to the other; spreading over the prairies, crowding up into the nooks and angles of the North, and taking the whole South as in his outspread arms."*

But James Russell Lowell jested:

> *That American Punch, like the English, no doubt,*
> *Just the sugar and lemons and spirit left out.*

Yankee Doodle *did not survive beyond 1847.*

Yankee Doodle, *Volume 1, Number 10, December 12, 1846. Special Collections, Lehigh University Libraries, Bethlehem, Pennsylvania*

NEW YORK, SATURDAY, DECEMBER 12, 1846.

[VOLUME I.] [NUMBER X.]

Published at *WILLIAM H. GRAHAM'S, 160 Nassau Street, Tribune Buildings.*
PRICE, SIX CENTS.—THREE DOLLARS PER ANNUM IN ADVANCE.

Persons in New York wishing "Yankee Doodle" left at their residences are informed that a Subscription Book is now open at the Publishing Office.

The Reverend John Atwood, chaplain at the state prison in Concord, New Hampshire, and his family posed in their parlor for Henry F. Darby, then but sixteen. The artist recalled afterward that he spent three months in the New Hampshire capital "to paint the Atwoods all on one canvas. The father was represented sitting in the midst of his admiring wife and children, expounding his Bible." On the wall hangs a memorial to two children who had died in infancy.

The Reverend John Atwood (1795–1873), his wife Lydia Dodge (1806–1866), and their children (left to right) Solomon Dodge (1839–1915), Mary Frances (1837–1892), Ann Judson (1835–1874), Sarah Elizabeth (1829–1916), Lydia Dodge (1827–1909), and Roger William (1833–1917) by Henry F. Darby (born circa 1831), oil on canvas, 1845. Museum of Fine Arts, Boston, Massachusetts; gift of Maxim Karolik for the M. and M. Karolik Collection of American Paintings

William Lawson (born 1800), listed among the "People of Color" in the Boston City Directory from 1841 to 1850, was the proprietor of a clothing store. His portrait—unusually documented in small block letters on the front as having been painted by W. M. Prior on May 2, 1843—suggests that he was a man of considerable stature and affluence, and successful in the face of discrimination that was the lot of free blacks even in Massachusetts.

Of the fashionably dressed Mrs. William Lawson (born 1803) little is known. All that can be said about her is that she was a native of Massachusetts and the mother of at least one daughter. William Matthew Prior, however, has painted her with meticulous detail and with the addition—rare in his work—of a landscape background. Prior, one of the most enterprising of the folk artists of the time, offered his clients the choice of an academic likeness or "a flat picture . . .

without shade or shadow at one quarter price." William Lawson chose the more expensive alternative.

Nancy Lawson by William Matthew Prior (1806–1873), oil on canvas, May 11, 1843. Shelburne Museum, Shelburne, Vermont

William Lawson by William Matthew Prior (1806–1873), oil on canvas, May 2, 1843. Shelburne Museum, Shelburne, Vermont

The most talked-about structure in 1846 was not a Gothic fantasy or a sumptuous hotel, but instead a palace for consumers—Alexander T. Stewart's white marble dry-goods establishment on Broadway. "There is nothing in Paris or London to compare with this dry goods palace," wrote Philip Hone in September. *My attention was attracted, in passing this morning, to a most extraordinary, and I think useless, piece of extravagance. Several of the windows on the first floor, nearly level with the street, are formed of plateglass, six feet by eleven, which must have cost four or five hundred dollars each, and may be shivered by a boy's marble or a snow-ball as effectually as by a four-pound shot; and I am greatly mistaken if there are not persons (one is enough) in this heterogeneous mass of population influenced by jealousy, malice, or other instigation of the devil, bad enough to do such a deed of mischief.*

"Mr. Stewart has paid the ladies of this city a high compliment in giving them such a beautiful resort in which to while away their leisure hours of a morning," wrote editor James Gordon Bennett in the *New York Herald*. "Half the time of the fashionable ladies of New York, at the lowest calculation," Bennett noted, "is spent in the dry goods stores, in laying out plans for personal decoration. Dress forms a subject of the most grave and serious contemplation."

Proper dress in a gentleman was also not something to be taken lightly in 1846. "Great men, statesmen, divines, eminent lawyers, physicians, and magistrates should dress well," noted Philip Hone. "It gives them consideration and raises their several professions in the eyes of their fellow men; black is safest—it is peculiarly the garb of a gentleman, and never goes out of style." Hone, one of the founders of the Whig Party in New York, confided in his diary that *in this matter of dress one of our great men (than whom there is none greater), Mr.* [Daniel] *Webster, has a strange fancy. He is not slovenly, but on the contrary tawdry, fond of a variety of colors. I do not remember ever to have seen him in the only dress in which he should appear—the respectable and dignified suit of black.*

Americans in general, Alexander Mackay summed up, *are excessively fond of being well dressed. The artisans amongst them are particularly so, not so much from personal vanity, as from the fact that they make dress a test of respectability. Almost every man who is not an emigrant wears superfine broad-cloth in America, if we except the hard-working farmer who generally attires himself in homespun. You seldom meet with a fustian jacket, except on an emigrant's back, in an American town.* Mackay concluded, "Canvass-back ducks they have in abundance, but no canvass-backed people."

Bets were placed that Alexander T. Stewart's magnificent dry-goods palace would be converted into a hotel in less than three years. "Stewart is worth, it is said, a half million of dollars, acquired by selling dry goods to the fashionables; but this is a dangerous experiment he has ventured upon," the New York correspondent of the Charleston News gossiped. "He has built this costly establishment on the unfashionable or shilling side of Broadway, relying on his name and fame to bring over the world from the other side of the way to buy goods at his magnificent counters, and of his handsome clerks."

The handsome clerks were all male, and Walt Whitman related that one woman had almost made up her mind never to do any shopping there again. "It puts me out of patience to see eighteen or twenty able bodied young men fussing about the ladies in the cloak room," she complained, "buttoning and unbuttoning, smoothing down folds, matching colors and arranging fringes—when the employment of females in those offices would be so much more appropriate and becoming."

Stewart's "dangerous experiment" propelled his fortune to new heights, and he enlarged his marble palace several times to keep up with the public demand.

Outside of Stewart's New Palace in Broadway, *from the* New York Herald, *September 26, 1846. The New-York Historical Society, New York City*

FASHIONABLE SHOPPING IN NEW YORK.
Outside View of Stewart's New Palace in Broadway.

Mackay was also struck by the prominent position of the periodical and newspaper press in American literature. "Periodicals, that is to say, quarterlies, monthlies, and serials of all kinds, issue from it in abundance." Arguably the most popular and influential periodical in the country was *Godey's Magazine and Lady's Book.* "From Maine to the Rocky Mountains," proprietor Louis Antoine Godey proclaimed, "there is scarcely a hamlet, however inconsiderable, where it is not received and read; and in the larger towns and cities it is universally distributed." *Godey's* "came as a pleasant friend to amuse as well as instruct," observed editor Sarah

Josepha Hale. "Some take it for the sake of the plates, some to read the stories, others because a friend writes for it."

Hale promised "literary excellence and artistic beauty, still keeping the moral tone onward and upward in its ennobling and purifying influence." She wrote in November 1846, "We seek to make ours emphatically *the Lady's Book*. No other periodical does or can compare with it in appropriateness for our own sex."

Even more pervasive than the periodicals were the extraordinary number of newspapers. Alexander Mackay found them at every turn, "on board the steamer and on the rail, in the counting house and the hotel, in the street and in the private dwelling, in the crowded thoroughfare and in the remotest rural district."

THE CELEBRATED TOM THUMB & HIS EQUIPAGE.

GODEY'S
LADY'S BOOK.

PHILADELPHIA, FEBRUARY, 1846.

THE FAIR CLIENT; OR, THE PACKET OF LETTERS.

(See Plate.)

"OH, dear! Cousin Carry, father is going to marry that horrid Mrs. Dayton! What shall we do?" said Alice Clinton, as she ran into Mrs. Somers' breakfast-room one bright summer morning, followed by her younger brother and sister. "Won't you speak to father, Cousin Carry?" continued she, coaxingly. "You know you have more influence with him than any one else."

"Yes, do—won't you?" chimed in George. "We don't dare to speak to him about it. That dreadful woman! I never could endure her. I am sure we can never stay at home if she comes. I will come and live with you."

"And so will I," sobbed little Mary, crying out of pure sympathy for her brother and sister.

"What is the matter?" asked Mrs. Somers. "Has anything happened lately? Only last week your father told me that the report of his intended marriage was false. It seems to me you alarm yourselves unnecessarily."

"Oh, no," replied Alice, a fair girl of sixteen; "she is coming here next week, and I heard father tell Uncle John this morning that he hoped his house would be a little more cheerful before long, for he thought of bringing home a bright presiding genius. Those were his very words;" and Alice leaned her head on Mrs. Somers' shoulder and sobbed bitterly.

"Well, well," said Mrs. Somers, at last, overcome by their united tears and entreaties, "I will exert all my influence in your favour, but I am afraid it will be useless when opposed by Mrs. Dayton's charms. How did your father become so infatuated by a woman he once disliked so excessively?"

"Oh," said George, bluntly, "she flattered him so much. I heard her tell him that he was one of the finest-looking men she ever saw; and she

called him so dignified and stately, and then she looked at Mrs. Dale and laughed, but father did not see her."

"Stay! that reminds me," exclaimed Mrs. Somers, "I have an idea in my mind; but I fear it will hardly be right to act upon it."

"Oh, yes," said Alice, raising her blue eyes filled with tears; "anything would be right, it seems to me. Pray, do all that you can."

"Well, dearest, dry your tears and go home, and I will think about it," said Mrs. Somers, kissing her brow. "There, I see your father coming; run home through the garden and I will speak with him."

And Mrs. Somers stepped into the little grass-plat in front of her house and called to Mr. Clinton, who readily obeyed her summons—for he had been waiting for an opportunity of informing his old ward and favourite of his determination, and of justifying himself in her eyes for what he feared she would consider a rash step.

Long and earnest was the conversation. She recalled to his mind the dislike formerly existing between himself and his now worshiped Mrs. Dayton; asked him if he had forgotten that he had once thought her so heartless and worldly that he had forbidden his wife to visit her, and reminded him of a conversation he had overheard between Mrs. Dayton and one of her friends, in which he was ridiculed so unmercifully as almost to produce an open quarrel. But it was all to no effect. He listened with ill-disguised impatience, and said that she had been very much misunderstood; she had explained everything to him, and in a village like theirs so many unfounded rumours were flying about that he thought a person of sense should pay no attention to them. For his part, his determination was taken, and once formed, Mrs. Somers

LE FOLLET

PARIS, *Boulevart S.t Martin, 61.*

Robe & pardessus ensembles de toilettes de M.me Thiery, bout Montmartre, 13.
Chapeaux de M.me Pratt bout de la Madeleine, 16, Cité Vindé. — Plumes de Mertens, r. Richelieu, 92.
Passementeries de Richout-Bayard, r. S.t Denis, 166. — Mouchoir de L. Chapron & Dubois, r. de la Paix, 7.
Essences & fleurs de Guerlain, r. de la Paix, 11. — Chaussures de Hoffmann, r. du Dauphin, 9.

Graham's Magazine.

Godey's *chief rival was George Rex Graham's* Graham's Magazine, *which had begun publication in 1841. The magazine featured French fashion plates, which the* Lady's Book *countered with an "Americanization" of Paris fashions.*

Graham's American Monthly Magazine of Literature and Art, *1846. Smithsonian Institution Libraries, Washington, D.C.*

Cornelia Wells Walter (1813–1898) began writing for the Boston Evening Transcript *to help out her brother, the founder and first editor of the newspaper, who was stricken with a lingering illness. After his death in 1842, Henry W. Dutton, the senior proprietor of the* Transcript, *sought out her father and through him offered her the editorship at $500 a year, the same wage paid her brother. Cornelia Walter was then less than thirty years old. She presided over the paper with vigor and determination, wielding a "trenchant and fearless" pen until her marriage to William Bordman Richards in 1847, when she thought it proper to resign.*

Thomas Ball, who painted miniatures, life-size portraits, and religious pictures in his studio on Tremont Row in Boston, would soon abandon painting in favor of sculpture.

Cornelia W. Walter by Thomas Ball (1819–1911), oil on canvas, circa 1846. Museum of Fine Arts, Boston, Massachusetts; gift of Elsie Bordman Richards

In Boston, Cornelia Wells Walter, editor of the *Boston Evening Transcript*, greeted the New Year with satisfaction. "Our friends and patrons were never more numerous than they are at the advent of '46." Her publisher, she told her readers, "voluntarily attributed our success to—to—we are somewhat diffident in proclaiming it—to *'the feminine rule!'*" But Walter, the first woman in America to preside over a daily newspaper, disclaimed, "Feminine ability is well enough in its way, but masculine aid is all-important, and as a family paper, the 'Transcript' has abundantly realized this fact." Particularly strong in covering literature, art, music, and drama, the *Evening Transcript* lived up to its reputation as the indispensable companion of the tea table.

"The 'simplicity of republican living,' is a phrase which is fast degenerating from former truthfulness into *present burlesque*," editorialized Walter in May. "In many cities . . . the appendages of an aristocracy of wealth have been introduced to the entire exclusion of aught that looks like simplicity."

Perhaps nothing symbolized the extravagant rush of the times more than the steamboat. And Cornelius Vanderbilt—known as the Commodore—a self-made, profane man without education or grace, saw to it that his steamboats were large and elegant, as well as fast. In 1846 Vanderbilt, who owned more steamboats than anyone else in the country, launched the finest boat (named for himself) yet seen on the Hudson. But in December, on a trip from Charleston, South Carolina, to Wilmington, North Carolina, the *Cornelius Vanderbilt* overturned in a heavy gale, and its rudder was "carried away, both wheel houses demolished and her masts broken off close to her deck." No lives were lost, but its cargo of mail was swept into the ocean. Subsequently righted and towed to port, the *Vanderbilt* was ready a few months later to participate in the great steamboat race against Commodore George Law's *Oregon*. "They went to Croton Point

Americans were fascinated with the pseudo-science of phrenology, whereby character could be read by studying the convexities of the skull. To assist the layman, the "organs" of the brain were marked off and labeled according to abstract qualities and tendencies such as compassion, caution, conscientiousness, love, and industry.

Phrenological head attributed to Asa Ames (1823–1851), polychromed pine, 1847–1850. Museum of American Folk Art, New York City; bequest of Jeanette Virgin (1981.24.1)

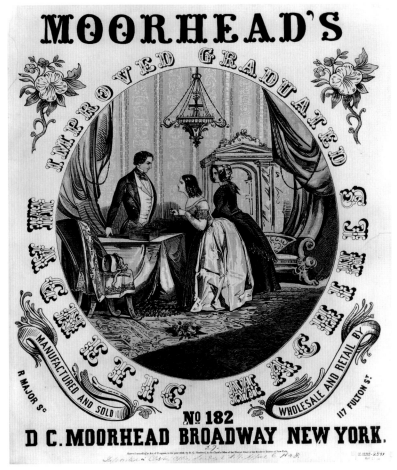

MOORHEAD'S

IMPROVED GRADUATED

MANUFACTURED AND SOLD

WHOLESALE AND RETAIL BY

R MAJOR Sᶜ

117 FULTON Sᵀ

No 182

D C. MOORHEAD BROADWAY NEW YORK.

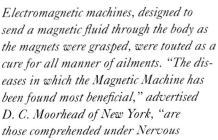

Electromagnetic machines, designed to send a magnetic fluid through the body as the magnets were grasped, were touted as a cure for all manner of ailments. "The diseases in which the Magnetic Machine has been found most beneficial," advertised D. C. Moorhead of New York, "are those comprehended under Nervous

Complaints: among which are Paralysis, Tic Doloreux, Fits, Rheumatism, acute and chronic: Headaches, Deafness, Bronchitis, Dyspepsia, Spinal affections, Palpitation of the Heart, General Debility and Deficiency of Nervous and Physical energy. Many of the cures performed are truly wonderful; some of them in diseases

of the most serious and obstinate character known to the medical profession."

Advertisement for "Moorhead's Improved Graduated Magnetic Machines" by Richard C. Major (active 1845–1868), wood engraving, 1848. Prints and Photographs Division, Library of Congress, Washington, D.C.

In 1846 Cornelius Vanderbilt (1794–1877) was fifty-two, with an estimated worth of $1.2 million. "Of an old Dutch root, Cornelius has evinced more energy and 'go aheadativeness' in business and driving steamboats, and other projects, than every one single Dutchman possessed," assessed a contemporary chronicler of the wealthy citizens of New York City.

Vanderbilt's portrait, painted by Nathaniel Jocelyn, a member of a Connecticut abolitionist family, was exhibited at the National Academy of Design in 1846. It became the property of Dr. Jared Linsly, who had been Vanderbilt's physician since 1833, when Vanderbilt was seriously injured in a railroad accident, an event that was said to have prejudiced him against railroad investment—ultimately the greatest source of his immense fortune—for many years.

Cornelius Vanderbilt by Nathaniel Jocelyn (1796–1881), oil on canvas, 1846. National Portrait Gallery, Smithsonian Institution, Washington, D.C.

Cornelius Vanderbilt listed himself as both the owner and master when he registered the Cornelius Vanderbilt *at the New York Customs House in 1846. Designed and constructed to Vanderbilt's specifications, the lavishly fitted-out steamship was nearly a thousand tons and could reach a speed of twenty-five miles an hour. No expense was spared in the appointments.*

The twins James and John Bard, both self-taught artists who worked together painting exact representations of steamboats, were employed by Commodore Van- derbilt to depict ships in which he had an interest. The *Cornelius Vanderbilt is here shown in the famous race up the Hudson with George Law's* Oregon *(the flag O), a contest that Law won by burning his costly interiors as fuel when his coal supply dwindled.*

🌾 The Cornelius Vanderbilt *by James Bard (1815–1897) and John Bard (1815–1856), oil on academy board, circa 1847. Shelburne Museum, Shelburne, Vermont*

and returned, seventy-five miles, in three hours and fifteen minutes—a rate of speed which would carry a vessel to Liverpool in five or six days," Philip Hone noted in his diary. The *Oregon* won the race, he continued, and "Vanderbilt was beaten for once."

Dangers were inherent in the fast-moving life of the "go-ahead" nation. Steamboat and railroad accidents were all too common. "I never take up a paper that does not contain accounts of loss of life, dreadful mutilation of limbs, and destruction of property, with which these reckless, dangerous, murderous modes of locomotion are attended," Philip Hone said. "The detail of loss of life by boiler-bursting, collisions, and snakesheads is as regular a concomitant of the breakfast-table as black tea and smoked beef."

Hone, a crusty, sixty-six-year-old conservative, often found cause to both marvel at and deplore the times. On April 17 he noted the arrival of the ship *Rainbow* from Canton in seventy-five days. The ship had made, he observed, "two complete voyages to and from Canton in the space of fourteen months, just about the time formerly consumed in one voyage." He added, "Everything goes fast now-a-days; the winds, even, begin to improve upon the speed which they have hitherto maintained; everything goes ahead but good manners and sound principles, and they are in a fair way to be driven from the track."

Symbolic of the "go-ahead" spirit of the times was the movement to build a railroad to the Pacific, which, James Gordon Bennett editorialized, would "place these United States in a position to control the trade of the whole world and make every nation on earth our tributary." A ship took fourteen to sixteen weeks to travel from New York to the Columbia River, whereas the three thousand miles across the continent by railroad could be traversed in eight days at a rate of sixteen miles an hour. American whalers in the Pacific would be able to send their cargoes from Oregon to market without delay; American manufacturers stood poised to monopolize the Chinese market.

George Wilkes, editor of the *National Police Gazette*, submitted a plan to Congress for building a railroad from some point on the Great Lakes to the Oregon territory under government auspices; Asa Whitney, a New York dry-goods merchant, offered a proposal for construction by private enterprise. Noting that Congress would decide between the two propositions, the *New York Herald* urged people to assemble and petition their representatives to support a transcontinental railroad. During the year, meetings

"The Americans have ever been a people peculiarly addicted to locomotion; so that, whilst the introduction of the railways was a welcome event, everything conspired to accelerate their multiplication in the United States," wrote Scottish barrister Alexander Mackay. "The extent to which the railway system has already developed itself there is truly surprising; whilst the schemes which are as yet only projected, are on a scale of vastness utterly bewildering to those who are unacquainted with the nature, the capacities, and the wants of the country."

Wrote Swiss naturalist Louis Agassiz, as he traveled by rail from Boston to New Haven at an average speed of fifteen to eighteen miles an hour, "The rapidity of the locomotion is frightful to those who are unused to it, but you adapt yourself to the speed, and soon become, like all the rest of the world, impatient of the slightest delay." He exclaimed, "There is something infernal in the irresistible power of steam, carrying such heavy masses along with the swiftness of lightning."

Opening of the Wilderness *by Thomas Prichard Rossiter (1818–1871), oil on canvas, circa 1846. Museum of Fine Arts, Boston, Massachusetts; bequest of Martha C. Karolik for the M. and M. Karolik Collection of American Paintings*

The success of the Rainbow *prompted her owners, William Edgar Howland and William H. Aspinwall, to have John W. Griffiths design a companion clipper ship for the China trade. "The splendid ship Sea Witch, whose peculiar model, and sharp bows, have for the last few months attracted so much attention was launched,"* the New York Herald *reported on December 8. "She is built of the very best material, and although present-ing such a light appearance, is most strongly constructed."* The Sea Witch, *sailing from Hong Kong to New York in seventy-seven days, would break all previous records.*

Clipper Ship Sea Witch Coming to Anchor at Whampoa *by an unidentified Chinese artist, oil on canvas, not dated. Peabody Essex Museum, Salem, Massachusetts; gift of Mrs. F. D. Elwell, 1942*

New York dry-goods merchant Asa Whitney (1797–1872), awakened by time spent in China to the advantage that America might have in that market with a railroad to the Pacific, began a campaign for its construction in 1844. After personally staking out the proposed route, Whitney submitted a plan to Congress for building a railroad on his own, in return for a strip of land sixty miles wide all along the way. His intended route from Milwaukee to Puget Sound, however, immediately aroused the opposition of Missouri Senator Thomas Hart Benton, who, although a strong railroad supporter, favored an eastern terminus in St. Louis. Other congressmen had their own preferred routes, and still others thought that the government itself should build the line. Whitney persisted in his efforts, but without success, until 1851.

Asa Whitney by an unidentified artist, oil on canvas, not dated. University of Pennsylvania Art Collection, Philadelphia

about the railroad were held in Cincinnati, Pittsburgh, Louisville, St. Louis, Terre Haute, Indianapolis, Dayton, Columbus, and Wheeling.

"We must again call upon Congress to give this subject some attention during the present session," Bennett wrote in December. *It is a matter infinitely of more importance to the United States than any question that has ever occupied the attention of the people, not even excepting the war with Mexico—the division of the Oregon territory, or the propriety of imposing specific ad valorum or high or low duties on our importations. It is a subject in which every State, every township, every American and well-wisher of America is interested, and we hope that the neglect with which it has been for so long a time treated will no longer be tolerated.* Not until 1853, however, when Secretary of War Jefferson Davis asked Congress for funds to survey the most feasible routes west, did the project for a transcontinental railroad begin to move forward.

"Gentlemen, this is no humbug"

Dr. John Collins Warren by Francis
Alexander (1800–1880), pastel on paper, circa
1845–1850. National Portrait Gallery,
Smithsonian Institution, Washington, D.C.

On October 16, 1846, at Massachusetts General Hospital, Dr. John Collins Warren (1778–1856), a major figure in American medicine for thirty years, agreed to participate in the first public demonstration of a substance that dentist Dr. William T. G. Morton (1819–1868) claimed would overcome pain. Morton, who had tried intoxicants, opium, and mesmerism, among other things, to alleviate the pain of tooth extractions, had turned, upon the suggestion of Dr. Charles T. Jackson, to experiments with sulfuric ether, at first inhaling it himself, and during July and August 1846 using it without ill effect on a goldfish, a hen, and his pet spaniel.

The patient on the morning of October 16, a young house painter by the name of Gilbert Abbot, was lost in sleep after the ether was administered and showed no signs of pain while Dr. Warren extracted a tumor

Operating room of the Massachusetts General Hospital, showing a reenactment of the first public demonstration of etherization, daguerreotype, circa 1846–1848. Massachusetts General Hospital, Boston, through the Harvard University Art Museums, Cambridge, Massachusetts

from his jaw. "Gentlemen, this is no humbug," pronounced Warren as Abbot regained consciousness. Another of those present exclaimed, "I have seen something today which will go around the world!"

"Everybody wants to have a hand in a great discovery," Dr. Oliver Wendell Holmes wrote to Morton. "All I will do is to give you a hint or two, as to names, or the name, to be applied to the state produced and the agent. The state should I think be called 'Anaesthesia.'. . . The adjective will be 'Anaesthetic.'"

Morton at once took out a patent on his innovation, and before the year was out became embroiled in a bitter dispute with Jackson over credit for the discovery of what Morton called "letheon." The trustees and surgeons of the Massachusetts General Hospital supported Morton, testifying that "in their opinion, Dr. William T. G. Morton first showed the world that ether would produce insensibility to the pain of surgical operations, and that it could be used with safety."

William T. G. Morton by an unidentified artist, watercolor on ivory, not dated. Division of Medical Sciences, National Museum of American History, Smithsonian Institution, Washington, D.C.

"Strange that so many of all kinds and classes of people should sell out comfortable homes, in Missouri and elsewhere, pack up and start across such an immense barren waste, to settle in some new place of which they have at most no certain information," reflected the famous mountain man James Clyman, coming upon the grave of an emigrant who had died along the way.

California pioneer Mary A. Jones recalled how it had been with her. "In the winter of 18 and 46 our neighbor got hold of Frémont's History of California and began talking of moving to the New Country & brought the book to my husband to read, & he was carried away with the idea too. I said O let us not go. Our neighbors, some of them old men & women, with large families, but it made no difference. They must go. . . . We sold our home . . . and what we could not sell . . . we gave away & on the 7th day of May 1846 we joined the camp for California."

Artist James F. Wilkins traveled the overland trail himself in 1849.

Leaving the Old Homestead *by James F. Wilkins (1808–1888), oil on canvas, circa 1853. Missouri Historical Society, St. Louis*

Chapter 4

Westward Ho!

In January 1846 John Augustus Sutter, the Swiss founder of the New Helvetia settlement in the Sacramento Valley of California, noted the recent arrival of Captain John Charles Frémont and Lansford Hastings. Frémont was on an exploring expedition for the United States; Hastings was a promoter and adventurer who had recently published *The Emigrants' Guide to Oregon and California*, "praising the country to the skies" in an effort to stimulate immigration. "Both of these Gentlemen bring us the news that it is a great excitement through the whole of the U. States to emigrate to Oregon and California," Sutter recorded in his diary, "and that we could expect several thousands of them here, and a good many of wealth and Capital."

Since 1843 several thousand Americans had ventured west over the Oregon Trail to settle in Oregon's fertile Willamette Valley. California was a newer destination; only about eight hundred Americans had so far chosen to settle in this salubrious land tenuously held by an erratic Mexican government. But 1846 was to be different. In the spring, as the wagon trains gathered at the jumping-off places in Missouri, the major talk was of California.

Andrew Jackson Grayson, a twenty-seven-year-old merchant from St. Louis whose passion was the study of nature, had long been tantalized by the flora and fauna he anticipated finding in the California climate. Grayson had been brought up on a plantation in northwestern Louisiana, where his greatest delight was to roam the fields with gun in hand. Sent to the College of St. Mary in St. Louis, he met mountain trappers bringing pelts to the American Fur Company.

Grayson used his inheritance from his father—the proceeds from selling three slaves—to open a country store in Columbia, Missouri. It failed within two years. By the time he married a local girl, Frances J. Timmons, he had determined "to dwell on the Pacific Shores of California," his wife later recalled. In 1844 the Graysons moved to St. Louis to plan their move west. Here Grayson again failed in business.

"Ho for California!" Grayson advertised on February 20, 1846. *At the suggestion and desire of a number of my friends, who propose emigrating with me to California, and deeming it actually necessary that some one should take the lead, whereby we may be able to organize an expedition and preserve good order while on the route, I have consented to take the charge upon myself, and pledge my life to the safe conduct of those who are disposed to join us in our journey to that country.* Because he was traveling with his young family—a two- or three-year-old son, Edward— Grayson expressed the hope "that we may have an orderly and well organized company." A columnist in the same issue of the *St. Louis Reveille* wrote that Grayson was "eminently qualified" to take charge of a proposed expedition to California, "being a young man of enterprise, courage and determination—one who has not been accustomed to the 'soft lap of luxury,' but who has rather courted, from his youth up, the excitement and dangers of an adventurous life in the extensive wilds of the South-west."

Those who wanted to join him should be in Independence on the Missouri River by April 1, Grayson specified. Timing was crucial to a twenty-five-hundred-mile journey across plains, mountain ranges, and deserts; a start could not be made until the spring rains had subsided, and California had to be reached before snow blocked passage over the Sierra Nevada.

"Emigrants should be well provided with arms and ammunition, good teams of mules or oxen, and provisions for at least six months," Grayson instructed. "It is better not to be burdened with any heavy and unnecessary articles of house furniture, but good assortments of farming implements, useful tools, garden-seeds, and such things only as will be serviceable in a new country, and not easily to be had in California." Many years later Mrs. Grayson recalled, "I was as full of romantic adventure as my

The Graysons broke off from the main group of the ill-fated Donner party and, according to Mrs. Grayson's account, "completed the last of the way over the mountains by themselves." She recalled, "Every step of the journey had been pleasant to Mr. Grayson, who had often wandered miles from the train on hunting excursions, observing birds."

In celebration of the family's safe arrival in California, Andrew Jackson Grayson (1819–1869) commissioned William S. Jewett to depict the family group on the very spot where, safely across the Sierra Nevada, they first glimpsed the Sacramento Valley. So meaningful was the moment that Grayson personally escorted the artist to the site, paying the expenses of the journey and two thousand dollars for the finished picture.

The Promised Land—The Grayson Family *by William S. Jewett (1792–1874), oil on canvas, 1850. Terra Museum of American Art, Chicago, Illinois; Daniel J. Terra Collection*

Whether bound for California, Oregon, or Sante Fe, the jumping-off place was Independence, Missouri, or Westport (present-day Kansas City), six miles upriver. "I can give you no idea of the hurry of this place at this time," wrote Mrs. George Donner from Independence on May 11. "It is supposed there will be 7000 waggons start from this place, this season." She expected the trip to California to be accomplished in four months. "I am willing to go & have no doubt it will be an advantage to our children & to us."

Independence Courthouse, *published in* The United States Illustrated *by Charles A. Dana. Prints and Photographs Division, Library of Congress, Washington, D.C.*

husband." She would even profess "that the trip across the plains was one of the most enjoyable episodes of my life."

The Graysons soon joined up with a group that included Colonel William Henry Russell, a flamboyant character who claimed to be a bosom friend of Henry Clay and of former Missouri Governor Lillburn W. Boggs. "Singular as it may appear, there is as much electioneering here for the captaincy of this expedition as it is for the presidency of the United States," wrote Edwin Bryant, a former Kentucky newspaper editor who also joined the party. In the course of the balloting, Grayson withdrew his name and threw his support to Russell, who was elected captain over Boggs.

Another of those who had made up his mind to head for California was James Frazier Reed of Springfield, Illinois. The forty-six-year-old Reed had come from Ireland as a child and settled in Illinois. As a private in the Black Hawk War, he had served alongside Abraham Lincoln. Reed had been in the mining business in Galena, Illinois, and then moved to Springfield, where he began a mercantile business and purchased a farm. Reed was a well-to-do man who expected to do even better in the California Eden.

Reed inspired his neighbors, the Donner brothers, George and Jacob, and their families to join him, and their advertisement reading "WESTWARD, HO! FOR OREGON AND CALIFORNIA!" appeared in Springfield's *Sagamo Journal* on March 26. *Who wants to go to California without costing them anything? As many as eight young men, of good character, who can drive an ox team, will be accommodated by gentlemen who will leave this vicinity about the first of April. Come, boys! You can have as much land as you want without costing you any thing. The government of California gives large tracts of land to persons who have to move there.*

James and Margaret Reed had four children—twelve-year-old Virginia, nine-year-old Patty, six-year-old James, and four-year-old Thomas. Also along was Mrs. Reed's seventy-five-year-old mother, Sarah Keyes, who, ill with consumption, would die early in the journey.

The Reeds and the Donners arrived in Independence during the second week of May. Here they were taken note of by a twenty-two-year-old gentleman from Boston who, identifying the immigrants as being from Illinois, recorded in his journal, "Some of these ox-wagons contained large families of children, peeping from under the covering. One remarkably pretty little girl was seated on horseback, holding a parasol over her head to keep off the rain." That description fit Virginia Reed, who took great pride in riding her pony, Billy. "All looked well—but what a journey before them!"

Young Francis Parkman, embarked on "a tour of amusement and curiosity," took no more than passing notice of his countrymen. His purpose was not with them, but with the Indians, whom he wanted to study before the forces of civilization changed them.

One hundred twenty miles outside of Independence, the Reed-Donner group joined the Russell company, which had been traveling at an average of fifteen miles a day. At its height, the Russell train, which included the Graysons, numbered three hundred people and seventy-odd wagons.

Parkman, disdainful of traveling with a wagon train, rode hour after hour over "a wide expanse of perfectly flat prairie . . . saw wolves—and where they had dug up a recent grave. Turkey buzzards and

Stirring in the mind of Francis Parkman (1823–1893)—a historian "in embryo" he called himself—was a plan to tell the story of England and France warring over Canada, a history that he ultimately expanded into the epic struggle for the North American continent. When his cousin Quincy Adams Shaw proposed a hunting trip in the Far West for health and recreation, Parkman, whose eyes were suffering from studying law at Harvard, readily agreed, seeing also a prime opportunity for "studying the manners and characters of Indians in their primitive state."

Francis Parkman, attributed to Albert Sands Southworth (1811–1894) and Josiah Johnson Hawes (1808–1901), daguerreotype, circa 1852. National Portrait Gallery, Smithsonian Institution, Washington, D.C.

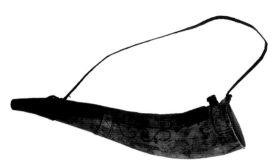

Francis Parkman related that for the first two months of his journey, he and Quincy Adams Shaw "wore the frock and trousers of civilization and when these wore out, we got the squaws to make us fringed buckskin frocks, and trousers to match, with moccasins of the Sioux pattern." As a memento of his two-thousand-mile adventure, Parkman hung the frock, along with his "old fashioned powder horn," Indian shield, and bow and arrows, on the walls of the room in which he slept and worked.

Parkman had obtained the shield from an Arapaho village near Bent's Fort, on the Arkansas River, in exchange for "a large piece of scarlet cloth, together with some tobacco and a knife."

✺ Parkman's powder horn. Private collection

✺ Parkman's shield, bow, and arrows. Massachusetts Historical Society, Boston

✺ Parkman's fringed buckskin frock. Wentworth Coolidge Mansion, New Hampshire Division of Parks and Recreation, Concord

frequent carcasses of cattle." In the later published account of his adventure, Parkman told his readers, let the traveler *be as enthusiastic as he may, he will find enough to damp his ardor. His wagons will stick in the mud; his horses will break loose; harness will give way; and axle-trees prove unsound. His bed will be a soft one, consisting often of black mud of the richest consistency. . . . The wolves will entertain him with a concert at night, and skulk around him by day, just beyond rifle-shot; his horse will step into badger-holes. . . . Add to this, that, all the morning, the sun beats upon him with a sultry, penetrating heat, and that, with provoking regularity, at about four o'clock in the afternoon, a thunderstorm rises and drenches him to the skin.*

Francis Parkman and his cousin, Quincy Adams Shaw, arrived at Fort Laramie, the isolated trading post in the foothills of the Rocky Mountains, on June 15. Parkman came upon "Russel's or Boggs' comp'y, engaged in drinking and refitting," and recorded in his journal on June 26 that "a part of Russe[ll]'s company . . . dissatisfied with their pragmatic, stump-orator leader, has split into half a dozen pieces."

From his camp, pleasantly situated on Laramie Creek eighteen miles from the fort, Parkman reported to his family, "We are living chiefly on buffalo and antelope." Their hunter, Henry Chatillon, he explained, "is to be implicitly relied on—intelligent, experienced, and knocks over buffalo whenever he chooses." Parkman added, "For a man of no education—(he cannot read or write), he is by far the most complete gentleman I ever saw."

The Oglala Sioux village of Old Smoke set up tents near Fort Laramie, and there Francis Parkman spent many of his evenings. "The Indians look upon us as great chiefs and entertain us with feasts of young puppies, which they consider the summit of luxury; and which, in fact are very good," Parkman wrote. *One old fellow was very anxious yesterday, that I should become his son-in-law; and offered his daughter at the cheap rate of one horse; but I explained to him that I loved my horses too well to part with them; with which excuse he seemed satisfied.*

On June 15, 1846, Francis Parkman reached Fort Laramie, where he reported, "The Oregon emigrants are arriving in large parties every day, and remain for several days to refit, buy supplies, etc; and the Indians are coming in from all quarters to meet them, and get presents, so that the whole fort is surrounded by waggons, tents, and Indian lodges."

The American Fur Company operated this trading post—the point beyond which there was no turning back—where they held "a most tyrannical monopoly." Parkman found prices to be "most extortionate. Sugar, two dollars a cup—5-cent tobacco at $1.50—bullets at $.75 a pound, etc."

Interior of Fort Laramie *by Alfred Jacob Miller (1810–1874), watercolor on paper, 1837. The Walters Art Gallery, Baltimore, Maryland*

Virginia Reed, writing in *Century Magazine* in 1891, remembered, "At Fort Laramie was a party of Sioux, who were on the war path going to fight the Crows or Blackfeet. The Sioux are fine-looking Indians and I was not in the least afraid of them. They fell in love with my pony and set about bargaining to buy him." But despite offers of buffalo robes, beautifully tanned buckskin, pretty beaded moccasins, and ropes made of grass, her father was not induced to part with her beautiful Billy.

An Oglala chief, the Whirlwind, was preparing to avenge his son's death at the hands of the Snakes, a branch of the Shoshones, and Parkman, enthralled by the opportunity to witness war ceremonies, followed Whirlwind and his warriors through the Black Hills. Disappointed when Whirlwind changed his mind about going to war, Parkman caught up with an encampment of Sioux who were hunting buffalo and lived with them for three weeks. Suffering from dysentery, Parkman became "so weak that, for a while, I could not saddle my horse without assistance, and an Indian village is no place for an invalid." He told his father, "I saw what I wanted to, however, and returned to the Fort in comparative health."

On September 1, en route to Santa Fe, John Mix Stanley's commanding officer, Lieutenant William Emory, recorded in his journal, "The first thing that caught my eye through the column of dust, was a fierce pair of Buffalo horns overlapped with long shaggy hair. As they approached, the sturdy form of a naked Indian re-vealed itself beneath the horns with shield and lance, dashing at full speed on a white horse, which like his own naked body was painted all the colors of the rainbow." Such was the scene that Stanley sketched, and he later worked it into a finished painting.

Buffalo Hunt on the Southwestern Prairies *by John Mix Stanley (1814–1872), oil on canvas, 1846. National Museum of American Art, Smithsonian Institution, Washington, D.C.; gift of the Misses Henry (daughters of Joseph Henry), 1908*

Parkman had not intended to travel further west than Fort Laramie—the point beyond which there was no turning back—and at the end of August he and Shaw moved south toward Bent's Fort on the Upper Arkansas River. All along the way, they ran into detachments of troops journeying to Santa Fe, which had just been occupied by American forces.

One of those in the military entourage shared Parkman's interest in the American Indian. John Mix Stanley, on his way to paint the Pueblo Indians in the spring of 1846, had attached himself to the trading caravan that was moving to Santa Fe under the protection of Colonel Stephen Watts Kearny. "We have one in our Company, Mr. Stanley rather celebrated for his Indian sketches," related Susan Magoffin, wife of one of the principal traders. Stanley was soon enlisted in the Topographical Corps of the Army of the West under the command of Lieutenant William Emory.

On September 26, as Stanley began the march from Santa Fe to California, Parkman reached Westport (now Kansas City), six miles from Independence, where he had begun his journey. He ended his Oregon Trail journal on October 1, while he was "stuck on a sandbar in the river" on the way to St. Louis.

Once Parkman returned to Boston, his health broke down completely. For weeks his eyes would not permit him to read or write, and his sleepless nights were spent in great pain. He persisted, nonetheless, in getting his Oregon Trail experiences into print, by having his journal entries read aloud and writing with a pen guided by a framework of wire. In February 1847 the first installment of "The Oregon Trail; A Summer's Journey out of Bounds" appeared in the *Knickerbocker Magazine.*

While readers in the East were being entertained with Parkman's adventure, the full saga of the 1846 westward emigration to California was still unfolding. Much had occurred since late June, when Parkman had witnessed the breakup of the Russell emigrant train at Fort Laramie. Andrew Jackson Grayson "had quarrelled with all his companions, and every one who could raise a horse had left him," Parkman reported.

Grayson himself recalled that his group left Fort Bridger (in the southwestern corner of what became Wyoming) on July 26, and when they arrived at the sink of the St. Mary's River, they met "a new species of trouble" when the Indians stole a number of their cattle and shot many more with poisoned arrows. Determined to teach the Indians a lesson—"they had raised the tomahawk against us, notwithstanding our kind treatment of them when they came about our camp"—Grayson led a company of about ten men to confront the Indians in their own village, "where they numbered upward of 300 fighting men and all arrayed for battle, whooping and yelling all kinds of defiance." Grayson recalled, *We charged upon them as fast as we were able but before we got within rifle shot they all disappeared behind the rocks, like so many squirrels into their holes. We still advanced upon them until within a few paces of where they were hit when they charged upon us with all the*

Francis Parkman was one of the first writers to have close contact with the Indians. In his foreword to the first edition of The California and Oregon Trail, *Parkman stressed that his account of the Indians' "wild and picturesque life" was based on what he himself had seen, whereas the depictions of the "romantic savage" by others, such as James Fenimore Cooper, "for the most part, are mere creatures of fancy."*

Felix Octavius Carr Darley (1822–1888), the most popular American illustrator of the period, drew the illustrations for Parkman's first edition.

The California and Oregon Trail: Being Sketches of Prairie and Rocky Mountain Life *by Francis Parkman Jr. (New York: George P. Putnam, 1849). Smithsonian Institution Libraries, Washington, D.C.*

This map, drawn by cartographer Charles Preuss, who was with John Charles Frémont on his three exploring expeditions, encompasses the territory west of Fort Laramie in today's southeastern Wyoming. The Donner party left the Oregon Trail near Fort Bridger on Black's Fork of the Green River in southwestern Wyoming. They took Hastings' Cutoff, which ran due west through the Wasatch Mountains, skirted the south end of the Great Salt Lake, crossed the Great Salt Lake Desert and the Rocky Mountains, and came to the Humboldt River, where it joined the old trail.

Map of Oregon and Upper California From the Surveys of John Charles Frémont and other Authorities *drawn by Charles Preuss (1803–1854), lithograph by E. Weber & Co., Baltimore, 1848. Geography and Map Division, Library of Congress, Washington, D.C.*

fury of savages. We met them, however, with steady aim, and every shot killed an Indian. They fell back in the rocks again and continued to pour their arrows at us faster than the hail from the clouds. We fought them from behind rocks all day shooting them through the head whenever we could catch one peeping over the rocks, until we finally routed them after killing 18 of their number. One of the Grayson party was killed, and three others were badly wounded.

The Graysons traveled on, reaching the Sierra Nevada in October, before the snows came. The Reeds and the Donners were not so fortunate. When the party now headed by George Donner reached Fort Bridger, they were persuaded to take Hastings' Cutoff, which left the Oregon Trail near the fort and ran straight west through the Wasatch Mountains, skirting the south end of the Great Salt Lake, crossing the Great Salt Lake

In 1852 John Mix Stanley placed his 152 Indian paintings on exhibition at the Smithsonian Institution in the hope that the government would purchase the collection. "Black Knife, An Apache Chief, reconnoitering the command of General Kearney on his march from Santa Fe to California," as Stanley described the painting in his catalogue, was one of only five of his canvases to survive the Smithsonian fire of January 24, 1865.

Black Knife, an Apache Chief *by John Mix Stanley (1814–1872), oil on canvas, 1846. National Museum of American Art, Smithsonian Institution, Washington, D.C.*

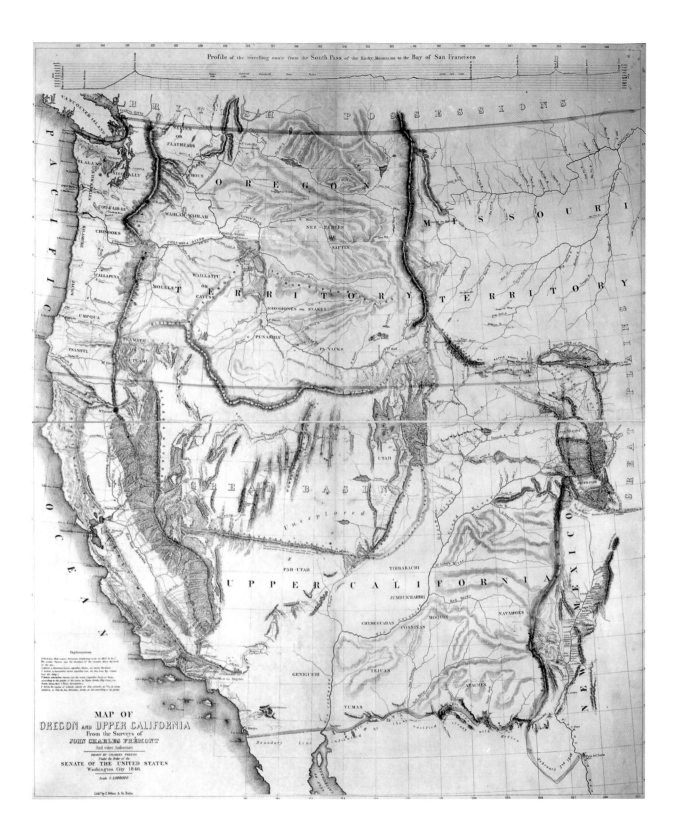

Profile of the travelling route from the South Pass of the Rocky Mountains to the Bay of San Francisco

MAP OF
OREGON AND UPPER CALIFORNIA
From the Surveys of
JOHN CHARLES FREMONT
And other Authorities
DRAWN BY CHARLES PREUSS
Under the Order of the
SENATE OF THE UNITED STATES
Washington City 1848.
Scale 1:3000000

Desert and the Rocky Mountains, and coming to the Humboldt River, where it joined the old trail.

"The new road, or Hastings' Cut-off is said to be a savings of 350 or 400 miles in going to California and a better route," wrote James Reed. *The rest of the Californians went the long route—feeling afraid of Hastings' Cutoff. Mr. Bridger informs me that the route we design to take, is a fine level road, with plenty of water and grass. It is estimated that 700 miles will take us to Capt. Suter's Fort, which we hope to make in seven weeks from this day.*

On July 31 the Donner party entered Hastings' Cutoff, traveling at a good pace of ten to twelve miles a day. At the bottom of Echo Canyon on August 6, they found a note, stuck in the top of some sage, from Lansford Hastings warning that the road ahead was virtually impassable. James Reed rode in search of Hastings, finding him after five days, but the promoter would do no more than point out a route from a high point above.

Making their way through the canyon, the Donner party could do no better than two miles a day. Virginia Reed wrote, "There was absolutely no road, not even a trail. The cañon wound around among the hills. Heavy underbrush had to be cut away and used for making a road bed."

The emigrants struggled out of the mountains on August 22 to find another note from Hastings, assuring them that the great desert could be crossed in two days and two nights. The trip proved to be more nearly eighty miles, rather than the forty Hastings had claimed, and on the third day the party's water ran out. The oxen, crazed with thirst, bolted away, and thirty-six were lost. Not until September 26 did the Donner party reach the Humboldt River, where the supposed shortcut—125 miles longer, in fact—joined the old trail.

On October 5, as double teams of oxen were pulling the wagons up a steep, sandy hill, two wagons became entangled, and in the resulting altercation James Reed drew out his hunting knife and killed a teamster. Reed was brought up for summary justice, and only his wife's pleading saved him from being hanged. He was banished from the company.

The Donner party continued down the Humboldt, most of its members walking beside the wagons to spare the oxen. On October 12 they met with further disaster when Indians killed twenty-one oxen with poisoned arrows. By this time, they had lost more than one hundred head of cattle. On October 30 they reached the final mountain, but as they rested their oxen to prepare for the ascent over the Sierra Nevada, five feet of snow fell, making it impossible for their wagons to get through. The Donner party—twenty-five men, fifteen women, and forty-one children—had no

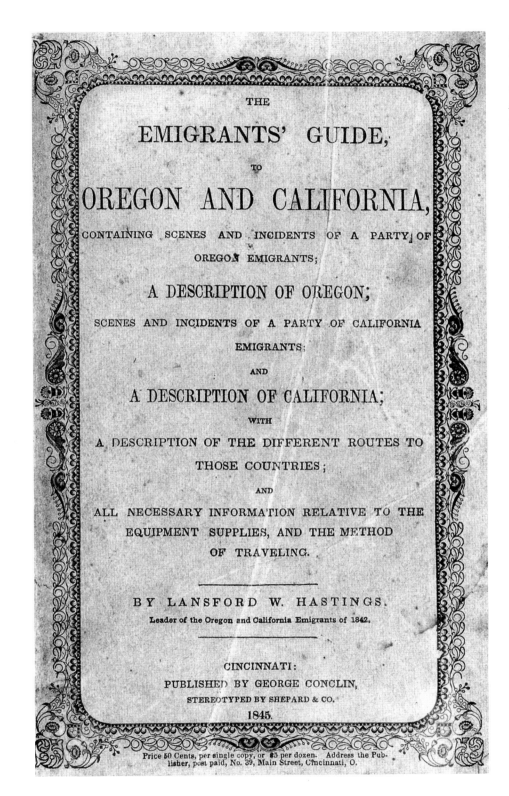

THE

EMIGRANTS' GUIDE,

TO

OREGON AND CALIFORNIA,

CONTAINING SCENES AND INCIDENTS OF A PARTY OF

OREGON EMIGRANTS;

A DESCRIPTION OF OREGON;

SCENES AND INCIDENTS OF A PARTY OF CALIFORNIA

EMIGRANTS;

AND

A DESCRIPTION OF CALIFORNIA;

WITH

A DESCRIPTION OF THE DIFFERENT ROUTES TO

THOSE COUNTRIES;

AND

ALL NECESSARY INFORMATION RELATIVE TO THE
EQUIPMENT SUPPLIES, AND THE METHOD
OF TRAVELING.

BY LANSFORD W. HASTINGS.

Leader of the Oregon and California Emigrants of 1842.

CINCINNATI:
PUBLISHED BY GEORGE CONCLIN,
STEREOTYPED BY SHEPARD & CO.
1845.

Price 50 Cents, per single copy, or $5 per dozen. Address the Publisher, post paid, No. 39, Main Street, Cincinnati, O.

Lawyer Lansford Hastings, ambitious to wrest California from Mexico and make it a republic (with himself as its first president, it was suspected), sought to lure emigrants through his book, which touted a new and shorter route of which he had no accurate knowledge.

The Emigrants' Guide to Oregon and California *by Lansford W. Hastings (Cincinnati: George Conclin, 1845). Yale Collection of Western Americana, Beinecke Rare Book and Manuscript Library, Yale University, New Haven, Connecticut*

choice but to move back to Truckee Lake to wait out the fierce winter of 1846 in makeshift camps, and without enough food to see them through.

On his own, James Reed had somehow made his way to California before the snow, staggering into Sutter's Fort in late October. Begging supplies and horses from Sutter, he rushed back to the mountains, only to be blocked by snow two miles from the summit.

Reed returned to Fort Sutter to raise money and men to attempt the rescue of his family, only to find that every able-bodied man in the valley—including Andrew Jackson Grayson and William Henry Russell—had gone South to retake Los Angeles from the Mexicans. Not until the fighting ended on January 10, 1847, did several relief parties set out. It was April 21 before the last of the Donner party was out of the mountains. Forty-one had died; forty-six survived. The Reeds were one of only two families without a loss.

From "Napa Vallie California," Virginia Reed wrote to her cousin on May 16, 1847, *O Mary I have not wrote you half of the truble* [we have had] *but I hav Wrote you anuf to let you* [k]*now what truble is but thank the Good god and the onely family that did not eat human flesh we have left everything but i dont cair for that we have got* [through with our lives but] *Dont let this letter dishaten anybody never take no cutofs and hury along as fast as you can.*

Nine-year-old Martha Reed, called Patty, kept a lock of her grandmother's hair and this doll with her throughout the horrendous ordeal of 1846. She survived to reach California, where she died in 1923 at the age of eighty-five.

Doll carried to California by Martha Reed in 1846. Sutter's Fort State Historic Park, California Department of Parks and Recreation, Sacramento

"We are all very well pleased with Cali-fornia," Virginia Reed wrote in May 1847. "It is a beautiful Country it is mostley in vallies it aut to be a beautiful Country to pay us for our trubel geting there."

The Reed family in front of their adobe house in California, by an unidentified photographer, photograph, not dated. Sutter's Fort State Historic Park, California Department of Parks and Recreation, Sacramento

The Mormon Exodus

The first of the emigrants to head west in 1846 were the Mormons, members of the Church of Jesus Christ of Latter-Day Saints, forced by circumstances to begin their exodus before the grass had grown high enough to feed their cattle.

Expelled from Missouri in 1839, the Mormons had built a city they called Nauvoo on the Illinois bank of the Mississippi River. Thanks to a vigorous missionary recruitment, Nauvoo's population had reached twelve thousand by 1846.

Hated by their neighbors because of some of their religious practices, especially polygamy, and resented because of their economic and political cohesion, the Mormons were subject to repeated mob action, which the Illinois militia could not contain. "Your religion is new, and it surprises the people as any great novelty in religion generally does," Governor Thomas Ford wrote to Brigham Young (1801–1877) in 1845. "They cannot rise above the prejudices excited by such novelty. . . . If you can get off by yourselves you may enjoy peace; but surrounded by such neighbors I confess I do not foresee the time when you will be permitted to enjoy quiet."

Brigham Young—elected to lead the Church of the Latter-Day Saints after founder Joseph Smith was murdered at the Carthage, Illinois, jail in 1844—had for some time recognized the expediency of migration to an unsettled area. Systematically, the Mormon leadership began a study of all the literature on the West—including John C. Frémont's reports—and came to the conclusion by mid-1845 that they should move to the basin of the Great Salt Lake or Bear River Valley, an area deemed inhospitable enough to discourage infringement from the Gentiles. Young

came to an agreement with Governor Ford that the Mormons would depart from Illinois in the spring.

The Mormon Temple in Nauvoo, which Young had determined should be finished even after it was clear that the town must be abandoned, was dedicated on November 30, and in the early days of 1846, Young noted in his diary that he had been giving himself "entirely to the work of the Lord in the Temple." By February ordinances—adoptions of children and the sealing of wives to husbands—had been administered to more than five thousand people.

April was the time set for the exodus, but in early February an attempt was made to arrest Young and others on the charge of harboring a counterfeiting operation. Amid rumors that federal troops in St. Louis were planning to intercept and destroy them, the first group of Mormons crossed the Mississippi River on February 4 and gathered in temporary camps in Iowa. Young remained behind until he could finish with the temple ceremonies, but departed with his family—twelve wives, nine children, and several foster children—on the evening of February 15.

Young organized the Saints into companies of fifty families, subdivided into ten, each led by a captain. On March 5 the first group, with five hundred wagons, started out from Sugar Creek, Iowa, singing as they went, "Come, Come Ye Saints" and "O Upper California, that's the land for me"—upper California being understood to mean anywhere south of Oregon and west of the Great Divide. Among the emigrants were Captain Pitts and his brass band, a group recruited en masse from England. Also along was William Warner Major, an artist who had come from England in 1844, and whose work included the por-

Brigham and Mary Ann Young and their children, by William Warner Major (1804–1854), oil on canvas, 1846. Museum of Church History and Art, Salt Lake City, Utah

Nauvoo, Illinois, *by an unidentified photographer, after a daguerreotype, circa 1846. LDS Church Archives, Salt Lake City, Utah*

trait of Brigham Young and his family in an ornate setting far removed from Nauvoo or Salt Lake City.

At Richardson's Point, fifty miles from Sugar Creek, the Saints built a permanent camp, where other companies could find supplies. They established another post at a crossing of the Chariton River, where they sowed crops.

Young and his followers intended that several hundred men would move to the Great Basin in 1846, but that plan changed when, after the outbreak of war with Mexico in May, President Polk authorized the enlistment of Mormons, who were to march to California with General Stephen Watts Kearny. Young, seizing the opportunity of moving five hundred Mormons to the West Coast at government expense, and at the same time giving the church the benefit of their pay and allowances, quickly moved from camp to camp, exhorting men and boys to enlist. On July 2 the Mormon battalion, accompanied by a number of wives, relatives, and children, moved out of the camps at Council Bluffs, Iowa, on their way to Fort Leavenworth, then on to Santa Fe, and eventually San Diego.

The Mormon battalion would see no military action; the only Saints to come under fire were those not yet able to leave Nauvoo, who were attacked during the summer and fall by anti-Mormon mobs.

By November all of the Saints were out of Nauvoo. The main body of the Mormons—some sixteen thousand strong—remained spread out during the winter, with the permission of army officers, over miles of Pottawattamie Indian land on the west bank of the Missouri River. In the spring of 1847 the first contingent would head for the Great Salt Lake.

With talk of war hero Zachary Taylor as a potential presidential candidate, Robert H. Gallaher, Whig proprietor of the Richmond, Virginia, Daily Republican, commissioned William Garl Brown to portray Taylor so that the public might see what the general—hidden away for most of his forty-year military career at frontier posts—looked like. Brown, welcomed at Taylor's Walnut Springs headquarters, just outside of Monterrey, Mexico, tarried for more than three months, painting not only a formal, life-size portrait, but also depicting "Rough and Ready" with his staff. Taylor's dress, wrote one of his men, "is that of a plain country farmer. He never wears a uniform; the neck-kerchief he has had on every time I have seen him has been of checked or striped cotton." One of the volunteers related, "general Tailor Come to see us he is averry old man and very sociable not only to officers but to buck soaldlers also he was not a proud man a tall when he Com to see us he road a muel."

Zachary Taylor at Walnut Springs by William Garl Brown Jr. (1823–1894), oil on canvas, 1847. National Portrait Gallery, Smithsonian Institution, Washington, D.C.

Chapter 5

War with Mexico

It is impossible to conceive of an administration less warlike, or more intriguing, than that of Mr. Polk," wrote Thomas Hart Benton in his memoir of thirty years of public life. *They were men of peace, with objects to be accomplished by means of war; so that war was a necessity and an indispensability to their purposes; but they wanted no more of it than would answer their purposes. They wanted a small war, just large enough to require a treaty of peace, and not large enough to make military reputations, dangerous for the presidency.*

The annexation of the Republic of Texas on December 29, 1845, after a long and heated debate over the admission of a vast slave territory into the Union,

made war with Mexico—which had denied Texas independence in 1836—all but inevitable. President Polk tried to avoid a confrontation, sending John Slidell as minister plenipotentiary in an attempt to settle the Texas boundary and the pent-up grievances of more than fifteen years between the two countries. But the Mexican government refused to receive Slidell.

Impotent though the government of Mexico might be, the threat to invade Texas had been made, and the United States was obligated to defend the territory that the state of Texas took to be hers, including the disputed area south of the Nueces River stretching to the Rio Grande. On January 13 General Zachary

Taylor, in charge of a small American army of some four thousand men, was directed to advance from Corpus Christi to the banks of the Rio Grande. Ulysses S. Grant, a young second lieutenant with the army, wrote to his sweetheart Julia Dent on February 5, "In all probability this movement to the Rio Grande will hasten the settlement of the boundary question, either by treaty or the sword."

Taylor began construction of a fort opposite Matamoros, a Mexican port at the mouth of the Rio Grande and the most important city of northern Mexico. "The troops are in good spirits and in the highest state of discipline; and at the head, we have a commanding general whose like is rarely seen," a letter intended for newspaper publication noted. "He is a 'plain,' unassuming, straight-forward, common-sense man—honest, upright, conscientious—with a judgment that rarely errs, and a sagacity that is never deceived."

In Washington on April 25 President Polk told his cabinet that attempts to conciliate Mexico were in vain, and the time had come to redress injuries. "We must treat all nations, whether great or small, strong or weak, alike, and . . . we should take a bold and firm course towards Mexico," he said. Although most of the cabinet members agreed that Congress should be asked for a declaration of war, Secretary of the Navy George Bancroft recommended that Polk wait for an open act of aggression by the Mexican army.

Even as the cabinet deliberated, the war was precipitated. On April 25 a Mexican detachment crossed the Rio Grande, surrounding two of Taylor's companies, and in the ensuing fight American lives were lost. Polk received word of the skirmish on Saturday evening, May 9. On Monday he informed Congress that Mexico had "invaded our territory, and shed American blood upon the American soil. She has proclaimed that hostilities have commenced, and that the two nations are now at war." Following a thirty-minute debate, the House of Representatives approved the President's recommendations to appropriate $5 million and call up to fifty thousand volunteers. Only fourteen congressmen, all Whigs, voted against the recommendations.

With John C. Calhoun expostulating at length, the Senate acted less promptly. "Mr. Calhoun denied that any war existed," the *New York Evening Post* reported. "A collision, he said, had occurred; but war could only be declared by Congress." But Sam Houston, former president of the Republic of Texas, said bluntly, "We have been at War with Mexico from the moment our Government consented to Annexation, and must fight it

THE ISSUE JOINED.

In late June 1846 Massachusetts Senator Daniel Webster publicly stated that the Mexican War was of James K. Polk's own making, engendering the confrontation imagined in this cartoon. Thomas Ritchie *(second from left), editor of the administration newspaper, the* Washington Union, *stands in support of the President. Behind him is editor James Watson Webb of the* Morning Courier and New-York Enquirer, *one of the few Whigs who supported the war. On Webster's side is an unidentified editor, along with Horace* Greeley of the New York Tribune, *an uncompromising critic of war in general and the Mexican War in particular. Greeley, an advocate of the dietary regime of Sylvester Graham, remarks, "I wish Dan had eaten more Graham bread he's too fat for Polk!"*

The Issue Joined *by H. R. Robinson (active circa 1837–circa 1851), lithograph, 1846. Prints and Photographs Division, Library of Congress, Washington, D.C.*

Fiery abolitionist and Ohio Representative Joshua Giddings (1795–1864) not only condemned the war with Mexico as "unjust, unholy and murderous," but went further, voting against supplying the troops. In July Giddings declared to his constituents that since the annexation of Texas was unconstitutional, the seating of Texas representatives in Congress had dissolved the Union, leaving Ohio at liberty to join a new arrangement or not. That said, he again declared himself a candidate for Congress, winning the Whig nomination, which was tantamount to election in his district.

Giddings "is a plain, blunt, speaking man, says what he thinks, and does not attempt to conceal his abolition jacket under a Whig overcoat," said the Democratic Plain Dealer. *"We hope he will explain how it is, if the Union is dissolved, as he claims, that he persists in going to a Congress which still recognizes the Union?"*

Joshua Reed Giddings by John Cranch (1807–1891), oil on canvas, 1855. National Portrait Gallery, Smithsonian Institution, Washington, D.C.

out." He declared, *The United States was, therefore, placed precisely in the situation in which Texas had been for the last ten years, subject to the aggressions, incursions, inroads, attacks, and outrages of the Mexican forces, acting in obedience to the commands of the constituted authorities of the Mexican government. Could any doubt exist that they were in fact and truth in a state of war?*

When the vote was finally taken on May 12, only Massachusetts Whig John Davis and Delaware Whig Thomas Clayton voted against declaring war. Calhoun abstained. "Mr. Polk and his party have accomplished their object: the war with Mexico is fairly commenced," Whig diarist Philip Hone wrote in disgust after the bill of war was signed on May 13. As Hone lamented, *The President (in violation of the Constitution, which gives to Congress the exclusive power to declare war) announces formally that a state of war exists, calls for volunteers and money, which Congress unhesitatingly grants; and if any old-fashioned legislator presumes to doubt the authority of Pope Polk, or questions the infallibility of his bull, he is stigmatized by some of the ruffians of the West as an enemy to his country, in league with the Mexicans.*

Agreeing with Ohio Representative Joshua Giddings, who had refused to vote for supplies for the war, militant abolitionist Charles Sumner told him, *Our position is an extreme one. We can preserve it only by standing on* principle. *With our feet there we shall be firm. If we abandon any* principle, *we shall lose the confidence of the country, & our own self-respect. Let the minority be small or great, I would oppose the war in every form.*

New England was a hotbed of dissent, but in the South and the West, the war was greeted with enthusiasm. "The war has begun in earnest," shrieked the headline in the *New Orleans Picayune.* "The Enemy is upon our soil!! Louisiana Volunteers, the Hour has arrived!!!" From Mississippi, Congressman Jefferson Davis heard, "We are in great excitement, drums beating, fifes playing, flags flying, meetings holding, and 'To Arms, To Arms,' in large Capitals stuck up at every corner of the streets, and at every fork of the roads." Davis was elected colonel of the First Mississippi Regiment and departed from Washington on July 4.

In Texas so many prominent citizens went to fight with Mexico that "it is with difficulty that a quorum of the Legislature can be kept together." Volunteers hurried to enlist, lest the war be over before they had their chance at glory. Illinois recruiters, assigned to raise four regiments, had enough volunteers to man fourteen. In Tennessee thirty thousand men answered the call. By December it was estimated that three hundred thousand men had volunteered.

on his way from his Walden Pond hut to town to retrieve a shoe from the cobbler's. He spent the night in the Concord jail for failing—as he had for six years past—to pay his poll tax.

"Mr. Webster told them how much the war cost, that was his protest, but voted [for] the war, and sends his son to it," Ralph Waldo Emerson recorded in his journal. "They calculated rightly on Mr. Webster. My friend Mr. Thoreau has gone to jail rather than pay his [poll] tax. On him they could not calculate."

Henry David Thoreau by Benjamin D. Maxham (active 1854–1859), daguerreotype, 1856. National Portrait Gallery, Smithsonian Institution, Washington, D.C.; gift of an anonymous donor

On July 23 Henry David Thoreau (1817–1862), disgusted by slavery and the war with Mexico, was arrested while

The administration newspaper, the *Washington Union*, urged Americans that "this is the time for action—bold, vigorous, decided action. Stroke should follow after stroke, and bring these vaunting, arrogant, obstinate Mexicans to terms. Let us, by our energy, conquer peace. Let us have a brisk and a short war of it." The war was expected to last no more than 90 to 120 days. But on the opposite side, Whig editor Horace Greeley was proud to proclaim the *New York Tribune*'s "open and fearless hostility" to war in general "and especially to the atrocious War waged upon Mexico."

While clamor against and in favor of the war raged on the home front, General Zachary Taylor had matters well in hand on the Rio Grande. Taylor's vastly outnumbered force first routed the Mexican army in Palo Alto, Mexico, on May 8 and again the following day at Resaca de la Palma. The Mexicans lost five hundred men; the Americans were left with four dead and forty-two wounded.

The country, awash with the fear that Taylor's little army was in grave danger, greeted the tidings of his victories with giddy relief. "The news from the seat of war on the Rio Grande and the army of occupation is the absorbing topic. 'General Taylor and the Army' is the toast which swells the ordinary allowance of wine in the glass to the generous overflowing of the bumper," wrote Philip Hone. "The squeaking voices of newspaper boys are modulated to the monotonous tune of 'Great News from Mex-

In an open letter, abolitionist Charles Sumner (1811–1874) accused Whig Representative Robert C. Winthrop of making the people of Boston "declare unjust and cowardly war, with superadded falsehood, in the cause of slavery. Through you they are made partakers in the blockade of Vera Cruz, the seizure of California, the capture of Santa Fe, the bloodshed of Monterey." Despite a series of rhetorical assaults on him, with whom he had gone to Boston Latin School, Sumner declined nomination to oppose him for reelection, leaving the challenge to Samuel Gridley Howe, whom Winthrop handily defeated.

Charles Sumner by Mathew Brady (1823–1896), albumen silver print, circa 1860. National Portrait Gallery, Smithsonian Institution, Washington, D.C.

Horace Greeley (1811–1872) was proud to proclaim the New York Tribune*'s "open and fearless hostility" to war in general and especially "to the atrocious War waged upon Mexico." He was not to be intimidated "by the scurrility of the cowardly ruffians who, either by anonymous letter or otherwise, attempt to appall or provoke us by abusive epithets or threats of personal violence." Greeley advised his readers, "Our course was taken in full view of all possible consequences and in the undoubting expectation that it would subject us to all manner of obloquy and execration from that class of patriots whose motto is 'Our Country Right or Wrong,' and who believe in butchering men and starving women and children in vindication of 'National Honor.'"*

Horace Greeley by an unidentified photographer, daguerreotype, circa 1850. National Portrait Gallery, Smithsonian Institution, Washington, D.C.

ico,' and you cannot pass the *pave* in front of the Exchange unprepared with an answer to the only question asked, 'What news from Mexico?'" Meanwhile, Polk sent a message to the Senate nominating Taylor for promotion to major general. Congress awarded him a gold medal bearing his portrait as soon as a proper likeness could be obtained.

On May 30 the President announced to his cabinet that he intended to acquire California, New Mexico, and perhaps other northern provinces of Mexico when peace was made, for it was clear that Mexico had no other means to compensate for the expenses of the war. To this end, Polk planned to order an expedition of mounted men to California to take immediate military possession of these provinces. The President called in Missouri Senator Thomas Hart Benton who, armed with John Charles Frémont's maps and reports, supplied detailed information and chose the route. Polk also recommended that Colonel Stephen Watts Kearny, in charge of the Third Military Department at Fort Leavenworth, command the expedition. In 1845 Kearny, assigned to dissuade the Indians from attacking the merchants traveling the eight hundred miles along the Santa Fe Trail, had undertaken an extraordinary march as far as the south pass of the Rocky Mountains, returning to Fort Leavenworth by way of Bent's Fort on the Arkansas River.

Kearny had already left Fort Leavenworth, under orders to protect the traders, who were moving out of Missouri on their annual spring trek to Mexico. Promoted to general on June 20, Kearny was instructed to take possession of Santa Fe and then proceed to California. To supplement Kearny's regular army force, two regiments of volunteers were ordered out of Missouri. "Several thousand can be readily raised," noted the *St. Louis Republican.* "Indeed, there will be difficulty in restraining them, rather than to fill up the ranks."

Marching along the Santa Fe Trail, Kearny's Army of the West easily moved into New Mexico on August 7. Eleven days later, the army entered Santa Fe to find that the New Mexican governor, General Manuel Armijo, had disbanded his small army and fled south to Chihuahua.

On the heels of Kearny's army, the traders entered Santa Fe on August 31. Among them was James Magoffin, a member of a family long prominent in Mexican commerce, and his eighteen-year-old bride Susan. Mrs. Magoffin wrote in her diary: *Though Gen. Kearny has come in and taken entire possession, seated himself in the former Governor's chair, raised the American flag and holds Santa Fe as a part of the United States, still he has not molested the habits, religion etc. of the people, who so far are well pleased with their truly republican governor.*

General Zachary Taylor, dressed for battle in simple farmer's garments and astride "Old Whitey," met the Mexican army drawn up across the plain at Palo Alto. An artillery duel lasted until dark, when, under cover of darkness, the Mexicans withdrew to a ravine known as Resaca de la Palma. Taylor followed and routed them in a brilliant charge, chasing the remnants of the army across the Rio Grande.

Battle of Palo-Alto *by Adolphe-Jean-Baptiste Bayot (1801–after 1866), after Carl Nebel, toned lithograph, 1851. Amon Carter Museum, Fort Worth, Texas*

Born in the District of Columbia, Samuel Ringgold (1800–1846) had been appointed to West Point from Maryland, and he graduated in 1818. In 1838 Ringgold organized an experimental company of flying artillery, training his men to advance their battery at a full gallop, unlimber, fire, remount, and whirl off to a new position.

Ringgold was one of the four American casualties at Palo Alto. Before he fell he had directed his pieces to within a hundred yards of the enemy. "He had infused his own spirit into the men under his command, who loved him as a father," wrote the New York Herald, "and so well were they disciplined, that they moved like a solid wedge and with the rapidity of a falcon swooping on his prey."

Samuel Ringgold by John Vanderlyn (1775–1852), oil on canvas, 1825. Estate of William Woodville VIII

Major Samuel Ringgold's death was lamented in poetry, music, and prints, and his remains were moved north with solemn pageantry. His funeral took place in Baltimore in December where "the city was thronged with troops and thousands of persons who had come up to honor the illustrious dead. . . . Flags and banners waved at half mast; martial music was heard on almost every square." The Baltimore Patriot reported, "The procession was very long, and made an imposing military display of unusual grandeur. The uniforms were elegant, and the troops exhibited a truly soldier-like appearance."

Major Ringgold's Funeral March, published by John Plumbe Jr. (1809–1857), lithograph, 1847. Contained in The National Plumbeotype Gallery (Philadelphia, 1847). National Portrait Gallery, Smithsonian Institution, Washington, D.C.

Artist *Richard Caton Woodville of Baltimore was studying in Düsseldorf, Ger-
many, during the Mexican War, but his*
War News from Mexico *reflects the
avidity with which Americans sought out
tidings from the battlefield. "The news
from the army on the Rio Grande has
caused more general excitement in this city*
than has before taken place, perhaps, during the present generation," a Baltimore
correspondent to the New York Herald
wrote early in the war. "People begin to
collect every evening, about 5 o'clock at the
telegraph and the newspaper offices, waiting for extras and despatches, where they
continue even to 12 or 1 o'clock at night,
discussing the news that may be received,
censuring the course of government, as well
as of the officer in command."

War News from Mexico *by Richard
Caton Woodville (1825–1855), oil on canvas,
1848. Manoogian Foundation*

General Zachary Taylor's victories on the Rio Grande warranted an acknowledgment from Congress, and General-in-Chief of the Army Winfield Scott argued for the award of a medal, a higher honor than the more traditional sword. By joint resolution on July 16, Congress authorized a gold medal based upon a profile portrait of Taylor that William Garl Brown drew while he was with the general at Walnut Springs, near Monterrey in Mexico.

As payment Brown asked for either $200 or a pair of dies, which he might use for striking medals in lesser metal for his own disposal. The pair of dies was agreed to, with the director of the mint declaring, "I think it desirable that copies of the medals be distributed as widely as possible." The mint itself later issued copies in bronze.

Zachary Taylor, bronze medal, 1846, based on a portrait by William Garl Brown Jr. (1823–1894). Numismatics Division, National Museum of American History, Smithsonian Institution, Washington, D.C.

Stephen Watts Kearny (1794–1848), who had left Columbia to fight in the War of 1812, had long experience with the army, most of it on the western frontier. Susan Shelby Magoffin, the young wife of a merchant who followed Kearny into Santa Fe, described him as "small of stature, very agreeable in conversation and manners, conducts himself with ease, can receive and return compliments, a few of which I gave him." Kearny related to Mrs. Magoffin that to give reassurance to the populace, he "paraded though some little village in the priests procession, carrying as did all his officers a lighted candle lightening the train of the Virgin Mary, and to use his own words 'making a fool of himself.'"

Stephen Watts Kearny by an unidentified artist, oil on canvas, not dated. Missouri Historical Society, St. Louis

In June 1846, as Susan Shelby Magoffin (1827–1855) left Independence, Missouri, on the way to Mexico with her husband's large merchant caravan, she began "El Diario de Dona Susanita Magoffin." On August 31 the traders followed the Army of the West into Santa Fe, and Magoffin recorded, "I have entered the city in a year that will always be remembered by my countrymen and under the 'Star-spangled banner' too, the first American lady, who has come under such auspices."

Susan Shelby Magoffin by an unidentified photographer, photograph after a daguerreotype, circa 1845. Missouri Historical Society, St. Louis

Susan Magoffin was present at a dinner attended by the local citizenry when General Kearny offered the toast, "The U.S. and Mexico—They are now united, may no one ever think of separating." After it was translated into Spanish, "the Mexican gentlemen around the table cried out *'viva' 'viva,'*" Mrs. Magoffin wrote.

Kearny organized the civil government of New Mexico, and on September 22 he departed from Santa Fe with three hundred men to secure California.

On the Rio Grande, General Taylor, hampered by a lack of supplies, delayed pushing further into Mexico and stayed put just outside of Matamoros. In September he finally moved toward Monterrey, the capital of the state of Nuevo León. The city of some twelve thousand was strongly fortified and defended by a force of ten thousand, commanded by General

1846: Portrait of the Nation

"There are few objects in nature resembling in sombre nakedness of aspect and lonely and isolated grandeur, a Mexican mountain," wrote an American volunteer as the army prepared to attack Monterrey. "Faint and famished as we were, we caught energy from our admiration of the sublimity which was unveiled before us."

Daniel Powers Whiting, who drew the scene from which the lithograph was made, was a captain in the United States Army. A graduate of West Point, he had received training in topographical drawing. In Monterrey General Taylor excused Whiting from his military duties and supplied him with a horse so he could record more views from the hills.

Heights of Monterey, from the Saltillo Road Looking Towards the City *by Frederick Swinton (active 1840s), after Daniel Powers Whiting, toned lithograph, 1847. Amon Carter Museum, Fort Worth, Texas*

Pedro Ampudia. After a bloody three days, which included street and house-to-house fighting, the Mexicans capitulated on September 23. For the first time in the war, American casualties had been heavy.

To Polk's dismay, Taylor agreed to an eight-week armistice. General Taylor, Polk grumbled, *had the enemy in his power & should have taken them prisoners, deprived them of their arms, discharged them on their parole of honour, and preserved the advantage which he had obtained by pushing on without delay further into the country, if the force at his command justified it. . . . It will only enable the Mexican army to reorganize and recruit so as to make another stand.*

Disappointed as Polk was with Taylor as a military commander, he was even further provoked by recurring mention of the general as a potential Whig presidential nominee. Just a few weeks after Taylor's victories on the Rio Grande, Thurlow Weed, the Whig editor of the *Albany Evening Journal*, casting about for a likely candidate to save the nation from the Democrats, had a chance encounter with Colonel Joseph P. Taylor, the general's brother. Colonel Taylor confirmed that Zachary Taylor had no politics—the general in fact had never voted—but was instinctively a Whig in his loathing of Andrew Jackson and in his support for a protectionist economic policy, indicated by his insistence on wearing American-manufactured clothes. The *Journal* predicted that one or two more victories would put Taylor—"Rough and Ready," as he was called by his soldiers—in the White House.

Polk, who had boldly decided to send an expedition to Veracruz and Mexico City, readily dismissed Taylor from his calculations. The cabinet agreed with Polk that General Taylor "was unfit for the chief command, that he had not mind enough for the station, that he was a bitter political partisan & had no sympathies with the administration."

Winfield Scott, a popular hero of the War of 1812, was General-in-Chief of the Army. Competent as a military man, Scott was also ambitious as a politician. In 1840 he had aspired—along with Henry Clay—for the Whig presidential nomination, which General William Henry Harrison had won. Before the sudden celebrity of Zachary Taylor, many had deemed Scott the most likely Whig choice for 1848.

When the war had begun in May, Polk had had little relish for giving Scott command of an expeditionary force to supplement General Taylor's small "army of occupation" in Mexico, but later conceded that his rank entitled him to it. "He has had experience in his profession," the President grumbled, "but I thought he was rather scientific and visionary in his views."

Left:
General-in-Chief of the Army Winfield Scott (1785–1866) stood six feet, five inches tall and was a magnificent figure in the full military dress he proudly wore. Famous for his insistence on proper military form, as well as for his appreciation of sashes, plumes, gold braid, and medals, Scott was dubbed "Old Fuss and Feathers."

Robert Walter Weir, familiar to Scott as the painter of The Embarkation of the Pilgrims *for the Capitol Rotunda and as professor of drawing at the United States Military Academy, undertook several portraits of the general. Scott posed for the artist about the time he was granted— after a seven-year delay because of political opposition—the rank of lieutenant general. Scott was the first man since George Washington to hold that office.*

Winfield Scott by Robert Walter Weir (1803–1889), oil on canvas, circa 1855. National Portrait Gallery, Smithsonian Institution, Washington, D.C.

DISTINGUISHED MILITARY OPERATIONS WITH A HASTY BOWL OF SOUP.

H.R.Robinson's Lith 142 Nassau St N.Y.

General Winfield Scott, surprised to receive a letter in May 1846 from Secretary of War William L. Marcy relieving him from command of the expedition to Mexico, replied to Marcy that his letter was received as "I sat down to take a hasty plate of soup," causing the Democrat press to deride him as "Soup." This cartoon suggests that Scott's reinstatement by the President in November was promoted by Polk's desire to quench General Zachary Taylor's presidential prospects.

Distinguished Military Operations with a Hasty Bowl of Soup *by H. R. Robinson (active circa 1831–circa 1851) after Edward Williams Clay, lithograph, 1846 or early 1847. Prints and Photographs Division, Library of Congress, Washington, D.C.*

When Scott—who insisted that equipping and moving the army would require at least three months—did not immediately leave Washington for the seat of war, Polk schemed for congressional authorization to supersede him by appointing a lieutenant general. Learning of the political intrigue, Scott fired off a letter to Secretary of War William L. Marcy, saying, "I do not desire to place myself in the most perilous of all positions: *a fire upon my rear, from Washington, and the fire, in front, from the Mexicans.*" Polk immediately directed the secretary of war to send a letter to Scott relieving him of command of the force intended to march against Mexico City.

By fall, in need of a commander to vigorously prosecute the war, Polk was forced to reconsider Scott. "I have strong objections to Gen'l Scott, and after his very exceptional letter in May last, nothing but stern necessity and a sense of public duty could induce me to place him at the head of so important an expedition," the President wrote. "Still I do not well see how it can be avoided." Scott was the only man who had the rank to command Taylor. To the President it was a choice between evils. Neither man, Polk believed, was a friend of the government. But on November 20 the President summoned General Scott and told him he "was willing that by-gones should be by-gones & that he should take the command." Scott, the President recorded, "was so grateful & so much affected that he almost shed tears. . . . He left, apparently the most delighted man I have seen for a long time, and as he retired expressed his deep gratitude to me." General Taylor, superseded, was ordered to give part of his force up to Scott.

Less than a year later, after Scott had fought and won six battles, he entered Mexico City at the head of the cavalry with the bands playing "Hail! Columbia," "Washington's March," "Yankee Doodle," and "Hail to the Chief." Scott noted in his official dispatch, "Even the inhabitants, catching the enthusiasm of the moment, filled the windows and lined the parapets, cheering the cavalcade as it passed at the gallop."

On February 2, 1848, the Treaty of Guadalupe Hidalgo—condemned both by those who wanted all of Mexico and by those who wanted none of it—was signed. America's title to Texas was confirmed, and for $15 million plus the assumption of claims against Mexico amounting to $3.25 million, the United States won a territory encompassing the present states of New Mexico, Arizona, Utah, Nevada, and California, as well as parts of Colorado and Wyoming. But the vast domain brought with it a ferment that would lead to the Civil War.

The Conquest of California

Mexico's far-away, sparsely settled, and scarcely governed department of California was clearly open to foreign intervention. It was not difficult to imagine that the restive Americans—a small contingent of some eight hundred—might see the opportunity to repeat the Texas pattern of rebellion, independent republic, and annexation to the United States.

When Secretary of the Navy George Bancroft and Thomas Hart Benton, in his capacity as chairman of the Senate Military Affairs Committee, planned John C. Frémont's third exploratory expedition, which would take him into California and Oregon, "the eventualities of war were taken into consideration," Frémont claimed in his memoirs.

John Charles Frémont by William S. Jewett (1812–1873), oil on panel, not dated. National Portrait Gallery, Smithsonian Institution, Washington, D.C.

tenant A. H. Gillespie, traveling with dispatches from Washington, found him on May 8. Gillespie gave Frémont letters from Benton and, according to Frémont, oral instructions from Secretary of the Navy Bancroft that implied that he should take and hold California "in the event of any occurrence." Frémont led his men back to Sutter's Fort.

As Thomas Hart Benton told the story, a deputation of American settlers feared that General José Maria Castro, who ruled in the northern part of the province, would march upon them, and also feared that the Indians would be incited to attack their families and burn their wheat fields. These settlers came to Frémont's camp and "implored him to place himself at their head and save them from destruction." Frémont thereupon boldly resolved "to overturn the Mexican government in California, and to establish Californian Independence."

Frémont (1813–1890) and his force of sixty-two well-armed men reached Sutter's Fort in December 1845 and planned to remain near San Jose through the winter, but by February the suspicious Californians ordered him out of the country. He moved north to Klamath Lake in the Oregon territory, where Lieu-

On June 14 a handful of Americans seized the small town of Sonoma and, raising a flag manufactured from unbleached cloth adorned with a grizzly bear facing a red star, proclaimed the Republic of California. Its existence proved to be necessary for less than a month.

Commodore J. D. Sloat, commander of the Pacific Squadron, who had orders to secure California should war with Mexico break out, reached the port in Monterey on July 2. A few days later, 250 seamen and marines marched in front of the old customhouse, and Sloat's proclamation, declaring "that he proposed to hoist the American flag at Monterey and carry it throughout California," was read to the Spanish-speaking residents, who understood not a word.

On July 8 the American flag replaced the Mexican colors on Yerba Buena Island in San Francisco Bay. Four days later, foreigners, principally Americans and Englishmen, flew the Stars and Stripes in San Jose.

Commodore Robert Field Stockton (1795–1866), who came to replace the retiring Sloat, reached Monterey on July 15. "I will now conquer all California," Stockton was reported as saying, "and Californians shall be free—on the ruins of Mexican folly and misrule will I establish a free government, and nothing but God's providence can prevent it."

When Stockton arrived at Yerba Buena, William Heath Davis was among the American traders who called to pay respects. "We were handsomely received by the commodore and were favorably struck with his appearance, which was that of a gentleman and thorough commander," wrote Davis in his memoirs. "He was fine-looking, of dark complexion; frank and offhand in manners and conversation; active and energetic."

Stockton, an organized man of quick decision, immediately enrolled John Charles Frémont's California

Lieutenant Colonel John Charles Frémont's personal flag, designed by Jessie Benton Frémont. Southwest Museum, Los Angeles, California

The Bear Flag, drawn by John Elliott Montgomery in a letter of June 25, 1846. Yale Collection of Western Americana, Beinecke Rare Book and Manuscript Library, Yale University, New Haven, Connecticut

Battalion in his force, and put them aboard ship en route to capture Los Angeles, then the capital of California. Los Angeles, a town of some fifteen hundred a few miles inland from its port of San Pedro, was defended by José Castro and Pío Pico, the governor of California. Upon the approach of Frémont's battalion, Castro and Pico disbanded their forces and sought to escape to Mexico. Los Angeles, the "City of the Angels," was captured on August 13. "The flag of the United States is now flying from every commanding position in the territory, and California is entirely free from Mexican dominion," Stockton declared in a proclamation on August 22.

The conquest was not quite settled, however. Captain Archibald Gillespie, who remained in Los Angeles with fifty men—rather than following Stockton's example in cultivating the wealthy rancheros—made himself obnoxious to the local populace and in late September was expelled by a force of several hundred under the command of José María Flores.

Meanwhile, Stephen Watts Kearny and his Army of the West, after traveling some thousand miles without firing a shot, were confronted, just as they reached California, by a band of eighty rebellious Californians under the command of Don Andres Pico. In the fight, which took place in the Indian village of San Pasqual on December 6, Kearny's men, mounted on mules, proved to be no match for the Californians astride powerful galloping horses and wielding long, sharp lances. Eighteen Americans were killed and eighteen more wounded; Kearny himself received lance wounds that temporarily retired him from command. Retreating to Escondido Mountain, the decimated force was surrounded by the enemy. On December 11 a force of 215 sailors and marines, sent by Stockton

from San Diego, rode to their rescue, and the Californians dispersed without a fight.

Stockton and Kearny—not without considerable rancor over who should be commander-in-chief—made plans to move on Los Angeles. Without waiting for Frémont, who had delayed bringing his battalion down from the north, they met the Californians on January 8 and 9 at San Gabriel and La Mesa, California, and with the loss of but one American life, finalized the conquest of California.

Robert Field Stockton by Thomas Sully (1783–1872), oil on canvas, 1851. Princeton Portrait Collection, Princeton University, New Jersey; commissioned by the American Whig Society

MONTEREY - CAPITOL OF CALIFORNIA.

Published by C. S. Francis & Co. N. York.

Sketched by J. W. Revere U. S. N.

Lith. of Wm. Endicott & Co N. York.

The Wilmot Proviso

Among the new members of Congress in 1846 was David Wilmot (1814–1868), a Democrat from rural Bradford County, Pennsylvania. "He is a man of much native talent, but acts on the spur of the moment—only great occasions arouse him, when, it is said, he is powerful," wrote one who knew Wilmot when he was but a country lawyer. *Mr. W. has the dignified bearing of a gentleman—converses charmingly, and it is a luxury to hear him laugh, but he is an inveterate chewer of tobacco—his hair hangs loosely about his eyes—he is almost slovenly in his dress and not over pious in his language. He is ambitious—is evidently more ambitious to shine as a politician than as a jurist, and may figure yet somewhere.*

When on August 8—two days before the date fixed for the adjournment of Congress—President Polk sent a message asking for a two-million-dollar appropriation to be used for unspecified purposes relating to negotiations with Mexico, Wilmot took the floor in the House of Representatives. Declaring that he believed the war to be necessary and proper and that "he was most earnestly desirous that a portion of territory on the Pacific, including the bay of San Francisco, should come into our possession by fair and honorable means," Wilmot offered a proviso that slavery be prohibited in any territory acquired from Mexico.

Wilmot's proviso was accepted with a vote of 83 to 64. "The slave-holders rallied, threatened, and implored; *but the proviso was carried by a decided majority*," exulted the abolitionist poet John Greenleaf Whittier. "The entire North, (with few exceptions), Whig and Democrat, voted for it." All representatives from the South voted against it. "For the first time since the fatal Missouri struggle in 1819–20, the Free States stood shoulder to shoulder for the limitation of slavery."

The two-million-dollar appropriation bill, with Wilmot's proviso attached, reached the Senate in the waning hours of the session. Most expected that the proviso would be removed and the remaining bill quickly passed. Massachusetts Whig John Davis, however, who had voted against the war, refused to yield the floor until the time for adjournment passed. "The cool self-possession with which Mr. Senator Davis literally talked the two million bill to death," wrote the Washington correspondent of the *Evening Post*, "was among the most amusing, as it certainly was the most provoking, thing that occurred during the session. 'Honest John' had imbibed the impres-

David Wilmot by M. H. Fraubel (lifedates unknown), lithograph, circa 1853. National Portrait Gallery, Smithsonian Institution, Washington, D.C.

John C. Calhoun by George Peter Alexander Healy (1813–1894), oil on canvas, circa 1846. National Portrait Gallery, Smithsonian Institution, Washington, D.C.

sion that here was an opportunity to deal the administration an effective blow." Wilmot's proviso would be brought up again, and it would "become the greatest topic of angry controversy which has ever agitated this country," even though "very little of the territory which might be acquired from Mexico is adapted to slave labor," the *New York Post* correctly predicted.

To John C. Calhoun (1782–1850), the proviso was a shot across the bow of the South. "What is to come of this only time can disclose," he wrote. "The present indication is, that the South will be united in opposition to the Scheme. If they regard their safety they must defeat it even if the Union should be rent asunder."

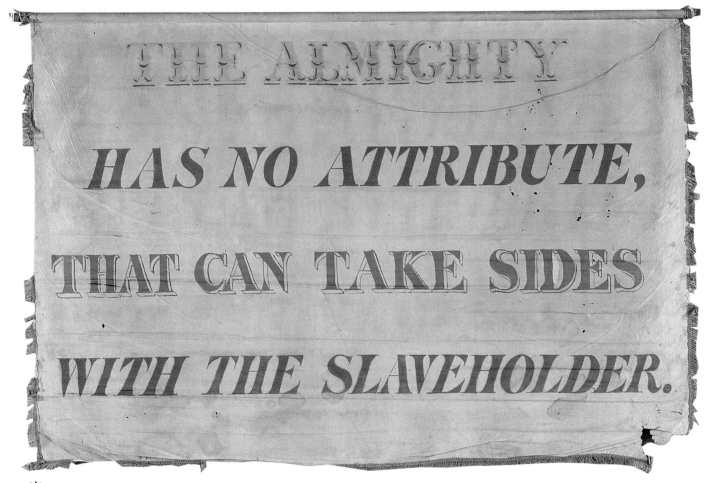

THE ALMIGHTY
HAS NO ATTRIBUTE,
THAT CAN TAKE SIDES
WITH THE SLAVEHOLDER.

Antislavery banner. Massachusetts Historical Society, Boston

Chapter 6

Voices of Reform

Many were the causes that called forth the energies of reformers in 1846—temperance, married women's property rights, the abolition of capital punishment among them—but overwhelming in importance was the abolition of slavery. "There is no one branch of Reform, in which we do not feel a lively interest," William Lloyd Garrison proclaimed in the year's first issue of the *Liberator*, but "first in the order of time, and we think first in importance, is the ABOLITION OF SLAVERY, the continuance of which constitutes the giant inequity, the withering curse, the one great peril of the land."

At the dawn of 1846, the antislavery lion was Cassius Clay, scion of a Kentucky plantation family who had come to denounce slavery after hearing Garrison speak during Clay's student days at Yale. Frustrated when the *Lexington Observer* refused his outpouring of spirited letters arguing that slavery was against the economic interest of non-slaveholding Kentuckians, Clay set up his own newspaper, called the *True Observer*, in June 1845. Threatened with mob action even before the first issue appeared, Clay armed his office with rifles, shotguns, Mexican cavalry lances, and two brass four-pounder cannons. In August, after an editorial—which Clay did not write—was perceived as an incitement to slave insurrection, a committee of citizens took it upon themselves to keep the peace by unceremoniously dumping his press across the river in Cincinnati. The incident caused no little stir in the northern papers.

Clay then set up his press in Cincinnati, and with his newfound fame traveled east to speak against slavery and drum up subscriptions for his newspaper. Horace Greeley introduced Clay to a crowd of three thousand assembled at the Broadway Tabernacle in New York, and the Kentuckian "enchanted the auditors for fully two hours." The correspondent for the Washington *National Intelligencer* reported, "There was much applauding and clapping, interspersed with a good share of hissing etc."

One of Clay's main themes was the superiority of the free states over the slave states. "Look to the Mechanic Arts," he said. "If you inquire at the Patent Office at Washington relative to those results of the extraordinary skill, ingenuity and inventive faculties of our countrymen, you will find that 99 out of a hundred are from Northern States." Clay continued, *Was I fond of the fine arts—of painting, of sculpture, of music, of poetry, of all that constitutes the embodiment of the beautiful and true! I saw that all these existed in a much higher degree of excellence in the free than in the Slave States! Did I look at the subject of Education!—I saw that the mind developed itself to a far greater degree in the free than in the Slave States.* Clay proclaimed to applause, "I love the South! And it is because I would make her great and glorious that I thus tell her of her faults."

To the surprise and dismay of his friends, Clay went off to fight in the Mexican War. He noted in the *True American*, "We have denounced unsparingly the Annexation of Texas, as a boldly flagitious scheme and a War with Mexico as kindred with that disgraceful and degrading act—degrading alike to the Government that consummated, and the People that submitted to it." But, he went on, "War *exists*. . . . Resistance to it now would be rebellion. . . . Our opinion is, that the war, so unjustly and wickedly begun, should be pressed with vigor." The antislavery *Pennsylvania Freeman* retorted, "Can it be that he is such a fool?"

From Great Britain came an account of the leading black abolitionist Frederick Douglass. In the spring of 1845, just prior to the publication of his autobiography, Douglass—still a fugitive slave—had left America upon the advice of friends, who doubted the power of Massachusetts to protect him from his former master. Douglass explained in a letter published in the *Liberator* in 1846, "Persecuted, hunted, and outraged in America, I have come to England; and behold the change! The chattel becomes a man. I breathe, and I am free."

No one has been more fiercely associated with the cause of abolition than William Lloyd Garrison (1805–1879), who in the first issue of the Liberator on January 1, 1831, had demanded the "immediate and complete emancipation" of slaves. "I am in earnest—I will not equivocate—I will not excuse—I will not retreat a single inch—and I will be heard." Although the newspaper's circulation never reached more than three thousand, Garrison's uncompromising gospel thundered across the land.

William Lloyd Garrison by an unidentified artist, oil on canvas, circa 1855. National Portrait Gallery, Smithsonian Institution, Washington, D.C.; gift of Marlies R. and Sylvester G. March

THE LIBERATOR

OUR COUNTRY IS THE WORLD--OUR COUNTRYMEN ARE ALL MANKIND.

BOSTON, FRIDAY, JANUARY 23, 1846.

Masthead of The Liberator, January 23, 1846. The Trustees of the Boston Public Library, Massachusetts

The Liberator *announced in April that a lithograph of "this intrepid friend of emancipation," Cassius M. Clay (1810–1903), could be obtained for seventy-five cents. "It is considered by all who have seen the original, to be one of the most perfect portraitures ever executed." The* Liberator *added, "The countenance of such a man should be made familiar to the rising generation."*

A month later, when Clay announced that he would go to fight in the Mexican War, his popularity evaporated. "The spectacle of Cassius M. Clay, the professed friend of freedom and emancipation, at the head of a cavalry company on their way to the seat of war, a war branded by himself as waged for the sole purpose of enlarging the slave market, and strengthening the despotism of the South—is a spectacle of unsurpassed inconsistency and revolting hypocrisy, (if not absolute insanity;)" resolved the Essex County Antislavery Society at a meeting presided over by free black C. Lenox Remond.

Cassius M. Clay by Albert Newsam (1809–1864) after Thomas P. Collins, lithograph, 1846. The Historical Society of Pennsylvania, Philadelphia

In early 1846 Douglass was in Scotland leading the American Anti-Slavery Society's campaign to persuade the British Presbyterians to denounce their slaveholding brethren in America. "Everything is so different here from what I have been accustomed to in the United States," Douglass wrote from Edinburgh. "No insults to encounter—no prejudice to encounter, but all is smooth—I am treated as a man and equal brother. My color instead of being a barrier to social equality—is not thought of as such."

There was no question about the fervor of antislavery sentiment in 1846, but the forces of emancipation were divided over the way to achieve their common goal. Presiding at the twelfth annual American Anti-Slavery Society meeting at Broadway Tabernacle in New York on May 12, 1846, Garrison reported, *The signs of the times were full of hope and good cheer. . . . In all the Free States but especially in New Hampshire, Massachusetts and Ohio, the cause had made great progress: and there were many indications that the public mind was rapidly being prepared to embrace the doctrine of "No Union with Slaveholders."*

Garrison's disdain for political action had put him into direct conflict with the Liberty Party, which fielded candidates for political office and denounced Garrison's plea for the union's dissolution. Garrison, who never harbored the slightest doubt about his own moral superiority, scoffed, "The truth is the misnamed 'Liberty party' is under the control of as ambitious, unprincipled, and crafty leaders as is either the Whig or Democratic party."

Quaker poet John Greenleaf Whittier, an early associate of Garrison's, had no difficulty using the political process. An unsuccessful candidate for Congress on the Liberty Party ticket in 1842 and an editor of the Liberty Party's *Essex Transcript*, Whittier referred to himself as a "humble and toiling member of that party of reform and progress."

Whittier was among those who maintained that the Liberty Party should concentrate on the single issue of abolition, rather than embracing other reforms to broaden its appeal. "Let us press forward as we have begun, requiring no new test of our members, content with our simple anti-slavery creed, leaving individuals to the free exercise of their own judgment as to what consistency requires of them in other matters."

At the end of December, Faneuil Hall was the site of the thirteenth Anti-Slavery Fair, an annual fundraising event instigated and organized by Maria Weston Chapman, William Lloyd Garrison's dedicated and devoted lieutenant. The fairs, which had begun in a private parlor and had netted

In his speeches in Great Britain, Frederick Douglass (1818–1895) dwelt upon slavery, but he also spoke out in favor of temperance and Irish home rule. "I cannot allow myself to be insensitive to the wrongs and sufferings of any part of the great family of man," he told William Lloyd Garrison.

The New York Express *denounced Douglass as a "glib-tongued scoundrel" and charged him with "running a muck in greedy-eared Britain against America, its people, its institution, and even against its peace." Douglass responded in a letter addressed to Horace Greeley's* Tribune, *noting that although he had given weight to the criticism "of exposing the sins of one nation in the ear of another," slavery "is of such a giant sin—such a monstrous aggregation of iniquity, so hardening to the human heart, so destructive to the moral senses, and so well calculated to get a character in every one around it favourable to its own continuance, that I feel not only at liberty but abundantly justified in appealing to the whole world to aid in its removal."*

Frederick Douglass by an unidentified artist, oil on canvas, circa 1845. National Portrait Gallery, Smithsonian Institution, Washington, D.C.

In New England the Hutchinson family singers sometimes performed at antislavery rallies where Frederick Douglass—"fluent, graceful, eloquent, shrewd, sarcastic"—held his audience spellbound for hours at a time. Jesse Hutchinson Jr., who put words to many of the tunes sung by his brothers and sisters, dedicated "The Fugitive's Song" to Douglass "for his fearless advocacy, signal ability and wonderful success in behalf of His Brothers in Bonds."

When Douglass came back to America from his trip to Great Britain, he was no longer a fugitive slave. His English friends, alarmed for his safety as he made plans to return to his wife and children, had purchased his freedom on December 12, 1846, and a deed of manumission was formally registered in the Baltimore County Courthouse. Many American abolitionists were horrified at actually paying a slaveholder, but Douglass asserted, "For myself, viewing it in the light of a ransom or as money extorted by a robber, and regarding my liberty of more value than one hundred and fifty pounds sterling, I could not see in it either a violation of the law of morality or economy."

"The Fugitive's Song" by Jesse Hutchinson Jr. (1778–1851), Henry Prentiss, Publisher (Boston, 1845). The Library Company of Philadelphia, Pennsylvania

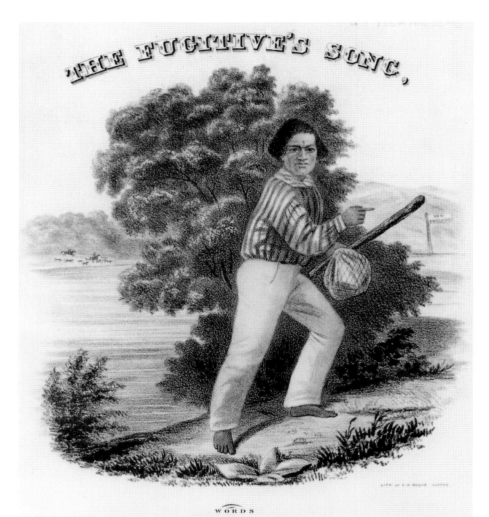

THE FUGITIVE'S SONG,

WORDS
composed and respectfully dedicated in token of confidial esteem to
FREDERICK DOUGLASS
A Graduate from the
"PECULIAR INSTITUTION"
For his fearless advocacy, signal ability and wonderful success in behalf of
HIS BROTHERS IN BONDS.
(and to the FUGITIVES FROM SLAVERY in the)
FREE STATES & CANADAS.
by their friend
JESSE HUTCHINSON JUN.r

BOSTON. Published by HENRY PRENTISS 33 Court St.

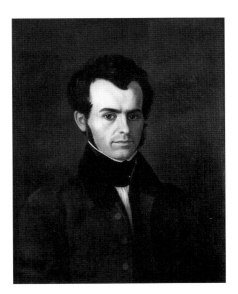

After Daniel Webster's arrival at the Massachusetts Whig Party's 1846 convention diverted the Massachusetts "Young Whigs" from their attempt to pass anti-slavery resolutions, John Greenleaf Whittier (1807–1892) asked in a verse, printed in the Boston Daily Whig:

Where's the man for Massachusetts
Where's the voice to speak her free?
Where's the hand to light up bonfires
*   from her mountains to the sea?*
Beats her Pilgrim pulse no longer?
Sits she dumb in her despair?
Has she none to break the silence?
Has she none to do and dare?

That September, Whittier had proposed the formation of a League of Freedom to provide a common ground for all who loved liberty and abhorred slavery. The league would be founded on three propositions: the abolition of slavery and vows not to vote for slaveholders or for those in fellowship with slaveholders. "We have eighty thousand Liberty voters to begin with, and a majority of both the old parties are well-nigh ready to join in such a movement," he wrote.

John Greenleaf Whittier by Robert Peckham (1785–1877), oil on canvas, 1833. Trustees of the Whittier Homestead, Haverhill, Massachusetts

only about three hundred dollars, now attracted great crowds and took in thousands of dollars. Evenings at the fair were "made interesting by the speeches of eloquent advocates of the cause," among them Garrison, just back from four months in England, and Boston Brahmin Wendell Phillips, a man who embraced many reforms.

Phillips was one of the very few bold enough in 1846 to envision political rights for women. In an article published in the *Liberator* on July 3, Phillips pointed out that many of the western states were ahead of Massachusetts in granting married women full control of their property. "I have always thought that the first right restored to woman would be that of the full and unfettered control of all her property and earnings, whether she were married or unmarried. . . . Next in order of importance and time, comes the ballot." Even Horace Greeley, the most reform-minded of men, who campaigned to let blacks in New York vote on the same basis as whites, confined himself to stating that *manhood* was the basis for suffrage. But under his own roof, Greeley harbored one of the seminal voices of feminism—Margaret Fuller, who came to work for the *Tribune* and lived for a time with the Greeleys in Turtle Bay.

In *Woman in the Nineteenth Century*, published in 1845, Fuller proclaimed, "We would have every path laid open to Woman as freely as to Man." Let men trust the woman entirely "and give her every privilege already

The pen of Maria Weston Chapman (1806–1885) "is more actively employed in behalf of the slave than that of any other person in the republic, both in the preparation of public contributions to the press, and in conducting an immense amount of private correspondence with the friends of emancipation on both sides of the Atlantic," William Lloyd Garrison declared in January 1846.

The success of the antislavery fairs was a tribute to Chapman's energy. "Hers was the spirit to suggest, to plan, to inform, to inspire, as it had been for many years; yet without bustle or parade, with unseen diligence, with sacred modesty, with entire self-forgetfulness," noted the Liberator. *James Russell Lowell wrote:*

> *There was Maria Chapman, too*
> *With her swift eyes of clear steel blue,*
> *The coiled-up mainspring of the fair*
> *Originating everywhere*
> *The expansive force without a sound*
> *That whirled a hundred wheels*
> *around.*

Maria Weston Chapman by an unidentified photographer, daguerreotype, circa 1846. The Trustees of the Boston Public Library, Massachusetts

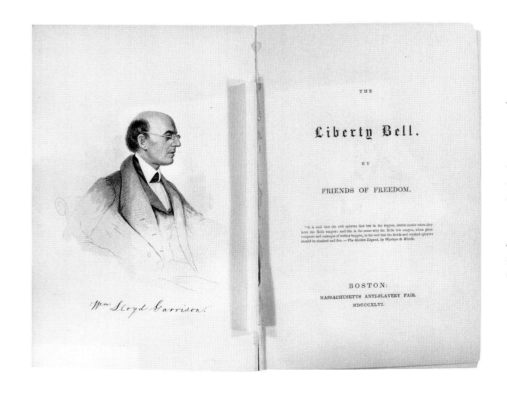

Since 1839 Maria Weston Chapman had edited an annual gift book, Liberty Bell, *as one of the most profitable activities of the antislavery fairs. For this she solicited poems, essays, and short stories. The book, available on the first morning of the fair in 1846, contained contributions from Cassius Clay, Margaret Fuller, William Lloyd Garrison, Joshua Giddings, James Russell Lowell, Lucretia Mott, and Wendell Phillips, among others.*

The Liberty Bell by Friends of Freedom, Massachusetts Anti-Slavery Fair (Boston, 1846). Special Collections, Wellesley College Library, Massachusetts

Boston Brahmin Wendell Phillips (1811–1884) was a man steeped in the reform spirit of 1846. "I am a teetotaler and against capital punishment. I believe in animal magnetism and phrenology. I advocate letting women vote and hold office," Phillips said, describing himself fifteen years after his 1831 graduation from Harvard. "My main business is to forward the abolition of slavery. I hold that the world is wrong side up and maintain the propriety of turning it upside down."

Wendell Phillips by Martin Milmore (1844–1883), bronze, 1869. National Portrait Gallery, Smithsonian Institution, Washington, D.C.

SON OF TEMPERANCE.

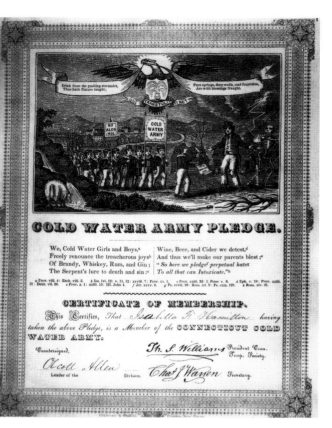

COLD WATER ARMY PLEDGE.

The most widespread of the reform movements in 1846 was aimed against the evils of drink. Hundreds of local temperance societies were active throughout America—holding meetings, conventions, and lectures; publishing pamphlets and newspapers; and promoting the signing of no-drinking pledges.

Son of Temperance *by John Hall (lifedates unknown), lithograph, 1846. Prints and Photographs Division, Library of Congress, Washington, D.C.*

Children organized into temperance societies dubbed the "Cold Water Army" paraded with banners on occasions such as George Washington's birthday and the Fourth of July, propagating total abstinence in song and ceremony. The "Cold Water Pledge" was absolute, spurning not only ardent spirits but also malt liquors, wine, and cider.

Cold Water Army Pledge, *Hitchcock & Stafford Printers, woodcut, not dated. The New-York Historical Society, New York City*

On August 1, 1846, Margaret Fuller (1810–1850) sailed to England after reaching an agreement that Horace Greeley would pay her ten dollars—twice the going rate—for each article she sent back to the Tribune. She was received in Britain, she wrote at the end of October, "with a warmth that surprized me; it is chiefly to Woman"—her Woman in the Nineteenth Century—"that I am indebted for this; that little volume has been read and prized by many."

In Italy Fuller was attracted to the young American artist Thomas Hicks, who resisted her affectionate advances by protesting that she "would find but a few embers on the hearth of a lonely ambitious man." Hicks painted her portrait sometime before Fuller married Giovanni Angelo, Marchese d'Ossoli, a Roman nobleman by whom she had a son in September 1848.

Margaret Fuller by Thomas Hicks (1823–1890), oil on canvas, 1848. Constance Fuller Threinen

acquired for himself—elective franchise, tenure of property, liberty to speak in public assemblies, etc." She added, "Those who think the physical circumstances of Woman would make a part in the affairs of national government unsuitable, are by no means those who think it impossible for negresses to endure field-work, even during pregnancy, or for sempstresses to go through their killing labors."

Horace Greeley praised *Woman in the Nineteenth Century*, but with the caveat that *so long as a lady shall deem herself in need of some gentleman's arm to conduct her properly out of a dining or ball-room—so long as she shall consider it dangerous or unbecoming to walk half a mile alone by night—I cannot see how the 'Woman's Rights' theory is ever to be anything more than a logically defensible abstraction.* In Fuller's own words, Greeley taunted, "Let them be sea captains if they will," as she waited for him to extend the expected courtesies.

Catharine Beecher was far better known among the general public than Margaret Fuller, and she had very different aspirations for the improvement of womankind. Beecher's *Treatise on Domestic Economy for the Use of Young Ladies at Home and at School*, first published in 1841, had since been reprinted annually and, followed by her *Domestic Receipt-Book*, provided the women of America with practical advice on every possible aspect of everyday life.

In 1846 Beecher was promoting "the cause of popular education, and as intimately connected with it, the elevation of my sex by the opening of a

"Two millions of American children are left without any teachers at all," Catharine Beecher pointed out, *"while, of those who go to school, a large portion of the youngest and tenderest are turned over to coarse, hard, unfeeling men, too lazy or too stupid to follow the appropriate duties of their sex."* At the same time, women, according to social custom, whiled away their time *"twining silk, working worsted, conning poetry and novels, enjoying life and its pleasures."* Beecher recognized in educated young women *"a restless, anxious longing for they know not what; while exciting amusements are vainly sought to fill the aching void."* Her proposed solution was to utilize these women as *"the best as well as the cheapest guardian[s] and teacher[s] of childhood."*

🌿 The Evils Suffered by American Women and American Children: The Causes and the Remedy *by Miss C. E. Beecher (New York: Harper & Brothers, 1846). Special Collections, Mount Holyoke College Library, South Hadley, Massachusetts*

THE EVILS SUFFERED

BY

AMERICAN WOMEN AND AMERICAN CHILDREN:

THE CAUSES AND THE REMEDY.

PRESENTED IN AN ADDRESS

BY MISS C. E. BEECHER,

TO MEETINGS OF LADIES IN CINCINNATI, WASHINGTON, BALTIMORE, PHIL-
ADELPHIA, NEW YORK, AND OTHER CITIES.
ALSO,
AN ADDRESS TO THE PROTESTANT CLERGY OF THE
UNITED STATES.

HARPER & BROTHERS, PUBLISHERS,
82 CLIFF STREET, NEW YORK.

profession for them as educators of the young." Her design—as she explained to church women in Pittsburgh, Baltimore, Washington, Philadelphia, New York, Troy, Albany, Hartford, New Haven, and Boston—was the formation of associations in those various cities. Each would raise one hundred dollars, to be placed in the hands of an organization that would send female teachers to the West. Before the women journeyed west, Beecher thought that they should be assembled for a few weeks so that she herself could instruct them "in the most important and yet neglected departments of education—*Moral Training* and *Domestic Economy*." In the course of the next decade, 450 teachers would be sent west under the auspices of Beecher's organization, though she herself would not stay the course.

Horace Mann, secretary of the Massachusetts Board of Education, in offering support for Beecher's endeavor, testified that "accomplished and highly gifted young women are the best school teachers in the world." Mann surpassed Beecher, however, in seeing that teachers were well trained, and he concentrated on the establishment of state teacher-training centers, called normal schools, for the purpose. "I believe Normal Schools to be a new instrumentality in the advancement of the race. I believe that, without them, Free Schools themselves would be shorn of their strength and healing power, and would at length become mere charity

Catharine Beecher (1800–1878), the oldest of Reverend Lyman Beecher's remarkable brood, devoted her life to female education. For twenty years she was in charge of female seminaries, first in Hartford and afterwards in Cincinnati. The lack of support in the western city and a breakdown of her health sent her journeying about the nation, where she observed "the deplorable amount of suffering endured in this country by young wives and mothers, especially in the more wealthy classes, from the combined influence of poor health, poor domestics, and a defective domestic education." To alleviate these many griefs, she prepared Domestic Economy, followed by her Domestic Receipt Book. "Had I been writing for fame I should have chosen some other than the humble subject of Domestic Economy," Beecher asserted. "Profit I expect not, and my highest ambition, in preparing these works, has been to raise an income by them," which would support an organization for sending female teachers to the West.

 Catharine Beecher by an unidentified photographer, daguerreotype, circa 1848. The Schlesinger Library, Radcliffe College, Cambridge, Massachusetts

schools, and thus die out in fact and form," Mann affirmed. "Neither the art of printing, nor trial by jury, nor a free press, nor free suffrage, can long exist to any beneficial and salutary purpose without schools for the training of teachers."

By 1846 Mann was confident that his normal-school plan was firmly in place. With the dedication of new buildings in Bridgewater and Westfield, Massachusetts, in the fall, three would be in operation. "I think the cause will be anchored when those are completed so that no storm . . . will drive it from its moorings," he wrote on July 25.

Summing up his labors during 1846 in a letter to a friend, Mann noted that he had prepared another volume of his *Annual School Abstracts*, which ran nearly 400 pages, spent seven or eight weeks on a tour of teachers' institutes, written and published his 170-page annual report, and overseen the general care and erection of two normal-school buildings. Mann, making reference to Thomas Hood's sentimental ballad describing the toil of the poor seamstress, once observed, "If Hood had known my case he would have written the 'Song of the Secretary,' instead of the 'Song of the Shirt.'"

Not to be outdone in laboring for a cause, Mann's friend Dorothea Dix tirelessly traveled the country inspecting the living conditions of the insane in jails, hospitals, poorhouses, almshouses, farmhouses, and private dwellings.

Dix had kept a school—the first one when she was fourteen—and had written a number of elementary-school texts and other books, but after a nervous and physical collapse in 1836, she found herself at loose ends. In 1841 she embarked on a crusade to bring the plight of the insane to public attention under the inspiration of the great Unitarian divine, William Ellery Channing, and with the support of Samuel Gridley Howe, Charles Sumner, and Horace Mann, who advised her in the writing of *Remarks on*

The first of the Massachusetts normal schools, initially set up in Lexington, was moved to a Greek Revival building in West Newton, which Horace Mann had persuaded a benefactor to purchase and which he himself had borrowed money to renovate, pledging his shares in the Boston and Worcester Railroad as security.

Circular and Register of the State Normal School *by William B. Fowle (Boston, 1846). Whittemore Library, Framingham State College, Massachusetts*

The communal association at Brook Farm, founded in 1841 by social reformer George Ripley and his wife Sophia, was meant to be a union of labor and culture with transcendental intellectuals sharing the drudgery of farm work during one half of the day and switching, during the other half, to cerebral pursuits. These included teaching pupils at the Brook Farm Institute of Agriculture and Education, an important source of income for what was intended to be a self-supporting society. Evenings were devoted to philosophical discussion and inquiry enlivened by visitors such as Ralph Waldo Emerson, and Margaret and Bronson Alcott.

Josiah Wolcott, a follower of the French reformer Charles Fourier, whose radical theories were embraced during Brook

Farm's waning years, painted the scene in an idealistic glow. On the extreme left is the old farm house called Hive, which housed the kitchen, office, and meeting rooms. Along the hilltop stood the Eyrie, the most desirable of the lodgings, the Cottage, and Pilgrim House, which had space for the laundry and printing presses. Yet to be built was the phalanstery, intended for the accommodation of much-needed workers. The phalanstery, still in an uncompleted state, burned to the ground on March 3, 1846, leaving the commune $7,000 in debt. The fire, in effect, spelled the end of the literary Utopia.

Brook Farm *by Josiah Wolcott (circa 1815–1885), oil on canvas, circa 1844. Mrs. Robert Blake Watson*

Prisons and Prison Discipline in the United States. Once she determined the facts through personal visitation, she drew up petitions of remedy and had some of her male acquaintances present them to the legislature. Dix did not speak at public gatherings but was persistent in talking privately to officials.

Dix's travel schedule for 1846 was prodigious. She set out from Louisville to New Orleans on a steamboat and at each landing seized the opportunity to assess conditions on shore. She spent four days in New Orleans visiting the Charity Hospital and other public institutions. Next she went to Mobile, and from there 260 miles up the Alabama River to Montgomery and then to Tuskegee, Alabama; Columbus, Ohio; Knoxville, Tennessee; Macon, Milledgeville, Augusta, and Savannah, Georgia; and then she took a boat to Charleston, South Carolina. Traveling west, she visited the state hospital in Columbia, took a return trip to New Orleans through Georgia and Alabama, then up the Mississippi to the Arkansas River, and into Arkansas as far as Little Rock. In the heat of summer, she sailed up and down the Mississippi from Vicksburg north to Dubuque, Iowa, and back to St. Louis, and then up the Ohio. She traveled around southern Illinois, visited prisons in Indiana, Illinois, and Ohio, and then proceeded across the Ohio into Kentucky and Tennessee.

In September, after a day's survey of prisons and poorhouses, she collapsed at the hospital in Columbus. "I do not regret having come. On the contrary am thankful for having attempted all that I have done," she wrote to a friend from Cincinnati in November. "Heaven has greatly blessed my labors and I feel truly more and more that a leading Providence defines my path in the dark valleys of the world."

Dix resumed her labors in December; she could not rest, for as she told the North Carolina legislature, "I am the Hope of the poor crazed beings who pine in cells, and stalls, and cages, and waste-rooms."

As an advocate for the insane, Dorothea Dix (1802–1887) in 1843 began a three-year survey that would take her more than three thousand miles throughout America. The forty-four-year-old Dix traveled, "without a gentleman protector," by whatever conveyance was available—train, stagecoach, steamboat, or wagon. By the time she was finished, she concluded that she had "visited eighteen state penitentiaries, three hundred county jails and houses of correction and more than five hundred almshouses and other institutions."

By 1846 Dix was travel worn. She related that a backcountry woman, after asking Dix how old she was and hearing the reply, said, "Well, now I should not think you was that old but it looks like age is breaking upon you powerful fast and you had a mighty heap of trouble."

Dorothea Dix by an unidentified photographer, daguerreotype, circa 1849. National Portrait Gallery, Smithsonian Institution, Washington, D.C.

When New York merchant James Brown told Thomas Cole that he was willing to pay $1,000 for a large Catskill landscape, the artist suggested a scene at a picnic, a popular activity that he himself enjoyed. Brown agreed to this, and a friend advised Cole that Brown would be most pleased if "the figures be made large enough to be easily seen, and as a group to tell the story but no larger, and let the main features of the picture be such as to be easily seen." The sensitive artist was assured, "Of course your own taste and judgment will be your guide, but a knowledge of the taste of the future owner of the picture may be of service."

Cole himself was satisfied with the finished picture. His cheerful canvas gave evidence that life could be joyous even, as Cole saw it, if civilization was threatened by the ascent of the Jacksonian Democrats. This was one of the four works Cole exhibited at the National Academy of Design.

The Pic-Nic *by Thomas Cole (1801–1848), oil on canvas, 1846. The Brooklyn Museum, New York; A. Augustus Healy Fund B (67.205.2)*

Chapter 7

Currents of Culture

We turn now from politics, war, and weighty problems unsolved to take a brief look at some of the pleasures of the time—art, literature, music, and the performing arts. By 1846 Americans had an appreciation not only for portraiture, the artist's traditional staple, but also for landscapes and scenes of everyday life. Associated with the year are two of the great masterpieces in American art—George Caleb Bingham's *The Jolly Flatboatmen* and William Sidney Mount's *The Power of Music*—as well as memorable landscapes by Thomas Cole and Asher Durand. In literature it was a golden age for poetry (although not without considerable dross); it was the era of Ralph Waldo Emerson's essays and Edgar Allan Poe's short stories; of experiments in native subject matter by William Gilmore Simms and others. Americans loved to sing—they were partial to sentimental ballads—and sheet-music manufacturers did a thriving business. Vocalists—particularly singing groups—pianists, violinists, and in a few cities, full orchestras found a ready audience. Theatrical entertainment of every description was relished, and enjoyed a popularity that rivaled that of presidential candidates and military heroes.

In 1846 a vast number of Americans, who had always favored portraiture over other genres, were having their visages recorded not only by painters and sculptors, but also through the emerging new photographic medium of the daguerreotype. Reporting on John Plumbe's New York gallery, Walt Whitman wrote, "You will see more *life* there—more variety; more human nature, more artistic beauty, (for what created thing can surpass that masterpiece of physical perfection, the human face?) than in any spot we know of." There, hundreds of portraits stretched from floor to ceiling. "We could spend days in that collection, and find enough enjoyment in the thousand human histories, involved in those daguerreotypes," proclaimed Whitman. *There is always . . . a strange fascination in portraits. We love to dwell long upon them—to infer many things, from the text they preach—to pursue the current of thoughts running riot about them. . . . For the strange fascination of looking at the eyes of a portrait, sometimes goes beyond what comes from the real orbs themselves.*

Cornelia Wells Walter's *Daily Evening Transcript* on May 6 carried a long article about portraiture, in which she pointed out that although there were forty portrait painters residing in Boston and an additional twelve who specialized in miniatures, "How few there are who understand the faces they would paint!" The writer observed, *Perhaps no people in the world have such a taste for portraits as the Americans. Go where you will, you find these memorials of affection hanging against the walls of their dwellings. There is of course every variety of style to be observed in them, from the daub of the itinerant artizan, who paints for his board and lodging, to the noble specimens from the pencil of superior artists. In the State of New York the feeling is so strong that the statute protects portraits from the profaning hands of the sheriff's officer, and when every thing else is gone, the likenesses of families are retained.*

Among the most talented of itinerant artists recording "the immortality of domestic life" was Sheldon Peck, who worked in rural Illinois, painting arresting full-length portraits surrounded by trompe l'oeil frames. In August he stayed for a week with the John J. Wagner family of Aurora, Illinois, and painted them in a group—eight of them, "not to mention the dog."

On Long Island, William Sidney Mount began the year by resolving to "fiddle less and paint more." Mount, already known for his scenes of everyday life in rural America, reflected in March, "I must leave these diggins for a season at least and paint portraits. They sometimes pay best." He resolved, "I must not undertake any more than I can do easily." He intended to paint only four hours a day, devoting "the rest of the time to exercise (in the open air), reading and playing the violin, sufficient to keep me in good spirits."

There was not a city in America without several competing daguerrian galleries, although few of the proprietors matched the expansive enterprise of John Plumbe Jr. "Among the 'sights' of the city, which strangers as well as residents will be gratified in visiting," the New York Herald asserted, "are the daguerrian rooms of Mr. Plumbe, 251 Broadway. There are exhibited an immense number of sun-portraits, including those of almost all distinguished persons, whose features every body wishes to know; and the fidelity of the resemblance as taken by the skillful method of Mr. Plumbe, gives assurance to the beholder that he sees the very image of the individual."

Advertisement for Plumbe's National Daguerrian Gallery, from the New York Mercantile Register, 1847–1848. General Research Division, The New York Public Library, New York City; Astor, Lenox and Tilden Foundations

Sheldon Peck began to work as a self-taught painter in Vermont around 1820 but then moved to Onondaga County in western New York. He reached Chicago just before the Panic of 1837 and then bought land twenty miles west at Babcock's Grove. Listed in the 1840 census as "employed in agriculture," Peck also traveled about in search of portrait commissions.

Maria Wagner Messenger, the child in the far right in the portrait of the Wagner family, recalled in 1913, "Mr. Peck sketched the faces from life, and then arranged the group.... It took him almost a week, during which time he stayed at our house." The portrait is dated 1846 or 1847 from the ages of the parents—fifty-three and forty-one—inscribed beside them on the canvas.

The John J. Wagner Family *by Sheldon Peck (1797–1868), oil on canvas, 1846 or 1847. Aurora Historical Society and Museum, Illinois*

For the most part, 1846 was a fallow year for Mount. He undertook a "sketch in oil of a little Girl after death" at a price of $12, and for $60 made a life-size portrait of a woman, which he had copied from a miniature. In return for several small cabinet portraits, Mount was paid in firewood. A portrait of a four-year-old child netted him $50, but Mount said that the child was "the last I hope to paint at that age." He executed a pair of portraits for a fee of $75 each and was delighted when his customer—as was sometimes the case—paid him more than he asked. Engaged to paint a posthumous portrait, Mount complied for $20 but decided that it would be his last: "While death is a patron to some painters, I had rather paint the living."

The American Art-Union, an association of professional artists and art patrons devoted to the encouragement of American art, was in a flourishing state. William Cullen Bryant, concluding his three years as its president, reported, "The season which now closes is altogether the most brilliant which the Institution has known." The free picture gallery at 497 Broadway, where members showed their work, was "crowded day after day and night after night with spectators."

"I sometimes feel as if I should give all my time to pictures, make character, expression and colour my only study," William Sidney Mount reflected in the summer of 1846. "Paint scenes that come home to everybody. That every one can understand." In November the opportunity came to do just that when he received an important commission from Mrs. Gideon Lee of Geneva, New York. Lee was the mother-in-law of Charles M. Leupp, a major collector of American and European art, for whom Mount had painted Dance of the Haymakers in 1845. "One picture for Mrs. Lee—good," Mount put down on November 20, "I must get my characters about me and go to work. Now's the time."

Mount executed a composition he had contemplated for more than a year. By March 7, 1847, The Power of Music was delivered to Leupp, and Mount related, "He stood a long time looking at it until I began to think I had made a failure and observed to him, 'If you think this picture will not suit Mrs. Lee, I will paint her another with pleasure.' 'Why man,' he said, 'I only wish the picture belonged to me.'"

The Power of Music *by William Sidney Mount (1807–1868), oil on canvas, 1847. The Cleveland Museum of Art, Ohio; Leonard C. Hanna, Jr., Fund, 91.110*

Each December works purchased by the Art-Union were distributed by lottery to the members. In addition, every member received a large print of one of the paintings with his $5 membership fee. Chosen as one of two pictures to be reproduced in 1846 was George Caleb Bingham's rendering of riverboat life, *The Jolly Flatboatmen.* The picture, etched on steel by Thomas Doney, was featured as the frontispiece of *Transactions of the American Art Union for 1846.* Some 9,500 prints of the large mezzotint were ultimately distributed to the Union members. And so it was that Bingham, dubbed "the Missouri artist," was encouraged to continue painting scenes of western life. Without the patronage of the Art-Union, Bingham later declared, "he would never perhaps have attempted that peculiar class of subjects which have given him all his reputation."

American artists unquestionably were coming into their own. "The encouragement of *good* native painters, we are glad to say, is constantly increasing. Our citizens begin to look *at home* for excellence," observed Lewis Gaylord Clark, editor of the *Knickerbocker Magazine* in January 1846. *Gentlemen of wealth among us begin to find it* fashionable *to order pictures of our own artists, at home and abroad, to decorate their parlors or galleries.* DURAND *is busy with his perfect transcripts from Nature; so is* COLE, *and a dozen others, whom we have no space to name.*

Thomas Cole had a prior claim as a landscape painter, having turned to that branch of art in the 1820s after failing as an itinerant portrait painter.

Hiram Powers, born in Vermont, brought up in Ohio, and since 1837 a resident in Italy, was saluted to great applause at a Washington dinner, reported the New York Tribune *on January 3, 1846, as "the first sculptor in the world, a son of the East a nurseling of the West." Later in the year, the* Boston Evening Transcript *announced the arrival of "A New Work by Powers," a bust of Proserpine, the Roman goddess of fertility. Originally created in response to a Philadelphia collector's com-*mission for an ideal head, Proserpine won immediate popularity—seven marble busts were on order by 1846—and before Powers was through, it was estimated that he had sold more than four dozen replicas of it at $400 each.

Proserpine *by Hiram Powers (1805–1873), marble, 1844. National Museum of American Art, Smithsonian Institution, Washington, D.C.; gift of Mrs. George Cabot Lodge*

Each year, on the Friday before Christmas, the works purchased by the American Art-Union during the past year were distributed by lottery. In 1846 145 paintings from 65 artists were raffled off to the 4,457 members. A year later membership had more than doubled. "Our artists," observed retiring President William Cullen Bryant, "paint with a freer hand and happier pencil, they give us more and better pictures, because they know that they have a resource in our Institution."

Distribution of the American Art-Union Prizes *by Sarony and Major Lithography Company (active 1846–1857), lithograph, 1847. The J. Clarence Davies Collection, Museum of the City of New York, New York (29.100.1513)*

In 1844, after four years spent painting portraits in Washington, George Caleb Bingham returned to Missouri, where, by the spring of 1846, the St. Louis Weekly Reveille proclaimed that the thirty-five-year-old artist was making "a brilliant reputation by the delineation of western scenes." Bingham, the newspaper reported, had completed "four really capital paintings," which were shown in St. Louis, and then sent to New York for exhibition at the American Art-Union. One of these, the piece Bingham called Dance on the Flat Boat, showed boatmen whiling away some tranquil moments as they floated down the Missouri for New Orleans. Purchased by the Art-Union in October for $290, including the frame, it was selected in November as one of two pictures to be mezzotinted for the members. The engraving process completed, the oil painting was auctioned off to New York grocer Benjamin Van Shiac and subsequently disappeared for more than a century. The widely distributed prints, however, kept the painting in public memory.

The Jolly Flatboatmen by George Caleb Bingham (1811–1879), oil on canvas, 1846. Private collection, on loan to the National Gallery of Art, Washington, D.C.

The Beeches, *exhibited at the National Academy of Design in 1846 as* Landscape Composition, *is believed to be Asher Durand's first landscape based on an outdoor sketch. "There is great individuality in Durand's trees," wrote Henry Tuckerman in his series on "Our Artists," which ran in* Godey's *during 1846. "This is a very desirable characteristic for an artist who deals with American scenery." Tuckerman was not alone in seeing in the atmosphere of Durand's landscapes a "coincidence of feeling" with the poetry of William Cullen Bryant. "Durand!—ah, here is an artist!" enthused the* Knickerbocker *reviewer. "What Bryant does with his pen, he effects with his pencil."*

The Beeches *by Asher B. Durand (1796–1886), oil on canvas, 1845. The Metropolitan Museum of Art, New York City*

Cole, however, had grander visions and preferred to devote himself to religious and historical allegories. In 1846 he had plans for a monumental series of five pictures on "the Cross and World," but he could find no patron for the ambitious project. "I long for the time when I can paint whatever my imagination would dictate without running into pecuniary difficulties," a disgruntled Cole wrote on the first day of the year. "Painting for money, and to please the many, is sadly repulsive to me."

In an 1846 lecture given at the Young Men's Association in Albany, Cole took issue with "the common remark, that America is too young and too poor to patronize the arts." He observed, *We give our money freely and admiringly to some foreign dancing girl, and shower golden favors on imported musicians—we build floating palaces, the admiration of the world, to busily ply upon our waters—and we indulge in the elegancies and luxuries of life more freely and extravagantly than any other nation—and are we too poor to give our patronage to the Painter and the Sculptor?*

In Bucks County, Pennsylvania, Edward Hicks, a Quaker preacher, made his living as a coach and sign painter. Hicks also painted pictures, taking repeatedly as his theme the "Peaceable Kingdom." He recorded in his diary on May 8 that he was "steadily engaged in my shop. My business, though too trifling and insignificant for a Christian to follow, affords me an honorable and I hope an honest living." Hicks's pictures were unknown in his lifetime outside of his self-contained Quaker world, but his distinctive signboards had warranted a mention in the *Historical Recollections of the State of Pennsylvania*, published in 1843.

From Paris, where he was touring with his Indian collection, George Catlin sent a memorial to Congress asking the government to purchase his assemblage of six hundred portraits and artifacts for $65,000. A petition of support came from his fellow artists, who declared that the collection should be "purchased and cherished by the Federal Government, as a nucleus for a National museum where American Artists may freely study that bold race who once held possession of the country, and who are so fast disappearing before the tide of civilization."

"Is it asking too much then that the government will take measures for the concentrated perpetuity of this great collection?" asked Walt Whitman in the *Brooklyn Daily Eagle*. "A great deal is said by American writers and orators about the duty and mission of America; *to the future*," Whitman editorialized. "And yet, when it comes to the scratch, people are not a bit too forward to invest any thing in behalf of the future."

Edward Hicks, whose life was directed by his Quaker religion, took the "Peaceable Kingdom" as the major theme of his art. Between 1820 and his death in 1849 he painted perhaps one hundred versions of the biblical injunction that the lion lie down with the lamb. Most of these pictures Hicks sold, bartered, or gave away to his fellow Quakers. "I am nothing but a poor old worthless insignificant painter," he recorded in his diary on April 18, 1846. Two days later, he was "industriously engaged at my trade or business—working with my own hands to provide things honest in the sight of all men, ministering to my own necessities and them that are with me, which always produces peace of mind to an humble, honest Christian."

The Peaceable Kingdom *by Edward Hicks (1780–1849), oil on canvas, 1846. The Phillips Collection, Washington, D.C.*

"You know what has been, and still is my first ambition—not money, but to build a Monument *to a dying race and to myself,*" proclaimed George Catlin (1796–1872) as his petition for the purchase of his Indian collection was before the Congress. "*I dread the idea of rearing it in a foreign land; nor will I do it, if I can have the good will of my countrymen, and the means enabling me to do it in my native country.*" Printing Catlin's letter on August 8, the New York Journal of Commerce *observed, "Many feel no little anxiety about the fate of the Smithsonian Bill and the works of our distinguished countryman and artist, Mr. Catlin."*

The Joint Committee of the Library recommended that the collection be purchased, but no action was taken. "Sooner or later, I trust, the thing will be done," a prominent member of Congress was quoted as saying, "and I can only say, that in my humble judgment Mr. Catlin's collection belongs to this country, and it ought to belong to the Government."

George Catlin's collection, stored for a quarter of a century by his Philadelphia creditor Joseph Harrison, was given to the United States Museum by Harrison's widow in 1879.

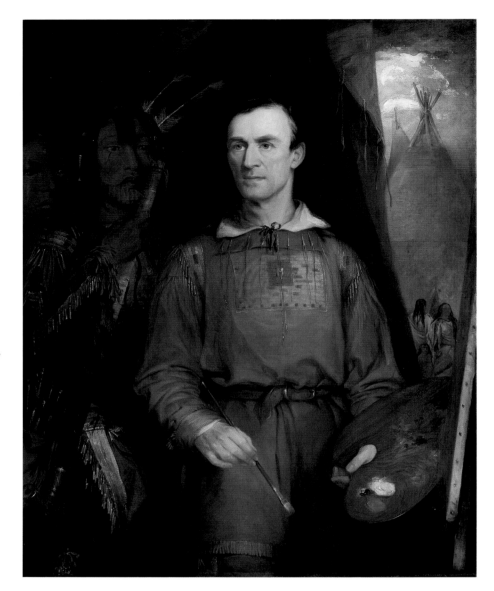

George Catlin by William Fisk (1796–1872), oil on canvas, 1849. National Portrait Gallery, Smithsonian Institution, Washington, D.C.; transfer from the National Museum of American Art, Smithsonian Institution; gift of Miss May C. Kinney, Ernest C. Kinney, and Bradford Wickes, 1945

Meanwhile, on other cultural fronts, America also forged ahead. No longer was it asked who in the four corners of the earth read an American book. The year 1846 saw the publication, simultaneously in England and America, of Herman Melville's first novel, *Typee: A Peep at Polynesian Life*, the story of four months spent among the natives of the Marquesas Islands after the author, who had gone to sea on a whaler at the age of seventeen, jumped ship. Margaret Fuller, referring to Melville's "pretty and spirited pictures" of the "Happy Valley of the gentle cannibals," opined that "the sewing societies of the country villages will find this the very book they wish to have read while assembled at their work."

No writer in America was busier in 1846 than South Carolinian William Gilmore Simms, whose "prolific and vigorous pen" gave literary voice to the South. His sonnets appeared in the *Democratic Review* from June through December. "Thoughts on Theatricals," three letters about drama, appeared in the *Southern Patriot* during July and September. *The Life of Captain John Smith* was published, as were *Grouped Thoughts and Scattered Fancies*, a collection of sonnets, and *Areytos, or Songs of the South*.

The erratic Edgar Allan Poe, who eked out a living writing prose for various magazines, had been acclaimed after the publication of *The Raven and Other Poems*. "Poe's masterly facility in diction may be supposed to have occasioned the only fault which we perceive in these poems, an appearance of careless wantonness in rhythm," pronounced *Godey's* in January, "which perhaps, after all, may be merely the independent freedom of one who cannot but feel his own power." Later in the year, Poe ruffled many feathers with a series of opinionated delineations about the persons and performances of "The Literati of New York," which appeared in the magazine from May to October.

Cornelia Wells Walter, offended when Poe insulted Boston audiences with a recitation of poems he had written as a youth, had no tolerance for him. Walter, whom Poe had dubbed "that most beguiling of all little divinities," reported in December that there were accounts that Poe "had been reduced to beg for sustenance, owing to improvidence and sickness," and that several newspapers had begun subscriptions for his relief. Walter, who of course knew that Poe was intemperate as well as imprudent, frankly said, *"Reformation of habits and proper principle exerted to others* is what is requisite to free him in future from the necessity of pity."

After four years of adventure on board ship and in the South Sea Islands, Herman Melville (1819–1891) returned to America in the fall of 1844, outfitted with a wealth of material that would last him the greatest part of his literary life. Typee, published early in 1846, brought the author so much attention that Harper & Brothers, which had turned down Typee, readily accepted Omoo: A Narrative Adventure in the South Seas, which Melville completed in December.

It was around this time that Melville traveled to Albany, where Asa W. Twitchell painted his portrait. Melville, at age twenty-seven, was at the height of his contemporary fame. Acclaim for his greatest book, Moby Dick, would not come until the twentieth century.

Herman Melville by Asa Weston Twitchell (1820–1904), oil on canvas, circa 1847. Melville Collection, Berkshire Athenaeum, Pittsfield, Massachusetts

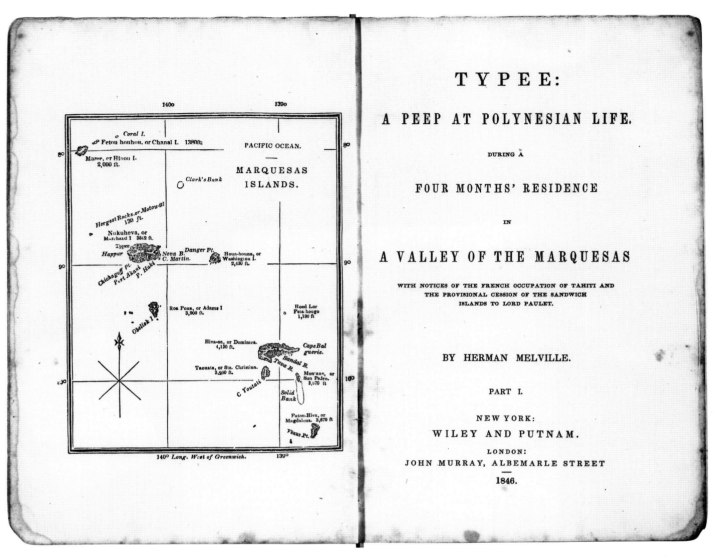

MARQUESAS ISLANDS.

PACIFIC OCEAN.

Coral I.
Fetou houhou, or Chanal I. 1380ft.
Masse, or Hiaou I. 2,000 ft.
Clark's Bank
Hergest Rocks, or Motou-iti 130 ft.
Nukuheva, or Marchand I 3842 ft.
Typee
Happar
Nova B.
C. Martin.
Danger Pt.
Houa-houna, or Washington I. 2,430 ft.
Chichagoff Pt.
Port Ahoui
P. Haki
Roa Poua, or Adams I 3,900 ft.
Obelisk I.
Hood Lor Feta-hougo 1,180 ft
Hiva-oa, or Dominica. 4,130 ft.
Taouata, or Sta. Christina. 3,980 ft.
Tawa B.
Standal B.
Cape Bal guerie.
Mon'ane, or San Pedro. 3,570 ft
C Youtati
Solid Bank
Fatou-Hiva, or Magdalena. 3,670 ft
Venus Pt.

140° Long. West of Greenwich.

T Y P E E:

A PEEP AT POLYNESIAN LIFE.

DURING A

FOUR MONTHS' RESIDENCE

IN

A VALLEY OF THE MARQUESAS

WITH NOTICES OF THE FRENCH OCCUPATION OF TAHITI AND
THE PROVISIONAL CESSION OF THE SANDWICH
ISLANDS TO LORD PAULET.

BY HERMAN MELVILLE.

PART I.

NEW YORK:
WILEY AND PUTNAM.
LONDON:
JOHN MURRAY, ALBEMARLE STREET
—
1846.

Typee *brought author Herman Melville (1819–1891) both praise and condemnation.* "A strange, graceful, most readable book this," *wrote Walt Whitman in* The Brooklyn Daily Eagle. "As a book to hold in one's hand and pore dreamily over of a summer day, it is unsurpassed." *But missionary magazines were outraged. The* New-York Evangelist *berated* Typee *as a* "racily-written narrative of a forecastle-runaway from an American whale ship. . . . He had life among Marquesan cannibals to his liking; a plenty of what pleases the vicious appetite of a sailor, or of sensual human nature generally. . . . The book abounds in praises of the life of nature, alias savageism, and in slurs and flings against missionaries and civilization."

"Mr. Melville's book is full of things strange and queer to the ears of Broadway and Chestnut Street," *pronounced* Graham's Magazine. *The author* "at times almost loses his loyalty to civilization and the Anglo-Saxon race. . . . So far he seems to think sailors and missionaries have carried little to the barbarious nations which have come under his notice, but disease, starvation and death." *The book sold for thirty-seven and a half cents.*

Typee: A Peep at Polynesian Life. During a Four Months' Residence in a Valley of the Marquesas *by Herman Melville (New York: Wiley & Putnam, 1846). Clifton Waller Barrett Library, Special Collections Department, University of Virginia Library, Charlottesville*

In addition to his literary labors, William Gilmore Simms (1806–1870) was on the stump in 1846 campaigning for reelection to the South Carolina House of Representatives. He found that there was "a most insane cry for rotation in office—as if office was a public cow at whose dugs everybody had a right to suck." He subsequently lost his seat by forty-five votes. Although his friends nominated him for lieutenant governor, he was again rejected by a slight majority. "Ours are a very simple sort of people, with all their chivalry & impracticability," he was told in explanation of his defeat. "You are a Novelist. As such only are you regarded by even the intelligent of our State. . . . Now our people do not comprehend your political aspirations, nor believe you really have any. They regard your excursion into politics as a sort of eccentric movement in search of excitement—having no purposes but momentary pleasure."

✹ William Gilmore Simms by an unidentified artist, oil on canvas, not dated. National Portrait Gallery, Smithsonian Institution, Washington, D.C.; donated in memory of the Charles Carroll Simms Family

"Poe, himself, is a very good looking fellow," observed William Gilmore Simms in 1846, who, as one of the few southern literary men, felt special kinship with the Virginia-born Edgar Allan Poe (1809–1849). "He is probably thirty three or four years old, some five feet, eight inches in height, of rather slender person, with a good eye, and a broad intelligent forehead. He is a man, clearly, of sudden and uneven impulses of great nervous susceptibility."

Samuel Osgood painted the only known life portrait in oils of Edgar Allan Poe. Osgood was a fashionable New York portrait painter and the husband of writer Frances Sargent Lockie. Mrs. Osgood and Poe met in March 1845 when Poe requested her opinion of The Raven. The two subsequently exchanged published poetry, and their relationship elicited gossip among the New York literati in 1846.

✹ Edgar Allan Poe by Samuel Osgood (1808–1885), oil on canvas, circa 1845. The New-York Historical Society, New York City

The *New Orleans Daily Picayune* sprang to Poe's defense, saying, "The public ought not and does not care to hear what may be the personal failings of those known to it but as authors." Poe's "tales have been extensively copied both here and in England. They are not only copied, but are read and remembered by thousands. They are written with such power, that you cannot forget them if you would."

Among those who had been subjected to the barbs from Poe's pen was America's most popular poet, Henry Wadsworth Longfellow. Longfellow's poems, issued in a sumptuous second edition by Ticknor & Company, brought forth from Poe the sarcastic observation that the author "is a poetical phenomenon, as entirely without fault as is the luxurious paper upon which his poems are invariably borne to the public eye." Poe, sneering at Longfellow's social position and influence, labeled him as nothing more than "a determined imitator and a dextrous adapter of the ideas of other people." Cornelia Walter retorted, "Whatever the miserable envy of trashy criticism may write against Longfellow one thing is most certain, no American Poet is more read."

Nathaniel Hawthorne and his wife Sophia—one of the three intellectual Peabody sisters—forced by the return of the owner to leave the Old Manse in Concord, had moved back to Salem. Hawthorne was desperate for employment and thought that his Democratic credentials entitled him to a political appointment. Sophia Hawthorne was pregnant, and her husband groaned, "What a devil of a pickle I shall be in if the baby should come, and the office should not!" On Hawthorne's behalf, Charles Sumner wrote to George Bancroft's wife to beg "for a friend of mine, & of your husband's; for a man of letters, of gentleness." Hawthorne, Sumner told Elizabeth Bancroft, "is an ornament of the country; nor is there any person of any party who would not hear with delight that the author of such Goldsmithian prose, as he writes, had received honor & office from his country."

George Bancroft, who was in charge of patronage in Massachusetts, replied to Sumner that he was "most perseveringly" Hawthorne's friend and jested that he was pleased to see his Whig friend Sumner "go for the good rule of dismissing wicked Whigs & putting in Democrats."

Finally, on April 3, President Polk signed Hawthorne's appointment as "Surveyor for the District of Salem and Beverly and Inspector of the Revenue for the Port of Salem." The post paid $1,200 a year. "It is no great affair," Hawthorne wrote, "but suits me well enough, as ensuring me a

Henry Wadsworth Longfellow (1807–1882), professor of modern languages and belles-lettres at Harvard, was married to Frances Elizabeth Appleton, the daughter of textile manufacturer Nathan Appleton. The pair lived comfortably in Craigie House, a Georgian mansion that had been the wedding gift of Longfellow's father-in-law.

In 1846 Longfellow was at work on Evangeline, *a poem based upon the English dispersal of the French Acadians in 1755. The story had been told to him by fellow writer Nathaniel Hawthorne, who thought that the topic was better suited to Longfellow's poetry than to his own prose.*

Longfellow found further stimulus for Evangeline *in John Banvard's three-mile panorama of the Mississippi River, which was exhibited in Boston in October.*

When Eastman Johnson opened a studio in Boston in the fall of 1846, Longfellow decided to have made a group of ten portraits of his family and some of his literary friends for the adornment of his home, of which this is one.

Henry Wadsworth Longfellow by Eastman Johnson (1824–1906), crayon and chalk on paper, 1846. National Park Service, Longfellow National Historic Site, Cambridge, Massachusetts

In 1846 Nathaniel Hawthorne (1804–1864) was appointed to a post at the Custom House in Salem, Massachusetts. His duties there were light, but he managed to write no more than a few reviews in 1846. "Whenever I sit alone, or walk alone, I find myself dreaming about stories, as of old," he told Henry Wadsworth Longfellow, "but these forenoons in the Custom House undo all that the afternoons and evenings have done." Nevertheless, in the Custom House Hawthorne came upon old documents and "a certain affair of fine red cloth," which would provide him with the inspiration for The Scarlet Letter.

On October 14 Hawthorne, responding to the request that he sit for his portrait, wrote to Longfellow, "If you will speak to Mr. Johnson, I will call on him the next time I visit Boston, and make arrangements about the portrait. My wife is delighted with the idea."

Nathaniel Hawthorne by Eastman Johnson (1824–1906), crayon and chalk on paper, 1846. National Park Service, Longfellow National Historic Site, Cambridge, Massachusetts

Ralph Waldo Emerson (1803–1882) complied with Henry Wadsworth Longfellow's request that he sit for his portrait on October 22, just after he had returned from a fortnight in Bangor, Maine, where he had delivered a course of five lectures at $25 each.

In December Emerson made haste to present Longfellow with a copy of his just-published Poems. *Longfellow received them "with the highest and keenest delight. A precious volume!" Mrs. Longfellow read the verses aloud, praising "the very Gold-coast of Song; along which we sailed, enjoying delicious sights and sounds of Nature and seeing the auriferous streams pour out their tribute into the sea." Longfellow told Emerson, "The only bad thing about it is, that I shall never get my wife to read any more of my poems, you have fascinated her so with yours."*

Ralph Waldo Emerson by Eastman Johnson (1824–1906), crayon and chalk on paper, 1846. National Park Service, Longfellow National Historic Site, Cambridge, Massachusetts

comfortable living, with a little margin for luxuries, and occupying only a moderate portion of time—so that I shall have as much freedom for literary employment as hitherto."

Meanwhile, the "sage of Concord," Ralph Waldo Emerson, was occupied with bringing out a volume of his poems for the Christmas trade. "Our people in Boston like a costly book," he noted. "So I think to get a good edition of the poems first; and if it seems advisable I will presently after print on coarser paper."

A share of Emerson's year was devoted to the lecture circuit, where he was always in demand. Scheduled to speak at the New Bedford Lyceum in March, Emerson canceled when he learned that the Lyceum had voted that blacks could not purchase tickets. "Now, as I think the Lyceum exists for popular education," Emerson wrote in explanation, *as I work in it for that, and think that it should bribe and importune the humblest and most ignorant to come in, and exclude nobody, or, if any body, certainly the most cultivated—this vote quite embarrasses me, and I should not know how to speak to the company.*

A correspondent to the *New York Tribune* related to New York readers that he had heard "the strong and eloquent Emerson" speak at the Mechanics' Lyceum in Lowell, and noted, "It is not in New England as with you; here lectures hold first rank and draw the best audiences." Emerson and Charles Sumner, the writer stated, "stand vastly higher than your De Meyers and Ole Bulls." Viennese pianist Leopold De Meyer was then touring the United States, and Norwegian violinist Ole Bull had recently left America after great success. "To our as yet uncultured people, they speak a better plainer and more desirable language; and sensible philosophy, happily is more palatable now than Music and the Arts."

New England had, nonetheless, come to accept the performing arts. Even so, "Many well-minded and conscientious individuals continue to regard the '*playhouse*' as a nursery for immorality, a hot-bed for vice, where ribaldry and profanity hold their court, and revel unrestrained," wrote Cornelia Walter in the *Evening Tribune*. "Let this stigma be effaced—let the supporters of the histrionic art, boldly and distinctly avow their belief that the legitimate drama is a mighty engine for the moral amelioration of the community."

"Two theatres in Boston in full blast. Concerts also have abounded," Longfellow wrote in October. "We heard the Hutchinsons the other night: and Leopold de Meyer, the Lion-pianist from Vienna, who when he plays seems to be dipping his hands into liquid music, and shaking the notes off the ends of his fingers like drops of water."

The Hutchinsons—Judson, John, Asa, and Abby—the four youngest members of a musical New Hampshire family, had recently returned from a triumphant tour of the British Isles. Longfellow had heard that in England "their Anti-Slavery songs commended them," but that his poem "Excelsior," which the oldest brother, Jesse Hutchinson, had set to music, "was more popular than all else."

French pianist Henri Herz began his yearlong tour of the United States in the fall of 1846. "You must still keep a place in your souls for Herz; or rather he will quietly *take* a place, whether you reserve it for him or not," wrote Lydia Maria Child, who heard him play in New York. Child, a popular author and former editor of the *National Anti-Slavery Standard*, then living in the city, continued, *I was sad when I went to the concert, but the graceful music touched my soul with fairy-wand, and it rose up buoyant and winged. Both his music, and his style of playing, are the expression of highly polished society, the musical utterance of drawing-room elegance! yet they charm me, simple recluse as I am.* She concluded, "To me there is something beautiful

Abby Hutchinson (1829–1892), the youngest of the Hutchinson singers and the only female among them, had been performing in public since the age of ten, and at thirteen she was invited to join her brothers in the first of the family traveling troupes—"a nest of brothers with a sister in it."

Much to the dismay of her brothers, Abby left the troupe after she was married in 1849, although from time to time she emerged from retirement to sing in support of causes dear to her heart, such as women's rights.

Abigail Jemima Hutchinson by Francis B. Carpenter (1830–1900), oil on canvas, not dated. The Lynn Historical Society, Massachusetts

The Hutchinsons' trademark song, "The Old Granite State," was set to the hymn tune "You Will See Your Lord A-Coming." It began: "We have come from the mountains of the 'Old Granite State,'" and continued, "Yes we're friends of emancipation," and "We are all teetotalers / And have sign'd the Temp'rance pledge."

"In patronizing the Hutchinson's," noted the Daily Advertiser of Rochester, "there is satisfaction in knowing that they are American vocalists, who breathe forth the music of their native Granite Hills, naturally and with unaffected grace, instead of throwing themselves into all sorts of shapes to squeak out some unintelligible foreign air. They are Yankee singers, with Yankee songs."

Judson, Abby, John, and Asa Hutchinson. "The Old Granite State: A Song Composed, Arranged and Sung by the Hutchinson Family" by G. and W. Endicott lithographers (active 1840s), lithograph, 1843. Music Division, Library of Congress, Washington, D.C.

Eleven of the "Tribe of Jessie," as the sons
of the Milford, New Hampshire, farmer
Jessie Hutchinson were called, performed,
in various combinations, solos and ensembles, songs both humorous and pathetic.
While Judson, John, and Asa—along with
sister Abby—were on a yearlong tour of
the British Isles, the "home branch" of the
family carried on in America. In February 1846 members of the Hutchinson family gave a concert in Rochester, and in

April they were at the Sing Sing prison,
where they sang separately to the males
and females and for prisoners in the hospital. There, reported the Brooklyn Daily
Eagle, "these Children of Song stood like
ministering angels, speaking in strains of
heavenly cheer to the desponding miserable
creatures there!" Later in the year,
Alexander Mackay met the Hutchinsons on
a steamboat en route from Washington to
Richmond and related that as they passed

Mount Vernon, the family came on deck
and sang "Washington's Grave." Wrote
Mackay, "The effect was good, for the
melody is touching, and the majority of the
audience were enthusiasts."

Hutchinson Family Singers—Asa,
Andrew, Jesse, Joshua, David, Caleb, Noah,
Judson, Zephaniah, and John by an unidentified
artist, full-plate daguerreotype, 1845. Gilman
Paper Company Collection, New York City

in the fact that while we send Europe our superior machines and tools, she
sends gifted minstrels to us, to impart her superior cultivation in Art."

The theatrical entertainment of distinctly American flavor was the minstrel show, a mixture of song, humorous patter, and dance performed by
troupes in blackface to the accompaniment of banjo, accordion, and bone
castanets. "Negro songs, glees, and other refinements of the same kind
helped along by worn-out conundrums, form this refined amusement,

"*Few names are better known in the musical world than that of Herz,*" Americans were told as the French pianist Henri Herz (1806–1866) arrived in New York, "*and it is a strong proof of the increasing taste for music among us, that it has drawn him to these shores from a country in which his fame has been so long established, and his merit so fully appreciated.*" Herz's tour took him as far south as New Orleans, where he orchestrated a program that featured twenty women performing on as many pianos. Two decades later Herz, discussing the 1846 tour in his memoirs, reflected that his southern audiences "*enjoyed compositions more elevated than the simple fantasies and variations on popular airs that crowded my earlier programs.*"

Henri Herz by Devérie (lifedates unknown), engraving, not dated. The Music Bio Files, Theatre Arts Collection, Harry Ransom Humanities Research Center, The University of Texas at Austin

In 1846 Stephen Collins Foster's (1826–1864) "There's a Good Time Coming," composed to a poem that had appeared in the London Daily News, *was published. The twenty-year-old self-taught musician, whose manuscript songs had been sung in the parlors of Pittsburgh, had recently moved downriver to Cincinnati to work for his brother's steamboat and commission firm. Among the songs he carried with him was "Oh, Susanna," which, pub-* lished in 1848, became an immediate favorite of the minstrel troupes and the marching song of those rushing to California in quest of gold.

Stephen Collins Foster attributed to Thomas Hicks (1823–1890), oil on canvas, circa 1850. National Portrait Gallery, Smithsonian Institution, Washington, D.C.; transfer from the National Gallery of Art; gift of Andrew W. Mellon, 1942

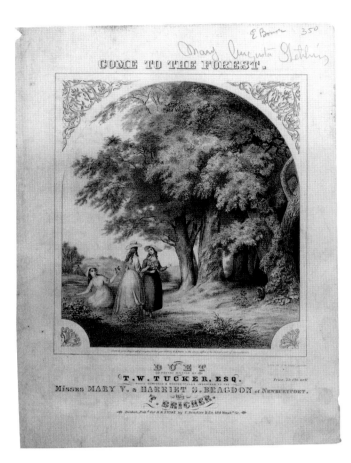

which is very popular and fills the theater," sneered the sophisticated Philip Hone. Walt Whitman allowed that he was beginning to agree with author James Kennard Jr., who in a recent article in the *Knickerbocker* sought "to prove that the negroes of the South were the originators of the true national music of the United States."

In April Edwin P. Christy's "original and far-famed band of Ethiopian Minstrels" opened at Palmo's Opera House in New York. "The soft touch of 'them bones' will ring in our ears so long as we have ears, and the sweet tones of that violin will ever awake within us some thought of melody," reported the *New York Herald*.

English actor Charles Kean and his wife Ellen Tree offered Americans a rich feast of Shakespearean fare during their farewell tour designed, Kean wrote, "to say Adieu in every city in which I have been kindly received." Kean, the son of the great English tragedian Edmund Kean, was not the actor his father was, however. Ellen Tree, whom he had married in January 1842, was an acclaimed actress, popular in America since her initial ap- pearance in 1836.

Jonas Chickering (1798–1853), who combined mechanical genius with a passion for music, had by 1846 made improvements in piano manufacturing—particularly the cast-iron frame—which increased the power and enriched the tone of the popular parlor instrument. Recognized as "The Minstrel's Friend," Chickering was untiring in the promotion of music and musicians. As president of Boston's Handel and Haydn Society, the pioneer association for the improvement of sacred music, he oversaw performances of Haydn's Creation, The Oratorio of David, *and* Moses in Egypt *during the 1846 season, himself sometimes beating time for the choruses. "Jonas Chickering," his health was once wittily given, "like his own pianos: Upright, Grand, and Square."*

Jonas Chickering by Albert Sands Southworth (1811–1894) and Josiah Johnson Hawes (1808–1901), daguerreotype, circa 1853. National Portrait Gallery, Smithsonian Institution, Washington, D.C.

On January 7 the Keans appeared at New York's Park Theatre in a magnificent production of *Richard III*, which boasted unprecedented attention to historical accuracy. The costumes and set were specially designed for the play and not merely taken from stock, as was the custom. The *New York Herald* declared the play to be "in truth the most extraordinary and interesting exhibition ever seen on the American stage. . . . Hundreds who never entered the walls of a theatre before, have been attracted by this celebrated dramatic spectacle." Theater aficionado Philip Hone commented, "The spectator seems carried back to the times of the white and red roses, and transported on one of Professor Morse's copper wires to Bosworth Field and Tamworth."

Hone also noted, "Mrs. Kean has a great advantage in appearing at this time, when she has no competitor for the histrionic crown in this country, nor, as far as I know, in her own." Ellen Tree had no rivals because Charlotte Cushman was out of the country, playing to great applause in London, Dublin, Edinburgh, and Liverpool, while her progress was proudly trumpeted in the American press, particularly in her hometown of Boston. At the Haymarket Theatre in London, Cushman took the role of Romeo and her sister that of Juliet. A letter from London reported, "Miss Cushman's fortune is made. The hall is at her foot. She is now incontestably by the suffrage of the British public, at the head of the British stage."

While Charlotte Cushman carried all before her, her compatriot Edwin Forrest was having mixed success. Forrest arrived in England in January 1846 and was well received in Shakespeare's *King Lear*, but when he presented *Metamora*, a drama that had won a prize for plays with an American theme, the *Times*'s critic declared that he had never seen "such utter rubbish."

When Forrest returned to New York in early September 1846, a public dinner was given in his honor. The first toast offered was to "Our Country" and the second to "The American Stage: its brilliant morning gives promise of a glorious day."

In Philadelphia actor James Edward Murdoch produced *Witchcraft or the Martyrs of Salem*, which he hoped would be the first of a series of American plays intended "to build up a *national drama* and interlinking with it the success of American authors and actors." Cornelia Walter applauded the undertaking as "a laudable and most excellent one," but added, "Let us have as many good American actors and authors as we may, there will yet be a proneness with our people to seize upon foreign talent in both capacities."

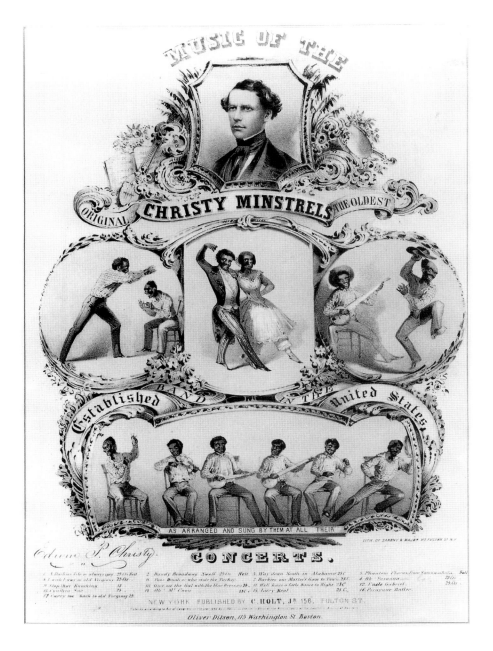

The Evening Transcript *pronounced that Edwin P. Christy (1815–1862)* "has introduced a new era in this kind of music," *when Christy's Minstrels performed at the Melodeon in Boston.* "The character of negro melodists has heretofore been greatly undervalued from inexperience and want of knowledge of melody, and we are happy to see that Mr C. has introduced a company who are not only musicale, but know how to appear as gentlemen." *In June Christy's Minstrels were in Cleveland, advertising* "Chaste and Inimitable Concerts, introducing a variety of Entirely New Songs, Choruses, Burlesques, etc." *Admission was twenty-five cents. In Buffalo they promised a change of program every evening.* "The Music (in part) from the most popular Operas of the Day—accompanied with the BANJO, VIOLIN, CONGO TAMBO, TAMBOURINE, and BONE CASTINETS."

Edwin P. Christy by Sarony and Major Lithography Company (active 1846–1857), after an unidentified artist, lithograph, 1848. National Portrait Gallery, Smithsonian Institution, Washington, D.C.

Mr. & Mrs. Cha.ˢ Kean as King John & Lady Constance.

Constance ——— "Thou monstrous injurer of Heaven & Earth"
K. John ——— "Bedlam, have done."   King John Act 3. Sc.1

PARK THEATRE.

Boxes $1.   Pit 50 Cents.   Gallery 25 Cents.

THE GREAT SHAKSPERIAN REVIVAL!!!

MRS. CHARLES KEAN & MR. CHARLES KEAN

IN SHAKSPERE'S TRAGEDY OF

KING JOHN.

To give additional effect to this Play

MR. GEO. VANDENHOFF

Has been expressly engaged to represent the Character of FAULCONBRIDGE.

IN ANNOUNCING THIS

GREAT SHAKSPERIAN REVIVAL!

The Manager begs respectfully to state, that no labour or expense
has been spared in endeavouring to attain the UTMOST FIDELITY
OF HISTORIC ILLUSTRATION!

☞ *In consequence of the enormous expense attending this perform-
ance, THE FREE LIST, with the single exception of the Public Press,
must be suspended, and no orders can on any account be admitted.*☜

Wednesday Evening, November 18, 1846, will be

Performed SHAKSPERE'S Historical Tragedy of

KING JOHN,

(Produced under the Immediate Direction and Superintendence of
Mr. CHAS. KEAN, at a cost and with a degree of Correct-
ness and Splendour, it is believed, hitherto not
witnessed in any Theatre.)

THE SCENES painted on upwards of 15,000 square feet of Canvas, by
Mr. HILLYARD, Mr. GRAIN, and Assistants.
THE COSTUMES, COSTLY ARMOURS, 176 in number, DECORATIONS and
APPOINTMENTS, from the Authorities named hereafter, by Mr.
DEJONGE.
THE MACHINERY, by Mr. SPEYERS.

☞ The indulgence of the audience is respectfully solicited between the first
and second Acts, as the whole of the previous scene has to be removed for
the purpose of exhibiting a Panoramic View of Angiers, the French Camp and
Distant Country: the Stage thrown open to the Walls of the Theatre.

---

*In November Charles Kean (1811–1868)
and his wife Ellen Tree (1805–1880)
opened at New York's Park Theatre in
Shakespeare's* King John. *The play, however, was not well known, and the audience was sparse. Kean complained that he
had* "expended $8000 out of my own
purse upon this revival you may imagine I
feel rather disgusted, for such an exhibition
was never witnessed before on an American Stage. . . . I have placed 150 persons
on the Stage in one scene alone, dressed
from head to foot in the accurate costume
of the period—& my efforts did not receive
the encouragement of one hand of
approbation."

✴ Mr. and Mrs. Charles Kean as King
John and Lady Constance *by Martin &
Johnson (active dates unknown), lithograph,
circa 1846. Folger Shakespeare Library,
Washington, D.C.*

✴ King John *Program, November 18,
1846. Folger Shakespeare Library, Washington, D.C.*

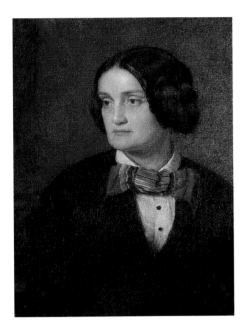

"Her gesture and utterance is somewhat angular and abrupt," wrote one who saw Charlotte Cushman (1816–1876) playing Lady Macbeth in London, "but this is amply compensated for by her intellectual conception and masterly realization of the character. Her figure is tall and erect, her features not handsome but expressive, her voice the most massive I ever heard in a woman."

Gansevoort Melville, secretary to the American legation, who was overseeing the publishing of his brother Herman's first book, visited her in London and observed, "Miss Charlotte Cushman is a woman of plain tho' expressive and intelligent features, tall and rather full person, full of conversation and vivacity and decidedly agreeable, tho' dashed strongly with masculineness."

Charlotte Cushman by William Page (1811–1885), oil on canvas, 1853. National Portrait Gallery, Smithsonian Institution, Washington, D.C.

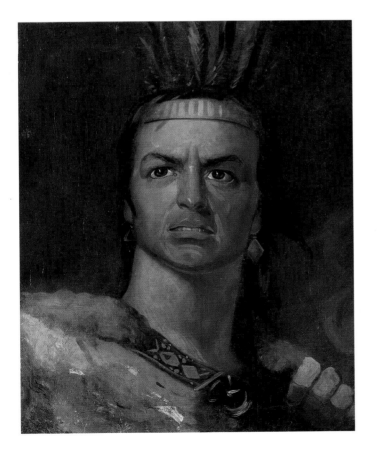

Edwin Forrest (1806–1872) bestowed his prize for the best play based on an American theme to John H. Stone's Metamora, the story of seventeenth-century Indian chief King Philip. The play's title role was one of Forrest's most popular representations in America. When Metamora opened in Boston, shortly after Forrest's return, it was reported that "many persons were disappointed in not being able to procure tickets—the great mass of them being taken up by speculators."

Forrest's acting style was summed up by his friend William Gilmore Simms: "Forrest . . . is the creation of the popular theatricals. . . . His bold personations, his daring reaches, his free, fearless execution, wild and startling transitions, great physique, and fresh, prompt resources— are due to, and illustrative of, the influence of the masses."

Edwin Forrest (as Metamora) by Frederick Styles Agate (1807–1844), oil on canvas, circa 1832. National Portrait Gallery, Smithsonian Institution, Washington, D.C.; gift of the Kathryn and Gilbert Miller Fund, in memory of Alexander Ince

Louis Agassiz Comes to America

Interest in science was high in America, but real "working men of science" were few. "There is in this country an astonishing dearth of any thing like a talent for original research in proportion of number to those who take an interest in science," complained Joseph Henry (1797–1878), a research scientist and professor of natural philosophy at Princeton, whose contributions in the field of electromagnetism had made Samuel F. B. Morse's telegraph possible. "Our newspapers are filled with the puffs of quackery and every man who can burn phosphorus in oxygen and exhibit a few experiments to a class of Young Ladies is called a man of Science."

It was with the greatest of pleasure that Benjamin Silliman (1779–1864), professor of chemistry and natural history at Yale and the patriarch of professional scientists, announced the anticipated visit of the distinguished Swiss naturalist, Professor Jean Louis Rodolphe

Agassiz (1807–1873), in the May 1846 *American Journal of Science* (the channel, since 1818, through which European research was reported in America). Agassiz, not yet forty, was famous for his work on modern and fossil fishes, his publications on Echinodermata, and his investigations of the glaciers of Switzerland. "His amiable and conciliating character," Silliman wrote, "will, without doubt, secure for him the cordial cooperation of our naturalists, and the favor of the public wherever he may travel over our vast territory."

Agassiz had been engaged to deliver a series of lectures at the Lowell Institute in Massachusetts, which had been set up according to an endowment from textile manufacturer John Lowell Jr. to provide free scientific lectures to the public.

Agassiz also intended to visit the most important centers of scientific endeavor throughout the country. "There is something intoxicating in the prodigious activity of the Americans which makes me enthusiastic," he wrote to Silliman. "I already feel young through the antici-

Joseph Henry by an unidentified artist, daguerreotype, circa 1845. Chicago Historical Society, Illinois

Jean Louis Rodolphe Agassiz by Fritz Züberbuhler (1822–1896), oil on canvas, 1844. Harvard University Portrait Collection, Cambridge, Massachusetts; gift of G. R. Agassiz, Max Agassiz, and R. L. Agassiz, 1910

Benjamin Silliman by Rudolf Hoffman (active 1840s–1850s), after photograph by Gibbs, lithograph with tinststone, 1857. National Portrait Gallery, Smithsonian Institution, Washington, D.C.

pated contact with the men of your young and glorious republic."

Upon Agassiz's arrival in Boston in early October, Asa Gray, professor of natural history at Harvard, volunteered to accompany him on his travels. Gray, the acknowledged leader of American botanists, was a man who had seen scientific opportunity in the Mexican War. He had arranged for a plant collector to travel to Santa Fe with the Army of the West, and was eagerly awaiting a harvest of plants, seeds, cacti, and bulbs, especially all the new things that he expected would be found in the mountains north of Santa Fe, which rose above the snow line.

After visiting Silliman, Agassiz traveled to Princeton, where he met Joseph Henry. "The physical department, under the direction of Professor Henry," Agassiz observed, "is remarkably rich in models of machinery and in electrical apparatus, to which the professor especially devotes himself." Henry, soon to become secretary of the Smithsonian Institution, and Agassiz, in due course elected to the Board of Regents, would have a long and close professional relationship.

In Philadelphia Agassiz met a young naturalist, Spencer Fullerton Baird, a professor at Dickinson College in Carlisle, Pennsylvania, who "offered me duplicates from his collections of birds and other animals." Baird would be hired in 1850 as Joseph Henry's assistant, bringing with him to Washington an enormous collection of specimens. In the course of his thirty-seven years at the Smithsonian—the last nine as secretary—Baird would ensure that there would be no turning back from the museum function of the Institution.

Proceeding to Washington, Agassiz hurried to the Patent Office to visit the National Museum, impatient to satisfy himself about the scientific value of the specimens gathered by the United States Exploring Expedition in the Pacific. "I confess that I was agreeably surprised by the richness of the zoological and geological collections," he wrote. "I do not think any European expedition has done more or better."

"I thought myself tolerably familiar with all that is doing in science in the United States, but I was far from anticipating so much that is interesting and important," Agassiz summed up at the close of his tour. "What is wanting to all these men is neither zeal nor knowledge. In both, they seem to compete with us, and in ardor and activity they even surpass most of our savans. What they need is leisure."

Agassiz planned to return to Europe in two years' time, but plans were afoot to keep him in America. Elected professor of zoology and geology at Harvard's newly established School of Instruction in Theoretical and Practical Science, funded by a fifty-thousand-dollar donation from Abbott Lawrence, Agassiz would remain in America for the rest of his life.

William J. Hough (1759–1869), the author of the final bill establishing the Smithsonian Institution, was elected interim secretary at the first meeting of the Board of Regents on September 9. After the regents adjourned, the press reported that "Mr. Hough will remain for several days, to transact business committed to his charge. He very generously undertook the task, re-fusing compensation." Hough also traveled around the country as a member of the building committee.

At the close of a single term in Congress, General Hough (his rank in the New York militia) returned to his law practice in Cazenovia, New York, where he was painted together with his wife, Clarinda Carpenter Hough (1799–1867), his son William Jerome (1821–1900), and his daughters, Helen Clarinda (born 1837) and Frances Jervis (born 1838).

William J. Hough and family (detail) by J. Brayton Wilcox (lifedates unknown), oil on canvas, circa 1848. National Portrait Gallery, Smithsonian Institution, Washington, D.C.; gift of Mrs. Violet Shepherd

Chapter 8

The Smithsonian Is Launched

Once Congress adjourned for its summer recess, most people who were free to do so abandoned the city during the sickly months of August and September. Those in charge of charting the course of the Smithsonian Institution, however—designated in the Hough bill as the Board of Regents—lost no time in beginning their work. On September 7 the regents, who had been appointed before adjournment, assembled for their first meeting in a room of the Post Office Building on F Street Northwest, across the street from the Patent Office Building, which occupied the two city blocks between Seventh and Ninth Streets. Before 1846 was out, the regents would decide the location and architect for the Smithsonian building and select the chief executive officer of the institution, called the secretary.

Named to the Board of Regents by the Speaker of the House of Representatives were Indiana Democrat Robert Dale Owen, New York Democrat William J. Hough, and Alabama Whig Henry W. Hilliard, one of the few southerners (along with future regent Jefferson Davis) to vote for the bill establishing the institution. Designated by the president of the Senate were Maine Whig George Evans, Illinois Democrat Sidney Breese, and Virginia Democrat Isaac Samuels Pennybacker, who would die early in January.

The six citizen members, chosen by joint resolution, were Alexander Dallas Bache, head of the United States Coast Survey, Joseph Gilbert Totten, chief of the Army Corps of Engineers—both fulfilling the statutory requirement for two resident members of the National Institute—Richard Rush, who had shepherded the Smithsonian bequest through Chancery, former Senators Rufus Choate and William Campbell Preston, and Gideon Hawley, state superintendent for public instruction of New York. Ex-officio members were Vice President George Mifflin Dallas, Chief Justice Roger B. Taney, and District of Columbia Mayor William Winston Seaton, who was incidentally one of the editors of the Whig newspaper, the *National Intelligencer.*

With the exception of Breese, who had departed for Illinois before he learned of his appointment, and Preston, who was detained by illness in South Carolina, all of the regents were present. "This general attendance of the Regents—some of them from great distance," reported the *National Intelligencer,* "evinces an appreciation of the duty committed to them honorable to the gentlemen selected, and auspicious, we think, for the success of the important Institution whose enduring foundation they are now met to lay." Hough was elected interim secretary. At a meeting the next day in the supposedly cooler Patent Office, Vice President Dallas was elected chancellor.

With the success of George Perkins Marsh's amendments allowing up to twenty-five thousand dollars for books, it was believed by many that the Smithsonian Institution was to be in fact no more than a great national library. But Robert Dale Owen had other ideas. The accrued interest was available for a building, and Owen intended to make the most of the opportunity. Owen, in fact, had started to make plans for the building shortly after the passage of the Tappan bill in 1845, asking his brother David Dale Owen to draw up specifications for a structure that would house the many activities he envisioned for the Smithsonian Institution.

"We shall have to select the location, and to make some preparations, I suppose, for the buildings," Owen wrote to Richard Rush a week after the Smithsonian bill had passed. "Upon judicious action on both these points much of the future character and utility of the Institution may depend." Owen's first consideration was to make sure that the building would be placed on the public ground called the Mall and not, as the act allowed, be connected to the Patent Office. Owen told Rush that he had already spoken to the President and the cabinet as well as the commissioner of

"The passage of the Smithsonian bill through the House was due to my efforts and the amendments to Owen's and Hough's bills, which changed every essential feature of them, were drawn and proposed by me," grumbled George Perkins Marsh (1801–1882), affronted when he was not named to the first Board of Regents. In December 1847, however, Marsh would replace Robert Dale Owen on the board.

Marsh, whose extensive print collection would be the first art purchased by the Smithsonian, had a great affinity for artists, welcoming them to his small house on F Street between Nineteenth and Twentieth Streets. He commissioned his portrait from George Peter Alexander Healy, whose skill "in seizing & portraying the best characteristic expression of his sitter" he much admired. Healy's "portrait of myself (the greater the subject the greater the work)," Marsh humorously pronounced, was "his magnum opus."

George Perkins Marsh by George Peter Alexander Healy (1813–1894), oil on canvas, circa 1845. Hood Museum of Art, Dartmouth College, Hanover, New Hampshire; bequest of Mrs. George Perkins Marsh

William Winston Seaton (1785–1866), coeditor of the National Intelligencer, *had taken a deep personal interest in the Smithson bequest from the beginning, publishing a series of long articles that discussed possible uses of the money. In his capacity as mayor of Washington, Seaton was zealous in urging Congress to take action on the matter. That Washington's mayor was by statute an ex officio member of the Board of Regents "was chiefly due to the zealous interest which Mr. Seaton had manifested in the advocacy of the measure." At the first meeting Seaton was appointed chairman of the executive committee and a member of the building committee. With the expiration of his term as regent, Seaton was elected treasurer of the institution and served until his death in 1866.*

William Winston Seaton by Leopold Grozelier (1830–1865), after George Peter Alexander Healy, lithograph, 1855. Published in Charles H. Brainard's Portrait Gallery of Distinguished Americans *(Boston, 1855). National Portrait Gallery, Smithsonian Institution, Washington, D.C.*

patents, who by law had to unanimously concur with the regents to determine the site. They were all opposed to any arrangement that would cut off the institution from "all ground for agricultural experiments, or even a botanical garden."

On September 9 the President, secretaries of state and war, attorney general, and mayor of the District of Columbia spent nearly an hour with the building committee of the regents, walking over the grounds on the Mall. "Opinions were freely expressed," President Polk recorded.

By early December the regents had decided to ask for about a hundred acres, comprising the greater part of the Mall, but Secretary of State James Buchanan, declaring that amount of land extravagant and unnecessary, refused to consent. The regents next suggested a site of about fifty-two acres between Seventh and Twelfth Streets, to which Buchanan again objected. Finally, on December 19 the regents offered a proposal for sixteen acres on the south half of the Mall between Ninth and Twelfth Streets, and all agreed to the plan.

In September Owen, Hough, and Totten had traveled to Philadelphia, Trenton, New York, Boston, and, in Owen's case, Cincinnati, visiting architects and viewing public buildings. A competition for the building design was announced, and all applicants were given a copy of the detailed floor plans and elevations that had been drawn up by David Dale Owen. Although the committee theoretically accepted entries until December 25, on November 30 they recommended to the regents the Norman design drawn up by the young architect of New York's Grace Church, James Renwick Jr.

On December 1 the committee on organization, headed by Owen and including Bache, Hilliard, Choate, and Pennybacker, issued its plan for carrying out the provisions of the legislation. The committee concluded that neither Smithson's will nor the legislation excluded any branch of human knowledge, but because of limited funds, the "efforts of the Institution [should] be chiefly directed to the increase and diffusion of knowledge in the physical sciences, in the useful arts, and in the theory and practice of public education, and, especially, of common school instruc-

tion." Clearly Robert Dale Owen was still intent on restoring his personal vision.

The regents postponed a final decision about the future activities of the Smithsonian until the secretary could be chosen, but they proceeded with their work, assuming, as did the committee, that the secretary, rather than the unpaid chancellor, would be the chief executive officer. Because there had been great uncertainty about the duties and responsibilities of the secretary—not to mention the activities of the institution—more than two dozen men of widely varying backgrounds and experiences became candidates for the position.

On December 3 the Board of Regents adopted the Owen committee's proposed resolution that the secretary *be a man possessing weight of character, and a high grade of talent; and that it is further desirable that he possess eminent scientific and general acquirements; that he be a man capable of advancing science and promoting letters by original research and effort, well qualified to act as a respected channel of communication between the institution and scientific and literary individuals and societies in this and foreign countries.* The hand of Alexander

This drawing is believed to be quite close to the submission that won James Renwick the commission as architect of the Smithsonian building, now known as the "Castle." Of all the entries, the building committee explained, only Renwick's design included "all the accommodations demanded by the charter." Provisions were made for a library on the first floor, a museum on the second, and an art gallery on the third.

Smithsonian Building, south elevation in the Romanesque style, by James Renwick Jr. (1818–1895), drawing, 1846. Smithsonian Institution Archives, Washington, D.C.

Dallas Bache—and the assent of Robert Dale Owen—are both evident in this list of qualifications, which certainly described very few men in the America of 1846.

Campaigning vigorously for the secretaryship was Francis Markoe Jr., clerk in the diplomatic bureau of the State Department and corresponding secretary of the National Institute. Markoe, associated with the National Institute during the heady days when the private organization had control of the specimens brought back by the United States Exploring Expedition, claimed to have the endorsements of President James K. Polk, former President John Quincy Adams, and others of influence.

Markoe recognized that he faced opposition from Alexander Dallas Bache, who he knew was hostile to the political and amateur elements of the National Institute, even though he himself was a corresponding member. "I regret that A. D. Bache is one of the Regents & it is quite absurd that he should be made a Regent, as one of the two members of the *National Institute*, wh. the law requires," Markoe wrote to Richard Rush in August. "He never did any thing to promote our views, & indeed is not a member, that is not a *Resident, paying member.* I fear him also, personally, because I have reason to believe that he will use all his exertions to secure the appt of Prof. Henry."

Bache—the great-grandson of Benjamin Franklin, the grandson of Alexander James Dallas, James Madison's secretary of the treasury, and the nephew of the Vice President—had the prestige of family connections, as well as the weight of his own accomplishments. A graduate of West Point, Bache had resigned from the army to become professor of natural philosophy and chemistry at the University of Pennsylvania. Named president of Girard College in 1836, which under the terms of the benefactor's will could not open until the building was finished, Bache spent two years abroad studying educational institutions. The opening of the college being further delayed, Bache spent his time reorganizing the public schools of Philadelphia and resumed teaching at the University of Pennsylvania. On December 12, 1843, he became superintendent of the United States Coast Survey.

One of Bache's closest friends was Joseph Henry, a pure-research scientist whose contributions in the field of electromagnetism had made Samuel F. B. Morse's telegraph possible. United in their dedication to advancing the cause of science in America through original discovery, the two rarely, if ever, found themselves in disagreement.

There was no doubt that Bache, with his usual good humor and tact, was manipulating with great skill to ensure that Henry would win appointment as the first secretary of the Smithsonian Institution. Henry's name had come up in the press and among his friends, but "Agreeably to your instructions on the subject of the Smithsonian," Henry informed Bache on November 16, "I have kept perfectly quiet."

Henry tended to be a prickly man, sensitive to slights; he was also a man who knew his own worth. "If the institution is to be of a scientific nature," he told his brother James, "and scientific reputation formed on scientific discoveries is to be the ground of choise then I am entitled to the situation."

On December 5 the regents met to select the secretary. Charles Pickering, who had been the chief zoologist of the Wilkes expedition and who had served briefly as curator of the National Institute, obtained one vote. Francis Markoe received four votes. Joseph Henry received seven votes and thereby was elected the first secretary of the Smithsonian Institution.

"Our Board of Regents adjourned to day," Bache immediately wrote to Henry, "in the best possible humour with themselves for having done so fine a thing as to elect you their Sec. thus paying homage to Science as the Chancellor expressed it."

Realizing that his friend had some qualms about leaving Princeton and taking on a mission yet to be clearly defined, Bache urged, "Redeem Washington. Save this great National Institution from the hands of charlatans." He pleaded, *Come you* must *for your country's sake. What if toils increase & vexations come. Is a man bound to do nothing for his country, his age. You have a name which must go down to History the great founder of a great Institution. The first Secretary of the American Institute.*

On December 8 Henry told his brother, *The die is cast and I have resolved to go to Washington. The proposition is one of great responsibility and difficulty but I have considerable confidence in my ability to render it subservient to the best interests of humanity. I have matured plans for the organization of the institution which if I am allowed to carry out will render the name of Smithson familiar to every part of the civilized world.*

Shortly after his election, Henry traveled to Washington and formally took up his duties. "I have succeeded beyond my most sanguine expectation in molding the opinions of the board of Regents into that of my plans," he reported to his wife, "but the difficulty is that we are hampered with the law of congress which directs that a building shall be erected with rooms suitable to con[t]ain on a liberal scale objects of natural history and particularly the collection of the exploring expedition."

"Professor Bache had a remarkable suavity of manner; a pressure in a hand shake that made you believe you were the chosen confidant, a smile of his liquid brown eyes that was irresistibly winning with both men and women," wrote one who first met Alexander Dallas Bache (1806–1867) in 1841. "His forcible manner of presenting his case abided with him through life."

Bache remained a valuable member of the Smithsonian's Board of Regents until the end of his life. Joseph Henry, in announcing his friend's death to the regents in 1867, recalled that "it had been principally through the influence of Professor Bache that he had been induced to venture to accept the appointment of Secretary of this Institution, and that with the sympathy, counsel and support of the deceased, he had been enabled, through all the eventful changes which had since taken place, to continue the discharge of the responsible duties of the office."

Alexander Dallas Bache by an unidentified artist, oil on canvas, not dated. University of Pennsylvania Art Collection, Philadelphia

On the last day of 1846, Henry outlined his concrete plans for the Smithsonian Institution. To increase knowledge, he would allot thirty thousand dollars to pay for "papers of an original character in the different branches of knowledge" from every part of the world to be published under the title "Smithsonian Contributions to Knowledge." Another part of the annual income would be used to support "lines of research in the way of observation and experiment; for example, in meteorology to settle the nature of our Atlantic storms, in terrestrial magnetism to determine the magnetic state of our continent, etc." To diffuse knowledge, he proposed the publication of journals "giving an account of the progress of the different branches of knowledge as compiled from all the journals of the world and containing particularly everything in the way of research in our own county." He also contemplated a short course of lectures for the edification of members of Congress. "I do not, however, consider this of much importance, but it will probably be found necessary to establish something of the kind." Henry concluded, "I am opposed to the scheme of forming a great miscellaneous library and also a museum, though these objects are interesting in themselves. I think their influence would be local and would not carry out the wishes of the Donor in the best manner."

To Rufus Choate's consternation, Henry shortly would succeed in divesting the Smithsonian of its library, but the congressional charge to care for "all objects of art and of foreign and curious research, and all objects of natural history, plants, and geological and mineralogical specimens belonging or hereafter to belong, to the United States, which may be in the city of Washington," remained. Once the Smithsonian building was completed, Joseph Henry could not avoid bringing the contents of the Great Hall of the Patent Office Building to the Smithsonian building, called the "Castle," on the Mall.

John Quincy Adams suffered a stroke in November 1846, and in the short time left to him, he would play no further role in the evolution of the Smithsonian Institution. "If I succeed in placing upon a firm and stable foundation the practical, permanent, progressive execution of the great design of James Smithson," Adams had written, "I shall depart for the sentence of my judge, with a blessing of more cheering hope for the future destiny of my country, and with the soothing consolation that I have not lived in vain."

Notes on Sources

Chapter 1: August 10, 1846

"Do what you have to do," *Brooklyn Daily Eagle*, July 9, 1846. "The adjournment was fixed," Charles Francis Adams, ed., *Memoirs of John Quincy Adams*, vol. 12, p. 270. "The most gratifying act," *New York Evening Post*, August 15, 1846. "Every whippersnapper vagabond," William Jones Rhees, ed., *The Smithsonian Institution: Documents Relative to Its Origin and History, 1835–1839*, p. 137. "The chief obstacle," Adams, *Memoirs*, vol. 12, p. 463. "With a heavy heart," Wilcomb E. Washburn, ed., *The Great Design: Two Lectures on the Smithsonian Bequest by John Quincy Adams*, p. 14. "Contemplated Institutes for education," *ibid.*, p. 73. "A botanical garden," Rhees, *Smithsonian Institution Documents*, p. 195. "Mean and selfish," Adams, *Memoirs*, vol. 10, p. 139. "Of plain and durable," Rhees, *Smithsonian Institution Documents*, p. 268. "A pretty energetic diffusing," *ibid.*, p. 284. "Accumulating a grand," *ibid.*, p. 286. "An absurd amendment," Adams, *Memoirs*, vol. 12, p. 199. "For universal education," *ibid.*, pp. 116–17. "Your child, which," Robert Dale Owen to Benjamin Tappan, October 30, 1845, Tappan Papers, Reel 8, Manuscript Division, Library of Congress, Washington, D.C. "The wildest and strangest of all," *Philadelphia North American*, December 5, 1846. "Opposed the bill in every shape," Rhees, *Smithsonian Institution Documents*, p. 261. "Point me to the power," Leonard Falkner, *The President Who Wouldn't Retire*, p. 297. "The money should properly," *New York Weekly Tribune*, May 9, 1846. "I hold it to be," Rhees, *Smithsonian Institution Documents*, p. 344. "Increase of Knowledge," Walter Karp, *The Smithsonian Institution*, p. 16. "The whole money thrown," Rhees, *Smithsonian Institution Documents*, p. 397. "In the first place Smithson's," *ibid.*, pp. 346–47. "Heard with great delight," *ibid.*, p. 397. "So, it was settled," *New York Weekly Tribune*, May 9, 1846. "Thus nearly the whole proceeds," Washburn, *The Great Design*, p. 27. "Will be

persisted in," Kenneth Hafertepe, *American's Castle*, p. 17. "In a moment Congress votes," John B. Pickard, *The Letters of John Greenleaf Whittier*, vol. 2, p. 25. "If they do not," *Washington Post*, August 5, 1846. "In a few well directed," *New York Herald*, August 12, 1846. "The great object," *ibid.*

Captions for Chapter 1: "So strange is this donation," Washburn, *The Great Design*, p. 13. "For the endowment of," *ibid.*, pp. 60–61. "It marks an era," reprinted in the *Albany Argus*, August 28, 1846. "Clever engraver of portraits," David McNeely Stauffer, *American Engravers upon Copper and Steel*, vol. 1, p. 218. "Does not the whole history," Samuel Gilman Brown, *The Works of Rufus Choate*, p. 256. "The House of Representatives," Joseph Jobe, *Extended Travels in Romantic America*, p. 63. "Were this book," *New York Herald*, February 20, 1846.

Chapter 2: President Polk's Washington

"Ladies and gentlemen," Milo Milton Quaife, *The Diary of James K. Polk*, vol. 2, p. 150. "Members of Congress," Adams, *Adams Memoir*, vol. 12, p. 229. "Mrs. P. came up dressed," James T. McIntosh, ed., *The Papers of Jefferson Davis*, vol. 2, p. 420. "A livery carriage," Varina Davis, *Jefferson Davis: A Memoir*, vol. 1, p. 266. "A large old-fashioned," *ibid.*, vol. 1, pp. 262–63. "It is an immensely large," Marc Rothenberg, ed., *The Papers of Joseph Henry*, vol. 6, p. 448. "The most abominable," McIntosh, *Jefferson Davis Papers*, vol. 2, p. 421. "We went down to-day," Davis, *Jefferson Davis*, vol. 1, p. 226. "Wandered in of her own account," Eastman Johnson to Charles Henry Hart, December 31, 1896, Charles Henry Hart Papers, Reel 934, frames 150–52, Archives of American Art, Smithsonian Institution, Washington, D.C. "The intended publication," *Boston Evening*

Transcript, July 20, 1846. "At best, Washington is," Alexander Mackay, *The Western World; or Travel in the United States in 1846–47*, vol. 1, p. 177. "Lives pleasantly in one," Allan Nevins, *The Diary of Philip Hone*, vol. 2, pp. 766–67. "The doughty knight," Adams, *Adams Memoirs*, vol. 11, p. 533. "Most happy lifes work," Pamela Herr, *Jessie Benton Frémont*, p. 82. "Fremont has particularly," *ibid.*, p. 83. "As for your Report," Mary Lee Spence and Donald Jackson, eds., *The Expeditions of John Charles Frémont*, vol. 2, p. 148. "Dressed in an odd looking," reprinted in the *Boston Evening Transcript*, April 6, 1846. "Was considerably over," Davis, *Jefferson Davis*, vol. 1, p. 282. "I found him thoroughly," Quaife, *Polk Diary*, vol. 1, p. 309. "Every Indian that comes," *Boston Evening Transcript*, October 8, 1846. "Between 40 & 50 chiefs," Quaife, *Polk Diary*, vol. 2, p. 3. "Great Mother," Herman J. Viola, *Diplomats in Buckskin: A History of Indian Delegations in Washington City*, p. 108. "John Ross, the Principal Chief," Quaife, *Polk Diary*, vol. 2, p. 81. "Almost every State," Davis, *Jefferson Davis*, vol. 1, pp. 253–54. "It is a vast," *New York Evening Transcript*, May 23, 1846. "For excelling all others," *Boston Evening Transcript*, June 24, 1846. "We believe the professor," *ibid.* "It is his intention," Alan Fern and Milton Kaplan, "John Plumbe, Jr., and the First Architectural Photographs of the Nation's Capitol," *A Century of Photographs, 1846–1946*, p. 5.

Captions for Chapter 2: "Could but illy spare," Quaife, *Polk Diary*, vol. 1, p. 193. "Mr. Healey, the artist," *ibid.*, vol. 1, pp. 473–74. "Among the pleasant recollections," Beverly Wilson Palmer, *The Selected Letters of Charles Sumner*, vol. 1, p. 164. "The glassware was," Margaret Brown Klapthor, *Official White House China*, p. 70. "In the midst of," Mackay, *The Western World*, p. 170. "Three weeks of peril," Davis, *Jefferson Davis*, p. 219. "I can assure you," McIntosh, *Jefferson Davis Papers*, vol. 3, p. v. "The front of the Capitol," Mackay, *The Western World*, vol. 1, p. 171. "All physical and scientific," Edward Lind Morse, ed., *Samuel F. B. Morse: His Letters and Journals*, vol. 2, p. 269. "Washington, Baltimore, Philadelphia," *National Intelligencer*, September 15, 1846. "An excellent likeness," William Kloss, *Samuel F. B. Morse*, p. 118. "The choicest architectural bijou," Mackay, *The Western World*, vol. 1, p. 169. "Brilliant soiree at the White House," *Boston Evening Transcript*, January 29, 1846. "Is one of the persons," reprinted in the *Boston Evening Transcript*, March 30, 1846. "Is one of," *Brooklyn Daily Eagle*, July 15, 1846. "From morning till night," Mackay, *The Western World*, vol. 1, pp. 182–83. "Is so much in vogue," Bayard Tuckerman, ed., *The Diary of Philip Hone*, vol. 2, p. 265. "This 'counterfeit presentment' of," Allan Nevins, *Hone Diary*, vol. 2, p. 761. "We could count on," Herr, *Jessie Benton Frémont*, p. 91. "He does not seem to have," *New York Evening Post*, July 10, 1846. "A new and useful machine," Elias Howe, Patent No. 4750, September 10, 1846. "Is said to be able," *Boston Evening Transcript*, June 2, 1846. "Cotton thread holds the Union," Edward Waldo Emerson, ed., *Journals of Ralph Waldo Emerson, 1845–1848*, p. 201. "This great and," *The Plumbeian*, January 6, 1847. "A daily portrait of," *ibid.*

54°40′ or Fight: "The great subject," Donald B. Cole and John J. McDonough, eds., *Benjamin Brown: French Witness to the Young Republic*, p. 183. "The truth is that," Quaife, *Polk Diary*, vol. 1, p. 345. "That he had two sons," *Albany Argus*, January 9, 1846. "The miserable traitor," *Cleveland Daily Plain Dealer*, February 15, 1846. "That new revelation," *National Intelligencer*, January 6, 1846. "That man must be poor," *ibid.* "We have now," reprinted in the *Boston Evening Transcript*, April 9, 1846.

A Visit to the Patent Office: "The Patent Office in Washington," Reverend G. Lewis, *Impressions of America and the American Churches*, p. 79. "The American people discover," Mackay, *The Western World*, vol. 3, p. 340. "The principal entrance," *Guide to the National Executive Offices and the Capitol of the United States*, 1842, p. 38. "Is the commission Washington," Lewis, *Impressions*, p. 80. "To be kept in custody," Adams, *Memoirs*, vol. 12, p. 15.

Chapter 3: Across the Fruited Plain

"But what prospects open before us!" *New York Herald*, January 2, 1846. "Our good city of New York," Nevins, *Hone Diary*, vol. 2, p. 785. "Is not a receding," *ibid.*, vol. 2, p. 185. "Now ships more cotton," *ibid.*, p. 282. "Sociable, easy, quiet society," Nicholas B. Wainwright, ed., *A Philadelphia Perspective: The Diary of Sidney George Fisher*, p. 190. "We perambulated the grounds," Robert C. Winthrop, *Memoir of the Hon. Nathan Appleton*, p. 25. "They dress well," Domingo Faustino Sarmiento, *Travels in the United States in 1847*, p. 246. "Into a form fit for chewing," Mackay, *The Western World*, vol. 2, p. 174. "They are everywhere," *ibid.*, pp. 183–84. "A thriving village," William Cullen Bryant II and Thomas G. Voss, eds., *The Letters of William Cullen Bryant*, vol. 2, p. 439. "To furnish entertainments," *Cleveland Daily Plain Dealer*, November 25, 1846. "Among a thousand other things," *ibid.*, December 4, 1846. "It is one of the most orderly," Mackay, *The Western World*, vol. 3, p. 79. "Has established in the eyes," *The Horticulturist and Journal of Rural Art and Taste*, August 1846, p. 80. "Doing more for the cause," Clara Longworth De Chambrun, *Cincinnati: Story of the Queen City*, p. 115. "Here is the sovereign people," Sarmiento, *Travels*, p. 141. "Every large city," *ibid.*, p. 143. "A large wing on one side," Mackay, *The Western World*, vol. 1, p. 20. "More money has been put," Sarmiento, *Travels*, p. 143. "This beats those tender-hearted," *Yankee Doodle*, December 12, 1846, p. 108. "Is the handsomest church," Kenneth Hafertepe, *America's Castle: The Evolution of the Smithsonian Building and Its Institution, 1840–1878*, p. 28. "There is nothing in Paris," Nevins, *Hone Diary*, vol. 2, p. 772. "Mr. Stewart has paid," *New York Herald*, September 18, 1846. "Half the time of the," *ibid.*, September 26, 1846. "Great men, statesmen, divines," Nevins, *Hone Diary*, vol. 2, pp. 728–29. "Are excessively fond," Mackay, *The Western World*, vol. 3, p. 340. "Canvass-back ducks," *ibid.*, vol. 1, p. 28. "Periodicals, that is to say," *ibid.*, vol. 3, p. 241.

"From Maine to the Rocky Mountains," Frank Luther Mott, *A History of American Magazines*, vol. 1, p. 141. "Came as a pleasant friend," *Godey's Magazine and Lady's Book*, November 1846, p. 236. "We seek to make ours emphatically," *ibid*. "On board the steamer," Mackay, *The Western World*, vol. 3, p. 241. "Our friends and patrons," Boston *Daily Evening Transcript*, January 3, 1846. "The 'simplicity of republican,'" *ibid*., May 6, 1846. "Rudder carried away," *New York Post*, December 21, 1846. "They went to Croton Point," Nevins, *Hone Diary*, vol. 2, p. 801. "I never take up," *ibid*., vol. 2, p. 825. "Two complete voyages," *ibid*., p. 760. "Place these United States," *New York Weekly Tribune*, September 28, 1846. "We must again call upon Congress," *ibid*., December 12, 1846.

Captions for Chapter 3: "If it were not for," *New York Herald*, January 11, 1846. "Daily ply the besom," *ibid*., November 12, 1846. "There must be something done," *ibid*. "All society was merged," Wainwright, *Fisher Diary*, p. 190. "It is a beautiful town," Nevins, *Hone Diary*, vol. 2, p. 748. "Like almost every New England," *New York Weekly Tribune*, March 7, 1846. "It is indeed a city," *New York Weekly Tribune*, February 13, 1846. "When the manufacture," Winthrop, *Appleton Memoir*, p. 24. "My mind has always," *ibid*., p. 60. "The general health of the," *New York Weekly Tribune*, March 7, 1846. "It has its long rows," Bryant and Voss, *Bryant Letters*, vol. 2, p. 446. "Put up at the Planters' House," Nevins, *Hone Diary*, vol. 2, p. 809. "There are few persons," *New Orleans Daily Picayune*, August 11, 1846. "Everywhere on both sides," *Horticulturist and Journal of Rural Art and Rural Taste*, July 1846, p. 10. "With the exception," Sarmiento, *Travels*, p. 142. "Seven hundred diners," *ibid*., p. 143. "There is not a city on earth," Mackay, *The Western World*, vol. 1, p. 85. "The American Continent," *Yankee Doodle*, vol. 1, no. 1, p. 3. "That American Punch," *Dictionary of American Biography*, vol. 6, p. 402. "Stewart is worth," *New Orleans Daily Picayune*, September 27, 1846. "It puts me out of patience," *Brooklyn Daily Eagle*, October 24, 1846. "We perceive that the," *Godey's Magazine and Lady's Book*, November 1846, p. 240. "Our corps of," Mott, *History of American Magazines*, vol. 1, p. 591. "What a high privilege," *Godey's Magazine and Lady's Book*, November 1846, p. 235. "Trenchant and fearless," obituary, *Boston Evening Transcript*, January 31, 1898. "Of an old Dutch root," Milo Y. Beach, *Wealth and Biography of the Wealthy Citizens of New York City*, quoted in Wheaton J. Lande, *Commodore Vanderbilt: An Epic of the Steam Age*, p. 77. "The Americans have ever been," Mackay, *The Western World*, vol. 1, p. 224. "The rapidity of the locomotion," Elizabeth Cary Agassiz, *Louis Agassiz: His Life and Correspondence*, p. 409. "The splendid ship," *New York Herald*, December 8, 1846.

"Gentlemen, this is no humbug": "Gentlemen, this is," Rhoda Truax, *The Doctors Warren of Boston*, p. 193. "Everybody wants to have," Mitchell Wilson, *Science and Invention: A Pictorial History*, p. 106. "In their opinion," Truax, *The Doctors Warren*, pp. 196–97.

"Praising the country," John Bidwell, "Life in California Before the Gold Discovery," *The Century Magazine*, December 1890, p. 176. "Both of these Gentlemen," Dale Morgan, *Overland in 1846: Diaries and Letters of the California-Oregon Trail*, vol. 1, p. 36. "Ho for California!" *ibid*., p. 480. "Emigrants should be well provided," *ibid*., p. 481. "I was as full of," Walter E. Bryant, "Andrew Jackson Grayson," reprint from *Zoe*, April 1891, p. 38. "Singular as it may appear," Lisa Ades and Ric Burns, "The Donner Party" in The American Experience series, Public Broadcasting Systems, 1992. "WESTWARD, HO! FOR OREGON AND CALIFORNIA," Morgan, *Overland in 1846*, vol. 1, p. 491. "Some of these ox-wagons," Mason Wade, ed., *The Journals of Francis Parkman*, p. 419. "A tour of curiosity and amusement," *ibid*., vol. 2, p. 386. "A wide expanse of perfectly flat," *ibid*., p. 429. "Be as enthusiastic," Francis Parkman, *The Oregon Trail*, pp. 32–33. "Russel's or Boggs' comp'y," Wade, *Parkman Journals*, p. 447. "We are living chiefly," Wilbur R. Jacobs, *Letters of Francis Parkman*, vol. 1, p. 41. "The Indians look upon us," *ibid*., p. 46. "At Fort Laramie," Virginia Reed Murphy, "Across the Plains in the Donner Party," *Century Magazine*, 1891, p. 414. "So weak that," Jacobs, *Parkman Letters*, vol. 1, p. 48. "We have one in our Company," Stella A. Drumm, *Down the Santa Fe Trail and into Mexico: The Diary of Susan Shelby Magoffin*, p. 19. "Stuck on a sandbar," *ibid*., p. 483. "Had quarrelled with all," Morgan, *Overland*, vol. 2, p. 623. "A new species of trouble," *ibid*., p. 775. "The new road, or Hastings' Cut-off," Ric Burns, "Never Take No Cutoffs," *American Heritage*, May–June 1993, p. 74. "There was absolutely no road," Murphy, "Across the Plains," p. 415. "Napa Vallie California," Morgan, *Overland*, vol. 2, p. 287.

Captions for Chapter 4: "Strange that so many," Morgan, *Overland*, vol. 1, p. 630. "In the winter of 18 and 46," Herr, *Jessie Benton Frémont*, pp. 120–21. "Completed the last," Bryant, "Andrew Jackson Grayson," p. 39. "I can give you no idea," Morgan, *Overland*, vol. 1, p. 527. "In embryo," Jacobs, *Parkman Letters*, vol. 1, p. 53. "Wore the frock and trousers," Francis Parkman to Frederic Remington, January 7, 1892, in Allen P. Splete and Marilyn D. Splete, *Frederic Remington: Selected Letters*, p. 243. "On the point of marriage," *ibid*. "The Oregon emigrants," Jacobs, *Parkman Letters*, p. 42. "A most tyrannical monopoly," Jacobs, *Letters*, vol. 1, p. 46. "Most extortionate," Wade, *Parkman Journals*, p. 440. "The first thing that," *New Orleans Daily Picayune*, November 15, 1846. "Wild and picturesque," foreword to the first edition of *The Oregon Trail*, quoted in Mason Wade, ed., *The Journals of Francis Parkman*, p. 391. "For the most part," Splete and Splete, *Remington Letters*, p. 243. "We are all very well pleased," Wade, *Parkman Journals*, vol. 2, p. 287.

The Mormon Exodus: "Your religion is new," Leonard J. Arrington, *Brigham Young: American Moses*, p. 123.

Chapter 5: War with Mexico

"It is impossible," Thomas Hart Benton, *Thirty Years' View*, p. 680. "In all probability" John Y. Simon, ed., *The Papers of Ulysses S. Grant*, vol. 1, p. 71. "The troops are in good spirits," *New York Evening Post*, May 15, 1846. "We must treat all nations," Quaife, *Polk Diary*, vol. 1, p. 354. "Invaded our territory," *New York Evening Post*, May 12, 1846. "Mr. Calhoun denied," *ibid*. "We have been at War," *New York Weekly Tribune*, June 13, 1846. "The United States was," *New York Post*, May 16, 1846. "Mr. Polk and his party," Nevins, *Hone Diary*, vol. 1, p. 763. "Our position is an extreme one," Beverly Wilson Palmer, ed., *The Selected Letters of Charles Sumner*, vol. 1, p. 184. "The war has begun in earnest," *New Orleans Daily Picayune*, May 13, 1846. "We are in great excitement," McIntosh, *Jefferson Davis Papers*, vol. 2, p. 594. "It is with difficulty," *Cleveland Daily Plain Dealer*, May 30, 1846. "This is the time for action," *Washington Union*, reprinted in the *National Intelligencer*, May 21, 1846. "Open and fearless hostility," *New York Weekly Tribune*, June 8, 1846. "The news from the seat," Nevins, *Hone Diary*, vol. 2, p. 765. "Several thousand can be readily raised," *St. Louis Republican*, May 22, 1846. "Though Gen. Kearny," Drumm, *Magoffin Diary*, p. 103. "The U.S. and Mexico," *ibid*., pp. 135–36. "Had the enemy," Quaife, *Polk Diary*, vol. 2, p. 181. "Was unfit for the chief command," *ibid*., "He has had experience," *ibid*., p. 401. "I do not desire," Charles Winslow Elliott, *Winfield Scott: The Soldier and the Man*, p. 427. "I have strong objections," Quaife, *Polk Diary*, vol. 2, p. 242. "Was willing that by-gones," *ibid*., p. 245. "Hail Columbia," Winfield Scott, *Memoirs of Lieut.-General Scott*, vol. 2, p. 535.

Captions for Chapter 5: "Is a plain, blunt, speaking man," *Cleveland Daily Plain Dealer*, September 9, 1846. "I simply wish to refuse," James Mackay, *Thoreau: Philosopher of Freedom*, p. 31. "Declare unjust and cowardly," Edward L. Pierce, *Memoir and Letters of Charles Sumner*, vol. 3, p. 135. "Open and fearless hostility," *New York Weekly Tribune*, June 8, 1846. "He had infused," *New York Herald*, May 24, 1846. "The news from the army," *New York Herald*, May 13, 1846. "I think it desirable," Georgia Stamm Chamberlain, *American Medals and Medalists*, p. 88. "The city was thronged," *New York Post*, December 23, 1846. "Small of stature, very agreeable," Drumm, *Magoffin Diary*, p. 106. "Paraded through some little village," *ibid*., pp. 129–30. "I have entered the city," *ibid*., p. 102. "There are few objects in nature," Robert W. Johannsen, *To the Halls of the Montezumas*, p. 79. "Is that of a plain country farmer," Holman Hamilton, *Zachary Taylor: Soldier of the Republic*, p. 230. "General Tailor Come to see us," Edward J. Nicholas, *Zach Taylor's Little Army*, p. 201. "I sat down to take a hasty bowl of soup," Elliott, *Winfield Scott*, p. 429.

The Conquest of California: "The eventualities of war," Russel B. Nye, *George Bancroft: Brahmin Rebel*, p. 152. "In the event of any occurence," *ibid*., p. 156. "Implored him to place himself," Thomas Hart Benton, *Thirty Years' View*, p. 691. "That he proposed," *Century Magazine*, September 1890, p. 776. "I will now conquer," *New York Herald*, December 6,

1846. "We were handsomely," Harold A. Small, ed., *Seventy-five Years in California*, p. 208.

The Wilmot Proviso: "He is a man of much," Charles Buxton Going, *David Wilmot: Free-Soiler*, pp. 35–36. "He was most earnestly desirous," *ibid*., p. 97. "The slave-holders," Pickard, *Whittier Letters*, vol. 2, pp. 30–31. "The cool self-possession," *New York Evening Post*, August 13, 1846. "Become the greatest topic," *ibid*., December 26, 1846. "What is to come of this," John C. Calhoun to Anna Maria Clemson, December 27, 1846, published in J. Franklin Jameson, ed., "Correspondence of John C. Calhoun," *Annual Report of the American Historical Association for 1899*, pp. 744–45.

Chapter 6: Voices of Reform

"There is no one branch," *The Liberator*, January 2, 1846. "Enchanted the audience," *New York Weekly Tribune*, January 17, 1846. "There was much applauding," *National Intelligencer*, January 15, 1846. "Look to the Mechanic Arts," *New York Weekly Tribune*, January 17, 1846. "We have denounced unsparingly," *The True American*, printed in the *New York Weekly Tribune*, June 27, 1846. "Can it be that," *Pennsylvania Freeman*, reprinted in *The Liberator*, July 3, 1846. "Persecuted, hunted, and outraged," *New York Weekly Tribune*, March 7, 1846. "Everything is so different," William S. McFeeley, *Frederick Douglass*, p. 132. "The signs of the times," *New York Weekly Tribune*, May 23, 1846. "The truth is the misnamed," Archibald H. Grimke, *William Lloyd Garrison: The Abolitionist*, p. 323. "Humble and toiling member," John B. Pickard, *The Letters of John Greenleaf Whittier*, vol. 2, p. 3. "Let us press forward," *ibid*., p. 22. "Made interesting by," *The Liberator*, November 27, 1846. "I have always thought," *The Liberator*, July 3, 1846. "We would have every path," Paula Blanchard, *Margaret Fuller: From Transcendentalism to Revolution*, p. 214. "And give her every privilege," S. Margaret Fuller, *Woman in the Nineteenth Century*, introduction by Madeleine B. Stern, p. xxvii. "So long as a lady," Laurie James, *Men, Women, and Margaret Fuller*, p. 369. "The cause of popular education," Kathryn Kish Sklan, *Catharine Beecher: A Study in American Domesticity*, p. 169. "In the most important," Catharine Beecher, *The Evils Suffered by American Women and American Children*, p. 34. "Accomplished and highly gifted," *Godey's Magazine and Lady's Book*, November 1846, p. 236. "I believe Normal Schools," Jonathan Messerli, *Horace Mann: A Biography*, p. 437. "I think the cause," Mary Peabody Mann, *Life of Horace Mann*, p. 249. "If Hood had known my case," *ibid*., p. 244. "I do not regret," Helen E. Marshall, *Dorothea Dix: Forgotten Samaritan*, p. 115. "I am the Hope," *ibid*.

Captions for Chapter 6: "Immediate and complete emancipation," *Dictionary of American Biography*, vol. 4, p. 169. "This intrepid friend," *The Liberator*, April 24, 1846. "The spectacle of Cassius M. Clay," *ibid*., May 23, 1846. "I cannot allow myself," Leon Litwack and August Meier, eds., *Black Leaders of the Nineteenth Century*, p. 66. "Glib-tongued scoundrel," *New York Weekly Tribune*, June 6, 1846. "For myself viewing it," Ellis Papson Oberholtz, ed., *Frederick Douglass*, p. 114. "Where's the man for Massachusetts," Pickard, *Whittier Letters*, vol. 2, p. 38. "We have eighty thousand," *ibid.*, p. 34. "Is more actively employed," *The Liberator*, January 23, 1846. "Hers was the spirit," *ibid.* "There was Maria Chapman," Walter McIntosh Merrill, *Against Wind and Tide*, pp. 196–97. "I am a teetotaler," Irving H. Bartlett, *Wendell Phillips, Brahmin Radical*, p. 114. "With a warmth that," Fuller, *Woman*, facsimile of the 1845 edition, introduction by Madeleine B. Stern, p. xxxv. "Would find but a few," James, *Men, Women, and Margaret Fuller*, p. 395. "The deplorable amount of," Beecher, *The Evils Suffered*, p. 13. "Had I been writing," *ibid.*, p. 14. "Two millions of American," *ibid.*, p. 5. "Twining silk, working worsted," *ibid.* "Visited eighteen state penitentiaries," *Dictionary of American Biography*, vol. 3, p. 324. "Well, now I should not think," Marshall, *Dorothea Dix*, p. 112.

Chapter 7: Currents of Culture

"You will see more *life*," *Brooklyn Daily Eagle*, July 2, 1846. "How few there are," *Boston Evening Transcript*, May 6, 1846. "the immortality of domestic," *ibid.* "Not to mention the dog," Richard Waller, *Antiques*, September 1984, p. 617. "Fiddle less and paint more," Alfred Frankenstein, *William Sidney Mount*, p. 141. "Sketch in oil," *ibid.*, p. 471. "The season which now closes," Mary Bartlett Cowdrey, *American Academy of Fine Arts and American Art-Union*, p. 249. "Crowded day after day," *ibid.*, p. 134. "He would never perhaps," *ibid.*, p. 159. "The encouragement of," *The Knickerbocker*, January 1846, pp. 90–91. "I long for the time," Louis Legrand Noble, *The Life and Works of Thomas Cole*, p. 274. "The common remark," *Albany Argus*, December 21, 1846. "Steadily engaged in my shop," Alice Elizabeth Ford, *Edward Hicks: Painter of the Peaceable Kingdom*, p. 102. "Purchased and cherished," *Boston Evening Transcript*, June 17, 1846. "Is it asking too much," *Brooklyn Daily Eagle*, July 9, 1846. "Pretty and spirited pictures," Jay Leyda, *The Melville Log: A Documentary Life of Herman Melville 1819–1891*, vol. 1, pp. 209–10. "Polite and vigorous pen," Elizabeth F. Hokie, *Notable American Women*, vol. 3, p. 536. "Poe's masterly facility," *Godey's Magazine and Lady's Book*, January 1846, p. 46. "That most beguiling," Hokie, *Notable Women*, p. 8. "Had been reduced to beg," *Boston Evening Transcript*, December 31, 1846. "The public ought not," *New Orleans Daily Picayune*, July 15, 1846. "Is a poetical phenomenon," *Godey's Magazine and Lady's Book*, May 1846, pp. 289–90. "Whatever the miserable envy," *Boston Evening Transcript*, January 19, 1846. "What a devil of a pickle," Edward Haviland Miller, *Salem Is My Dwelling Place: A Life of Nathaniel Hawthorne*, p. 242. "For a friend of mine," Edward L. Pierce, *Memoir and Letters of Charles Sumner*, vol. 3, pp. 161–62. "Most perseveringly," Arlin Turner, *Nathaniel Hawthorne: A Biography*, p. 162. "It is no great affair," Miller, *Life of Nathaniel Hawthorne*, p. 242. "Our people in Boston," Ralph L. Rusk, ed., *The Letters of Ralph Waldo Emerson*, vol. 3, p. 351. "Now, as I think the Lyceum," *New York Weekly Tribune*, January 31, 1846. "It is not in New England," *ibid.*, March 7, 1846. "Many well-minded," *Boston Evening Transcript*, September 17, 1846. "Two theatres in Boston," Andrew Hilen, ed., *The Letters of Henry Wadsworth Longfellow*, vol. 3, p. 121. "Their Anti-Slavery songs," Beverly Wilson Palmer, ed., *The Selected Letters of Charles Sumner*, vol. 1, p. 174. "You must still keep a place," *New York Weekly Tribune*, November 21, 1846. "Negro songs, glees," Nevins, *Hone Diary*, vol. 2, p. 710. "To prove that the negroes," *Brooklyn Daily Eagle*, January 29, 1846. "Original and far-famed band," George C. O. Odell, *Annals of the New York Stage*, vol. 5, p. 226. "The soft touch of," *New York Herald*, May 2, 1846. "To say Adieu in every city," William G. B. Carson, *Letters of Mr. and Mrs. Charles Kean Relating to their American Tours*, p. 64. "In truth the most extraordinary," *New York Herald*, January 22, 1846. "The spectator seems carried back," Nevins, *Hone Diary*, vol. 2, p. 753. "Miss Cushman's fortune," *Boston Evening Transcript*, March 28, 1846. "Such utter rubbish," quoted in Richard Moody, *Edwin Forrest: First Star of the American Stage*, p. 220. "Our country," *ibid.*, p. 237. "To build up a *national drama*," *Boston Evening Transcript*, May 4, 1846. "A laudable and most excellent one," *ibid.*

Captions for Chapter 7: "Mr. Peck sketched," Richard Miller, *Antiques*, September 1984, p. 617. "I sometimes feel," Frankenstein, *William Sidney Mount*, p. 143. "One picture for Mrs. Lee," *ibid.*, p. 145. "He stood a long time," quoted in Bruce Robertson, *The Bulletin of the Cleveland Museum of Art*, February 1992, p. 49. "It is an honor and a pride," Bryant and Voss, *Bryant Letters*, vol. 2, p. 472. "Virulent and malignant," Nevins, *Hone Diary*, vol. 2, pp. 686–87. "There is more of," *Literary World*, May 18, 1850. "A brilliant reputation," John Francis McDermott, *George Caleb Bingham, River Portraitist*, p. 54. "Our artists," Cowdrey, *American Academy*, p. 170. "The figures be made," Ellwood C. Parry III, *The Art of Thomas Cole*, p. 312. "I am nothing but a," Edward Ford, *Peaceable Kingdom*, p. 101. "Industriously engaged at my trade," Eleanore Price Mather, *Edward Hicks: A Peaceable Season*, n.p. "You know what has been," reprinted in the *Boston Evening Transcript*, August 8, 1846. "Sooner or later," *Brooklyn Daily Eagle*, July 29, 1846. "A strange, graceful," Jay Leyda, *The Melville Log*, p. 211. "A racily-written narrative," *ibid.*, pp. 210–11. "Mr. Melville's book," *ibid.*, p. 216. "A most insane cry for," Mary C. Simms Oliphant et al., eds., *The Letters of William Gilmore Simms*, vol. 2, p. 194. "Ours are a very simple," *ibid.*, p. 237. "Poe, himself, is a," *ibid.*, p. 174. "If you will speak to him," Rita K. Gollin, "Standing on the Green Sward: The Veiled Correspondence of Nathaniel Hawthorne and Henry Wadsworth Longfellow," *Papers Presented at the Longfellow Commemorative Conference*, April 1–3, 1982, p. 25. "Whenever I sit alone," Arlin Turner, *Nathaniel Hawthorne, A Biography*, p. 175. "With the highest and keenest," Hilen, *Longfellow Letters*, vol. 3, pp. 127–28. "In patronizing the Hutchinson's," *Rochester Daily Advertiser*, February 26, 1846. "Few names are better known," *New York Evening Post*, October 28, 1846. "Enjoyed compositions more elevated," Ronald L. Davis, *History of Music in American Life*, p. 107. "Has introduced a new era," *Boston Evening Transcript*, April 21, 1846. "Chaste and Inimitable," *Cleveland Daily Plain Dealer*, June 13, 1846. "The Music (in part)," *Rochester Daily Advertiser*, February 7, 1846. "Expended $8000 out of,"

William G. B. Carson, *Letters of Mr. and Mrs. Charles Kean Relating to their American Tours*, p. 66. "Her gesture and utterance," *Boston Evening Transcript*, January 27, 1846. "Miss Charlotte Cushman," Joseph Leach, *Bright Particular Star: The Life and Times of Charlotte Cushman*, p. 179. "Many persons were disappointed," *Boston Evening Transcript*, November 19, 1846. "Forrest...is the creation," Oliphant et al., *Simms Letters*, vol. 2, p. 192.

Louis Agassiz Comes to America: "There is in this country," Rothenberg, *Henry Papers*, pp. 383–84. "His amiable and conciliating," *The American Journal of Science and Arts*, May 1846, p. 451. "There is something intoxicating," quoted in Edward Lurie, *Louis Agassiz, A Life in Science*, p. 118. "The physical department," Agassiz, *Louis Agassiz*, vol. 2, p. 416. "Offered me duplicates," *ibid.*, p. 424. "I confess that I was," *ibid.*, p. 421. "I thought myself tolerably," *ibid.*, p. 419.

Chapter 8: The Smithsonian Is Launched

"This general attendance," *National Intelligencer*, September 8, 1846. "We shall have to select," Hafertepe, *America's Castle*, p. 18. "Opinions were freely expressed," Quaife, *Polk Diary*, vol. 2, p. 124. "Efforts of the Insti-tution," Rothenberg, *Henry Papers*, vol. 6, p. 557. "Be a man possessing weight," *ibid.*, p. 551. "I regret that A. D. Bache," *ibid.*, p. 485. "Agreeably to your instructions," *ibid.*, p. 538. "If the institution is to be," *ibid.*, p. 543. "Our Board of Regents," *ibid.*, p. 570. "Redeem Washington," *ibid.*, p. 566. "The die is cast," *ibid.*, p. 578. "I have succeeded beyond," *ibid.*, p. 604. "Papers of an original character," *ibid.*, pp. 623–24. "All objects of art," *ibid.*, p. 466. "If I succeed in placing," Washburn, *The Great Design*, p. 88.

Captions for Chapter 8: "Mr. Hough will remain," *New York Herald*, September 11, 1846. "The passage of the Smithsonian," Washburn, *The Great Design*, p. 29. "In seizing & portraying," David Lowenthal, *George Perkins Marsh: Versatile Vermonter*, p. 51. "Portrait of myself," *ibid.* "Was chiefly due," *Annual Report of The Board of Regents, of the Smithsonian Institution*, 1866, p. 73. "All the accommodations," Cynthia R. Field, Richard E. Stamm, and Heather P. Ewing, *The Castle: An Illustrated History of the Smithsonian Building*, p. 11. "Professor Bache had," Merle M. Odgers, *Alexander Dallas Bache: Scientist and Educator*, p. 132. "It had been principally," *Smithsonian Annual Report*, p. 73.

For Further Reading

Adams, Charles Francis, ed. *Memoirs of John Quincy Adams Comprising Portions of His Diary from 1795 to 1848.* 12 vols. Philadelphia, 1876.

Agassiz, Elizabeth Cary, ed. *Louis Agassiz: His Life and Correspondence.* 2 vols. Boston, 1885.

Balazs, Marianne E. "Sheldon Peck." *Antiques* 118, no. 2 (August 1975): 273–84.

Bryant, William Cullen II, and Thomas G. Voss, eds. *The Letters of William Cullen Bryant.* Vol. 2. New York, 1977.

Burns, Ric. "Never Take No Cutoffs." *American Heritage* 44, no. 3 (May/June 1993): 62–76.

Davis, Varina. *Jefferson Davis: A Memoir.* Vol. 1. 1890. Reprint, Baltimore, 1990.

De Voto, Bernard. *The Year of Decision: 1846.* Boston, 1943.

Dippie, Brian W. *Catlin and His Contemporaries: The Politics of Patronage.* Lincoln, Nebr., and London, 1990.

Drumm, Stella A., ed. *Down the Santa Fe Trail and into Mexico: The Diary of Susan Shelby Magoffin, 1846–1847.* 1926. Reprint, Lincoln, Nebr., 1982.

Emerson, Edward Waldo, and Waldo Emerson Forbes, eds. *Journals of Ralph Waldo Emerson.* Boston and New York, 1912.

Evelyn, Douglas E. "The Washington Years: The U.S. Patent Office." In *Robert Mills,* edited by John M. Bryan, 106–40. Washington, D.C., 1989.

Fern, Alan, and Milton Kaplan, "John Plumbe, Jr., and the First Architectural Photographs of the Nation's Capitol." In *A Century of Photographs, 1846–1946,* compiled by Renata V. Shaw, 5–13. Washington, D.C., 1980.

Ford, Alice Elizabeth. *Edward Hicks: Painter of the Peaceable Kingdom.* Philadelphia, 1952.

Frankenstein, Alfred. *William Sidney Mount.* New York, 1975.

Fuller, S. Margaret. *Woman in the Nineteenth Century.* A facsimile of the 1845 edition with an introduction by Madeleine B. Stern. Columbia, S.C., 1980.

Hafertepe, Kenneth. *America's Castle: The Evolution of the Smithsonian Building and Its Institution, 1840–1878.* Washington, D.C., 1984.

Jacobs, Wilbur R. *Letters of Francis Parkman.* Vol. 1. Norman, Okla., 1960.

Johannsen, Robert W. *To the Halls of the Montezumas: The Mexican War in the American Imagination.* New York, 1985.

Leyda, Jay. *The Melville Log: A Documentary Life of Herman Melville, 1819–1891.* Vol. 1. New York, 1969.

McIntosh, James T., ed. *The Papers of Jefferson Davis.* Vols. 2 and 3. Baton Rouge, La., 1974.

Mackay, Alexander. *The Western World; or Travels in the United States in 1846–47.* 3 vols. 1849. Reprint, New York, 1968.

Morgan, Dale. *Overland in 1846: Diaries and Letters of the California-Oregon Trail.* 2 vols. Georgetown, Calif., 1963.

Nevins, Allan, ed. *The Diary of Philip Hone, 1828–1851.* 2 vols. New York, 1927.

Oliphant, Mary C. Simms, Alfred Taylor Odell, and T. C. Duncan Eaves, eds. *The Letters of William Gilmore Simms.* Vol. 2. Columbia, S.C., 1953.

Parry, Ellwood C. III. *The Art of Thomas Cole: Ambition and Imagination.* Newark, Del., 1988.

Palmer, Beverly Wilson, ed. *The Selected Letters of Charles Sumner.* Vol. 1. Boston, 1990.

Parkman, Francis. *The Oregon Trail.* Reprint, New York, 1931.

Pickard, John B. *The Letters of John Greenleaf Whittier.* Vol. 2. Cambridge, Mass., and London, 1975.

Quaife, Milo Milton. *The Diary of James K. Polk.* 4 vols. Chicago, 1910.

Rash, Nancy. *The Paintings and Politics of George Caleb Bingham.* New Haven, Conn., and London, 1991.

Robertson, Bruce. "The Power of Music: A Painting by William Sidney Mount." *Bulletin of the Cleveland Museum of Art* 79, no. 2 (February 1992): 38–62.

Rothenberg, Marc, ed. *The Papers of Joseph Henry.* Vol 6. Washington, D.C., 1992.

Sandweiss, Martha A., Rick Stewart, and Ben W. Huseman. *Eyewitness to War: Prints and Daguerreotypes of the Mexican War, 1846–1848.* Washington, D.C., 1989.

Sarmiento, Domingo Faustino. *Travels in the United States in 1847.* Translation and introductory essay by Michael Aaron Rockland. Princeton, N.J., 1970.

Small, Harold A., ed. *Seventy-five Years in California: Recollections and Remarks by . . . William Heath Davis.* San Francisco, 1962.

Spence, Mary Lee, and Donald Jackson, eds. *The Expeditions of John Charles Frémont.* 4 vols. Urbana, Chicago, and London, 1970–1984.

Thomas, Dwight, and David K. Jackson. *The Poe Log: A Documentary Life of Edgar Allan Poe, 1809–1849.* Boston, 1987.

Viola, Herman J., and Carolyn Margolis, eds. *Magnificent Voyagers: The United States Exploring Expedition, 1838–1842.* Washington, D.C., 1985.

Wade, Mason, ed. *The Journals of Francis Parkman.* Vol. 2. New York and London, 1947.

Washburn, Wilcomb E., ed. *The Great Design: Two Lectures on the Smithsonian Bequest by John Quincy Adams.* Washington, D.C., 1965.

Photography Credits and Copyrights

Index

This book was edited by Frances K. Stevenson, Dru Dowdy, and Kirsten Williams at the National Portrait Gallery. The text was composed and film preparation completed by Monotype Composition Company in Baltimore. The book was printed on 80 lb. Warren Web Dull and bound by R. R. Donnelley and Sons Company in Willard, Ohio. The cover was printed by Phoenix Color Corporation in Hagerstown, Maryland.